RISKY BUSINESS

RISKY

BUSINESS

How Indonesia's
economic nationalism is hurting foreign
investment – and local people

ARI SHARP

connorcourt
PUBLISHING

Connor Court Publishing Pty Ltd

Copyright © Ari Sharp 2014

PO Box 224W
Ballarat VIC 3350
sales@connorcourt.com
www.connorcourt.com

ISBN: 9781925138320(pbk.)

Cover design by Ian James

Printed in Australia

CONTENTS

Author's Note   vii

A Note on Style   xiii

1. Introduction   1

2. Breaking Down the Problems   25

3. A Riot at the Gates   50

4. Time to Pack Your Bags   67

5. Legal Tangles   79

6. Zealous Prosecution   97

7. The Battle for Mahakam   115

8. A Port in a Storm   138

9. Facing Jail for Doing Business   153

10. Hunger Pangs   167

11. Bankers' Bluff   185

12. Not Ready for the World   206

13. Caging the Golden Goose   224

14. Conclusion   253

Endnotes   273

Bibliography   301

Acknowledgements   303

About the Author   305

Index   307

Author's Note

Were it not for the freedom of the press in Indonesia, I probably would never have come to live here. In 2010 my partner Melanie and I were keen to leave our home in Canberra for a stint somewhere more exotic. As an employee of the Australian government agency responsible for international development, Melanie had a slew of job opportunities open to her in developing countries. I had recently left a job covering politics for a couple of newspapers and was hungry for a new challenge. And so we unrolled a map of the world and looked at where we would go.

Each of us set some rules about where we would and would not move to. Melanie made clear that she would not go anywhere dangerous, so postings in Baghdad, Kabul and Islamabad were ruled out. I made clear that I was keen to continue working in journalism, so places that were quiet (like some Pacific islands) or imposed too many restrictions on reporters (like Harare and Beijing) were off limits. Left in the middle were a collection of safe but lively cities that could keep both of us satisfied professionally and sane at home. As we often heard, a happy spouse means a happy posting.

Top of the list was Jakarta, a place I knew had a thriving English-language media scene and was accommodating to journalists practising their craft. We secured a three-year posting there. Throughout the 2000s in Australia, our perceptions of Indonesia were often negative – of religious extremists carrying out terror attacks, trees in orangutan-filled forests being felled and crooked politicians having their scams exposed. We knew there must be so much more to the place and were keen to discover it for ourselves.

When we arrived in Jakarta we were overwhelmed by the pulsating energy of the city. Around the clock the streets were filled with cars and people bustling about a metropolis whose skyline was dominated by cranes and skyscrapers. Creative people were filling galleries with provocative work that hinted at a thriving counter-cultural scene, and entrepreneurs were swapping ideas at smoky street-side cafes. Jakarta made you feel thankful you were alive.

Not too long after I arrived I secured a job on the copy desk at the *Jakarta Globe*, one of the city's two English-language daily newspapers, working with the team of native speakers responsible for bringing the prose up to a high standard and inserting the occasional pun in a headline. Over the two and a half years that followed I was involved in editing stories on every subject that the paper covered, making me an armchair expert in topics ranging from the progress of the Jakarta monorail, the corruption scandals ensnaring local politicians, the thriving bond market, the underperforming national badminton team and the marriages and divorces of sinetron stars.

One area that repeatedly caught my eye was corporate news. I'd reported on business for a few years in Australia, and had a pretty solid understanding of economics. My perception of a prosperous and growing Indonesia chimed with the frequent blue-sky reports that I was editing on the country's lucrative investment prospects. Stories on new floats on the stock exchange, multi-million dollar corporate bond issues and exploitation of natural resources reserves filled the business pages.

But every so often there would be a grey cloud – a story that bucked the trend and showed things not going to plan. Like one involving the tender for a big infrastructure project that never got off the ground. Or an executive pleading their innocence as they were arrested. Or an overzealous local government official impeding the development of a project. At first I was dismissive of the significance of these stories. After all, in an economy of this size and this complexity, it is only natural that some things turn bad. There were still plenty of people making plenty of money and the sun was still shining bright.

Over time these grey cloud became heavier and more frequent, forcing me to reassess my thinking. Any one of these stories on their own could be considered an aberration, but when they are piled one of top of the other they indicate something else. Time and time again foreign investors were getting into trouble and it seemed to me that these stories represented a trend that, when looked at dispassionately, undermined much of the enthusiasm reflected in the blue-sky stories.

This book represents my effort to get to the bottom of what is going on. In it, I look at the history, politics and economics of Indonesia for clues as to why this trend has emerged. I look at the substance of each major instance of a foreign company encountering problems to see what was going on behind the scenes. I look at major policy debates to see how big decisions are made. And after all that, I look at what foreign investors and reform-minded government leaders can do to improve things.

In writing this book, I know that some people might misconstrue my message as being critical of Indonesia. This is far from the truth. I am in no doubt that Indonesia is a great democratic success story and that its economy has enormous potential. But through the greed and mismanagement of some people in positions of influence, the country has became a hostile place for outside investors. This puts at risk the likelihood that the country will realise its potential, leaving ordinary people – in their roles as consumers, employees, investors and citizens – worse off.

With national elections taking place in 2014, many people are wondering whether the recent economic nationalism will continue under the new president, Joko Widodo. I address this question more fully in the conclusion, but it's worth noting here that the forces at play appear to be underlying structural ones that go beyond individual personalities. Laying blame at the feet of President Susilo Bambang Yudhoyono and his ministers, who have been in power since 2004, would be misguided.

To bring to life the case studies at the heart of the book, I have had contact with many of the key people involved. Most investors have been reluctant to speak on the record about their negative experiences because they continue to do business in Indonesia and do not want to reopen old wounds. Government figures are also guarded in what they will say because of the sensitivities involved. As best as I can, I have sought to convey their perspective on events without breaching trust. Comment was sought from each of the key participants in the case studies, and the responses received have been included.

In writing this book I am greatly indebted to the Indonesian journalists who have covered the political and economic developments in their country with distinction. Indonesia is home to one of the freest presses in Asia, and the Reformasi generation of journalists are taking full advantage of this freedom to hold to account powerful figures in business and government. The country is the richer for their efforts.

I have drawn frequently (with attribution) from reporting in the *Jakarta Globe*, *Jakarta Post* and *Tempo* to chart the progress of the case studies in the book. The dedication, resources and language skills of those media outlets have made it far easier for outsiders like me to understand what is going on. As well, I have drawn from the reporting of international news agencies operating in Indonesia (particularly *Reuters*, *Agence France-Presse* and *Bloomberg*), who produce great material under considerable pressure.

In conducting research for this book I came to read the works of some of the Indonesian studies academics from around the world who have dedicated their professional lives to understanding the intricacies of this place. I was awestruck by the work of these thinkers, and I urge anyone curious to learn more about the place to dive into their books and essays, some of which are listed in the bibliography.

I do not claim to have anything like the level of Indonesian expertise that these writers have. Instead, I come to the subject as a journalist who covered business and politics elsewhere and spent three years of my life in Jakarta. With an understanding of the conceptual basics and an inquiring mind, I have sought to bring together a series of case studies and searched for common themes. Helping me along the way were many experts on different aspects of the Indonesian economy, both foreigners and locals.

The book aims to be reader-friendly, avoiding jargon where possible and keeping facts and figures to a useful minimum. I have used footnotes so that readers can verify the claims made and can find out more about topics that interest them.

My intention is for the book to act as a sobering reminder to two key categories of people. I hope that potential foreign investors appreciate the risks that they face in doing business in Indonesia, and calibrate their actions accordingly. And I hope that Indonesian decision-makers appreciate the consequences of their collective actions and renew their efforts to create institutions that have capacity, stability and integrity.

Indonesia has the potential for a bright and prosperous future, and I hope my small contribution can help it realise that potential.

Selamat membaca.

Ari Sharp, September 2014

A Note on Style

Knowing what name to use in referring to an Indonesian person on a second and subsequent reference can be tricky. Some publications follow the common Indonesian practice of using a given name on second reference, while others opt for the final name in line with Western convention. Given the presence of both Indonesians and foreigners in the book, I have opted to use last names to ensure consistency and avoid the unwarranted sense of familiarity that the use of first names can convey.

Indonesian company names formally carry the PT designation at the start, while state companies carry the designation (Persero) at the end. I have left those elements out because they often clutter text and have little informational value.

Key figures in rupiah have been converted into US dollars at a rate of Rp 12,000 to the dollar, the prevailing rate in early 2014.

1

Introduction

When it started a few years ago, Car-Free Sunday on Jakarta's majestic Jalan Sudirman and Jalan Thamrin boulevards was a place for leisurely wandering, for riding of bikes and for spending time with friends while enjoying the novelty of the usually clogged thoroughfare offering clean air to breathe and a sense of calm. Nowadays, the street on Car-Free Sunday is almost as busy as it is on weekdays, the road congested with amateur athletes trying their luck in the frequent fun-runs and more serious cyclists donning lycra as they tackle the smooth bitumen.

Many walkers, runners and cyclists crane their necks upward at the corporate offices that exemplify sleek modernity: the UOB Plaza building with whole floors jutting out as if it were made of children's building blocks, the gently curved roof of the sailboat-inspired Wisma 46 building, the statuesque grace of Menara BCA. Others have opted for a more classic style, like the faux-European palace look of Sampoerna Strategic Square and the kitsch gaudiness of the Da Vinci building.

Closer to the ground, a cottage industry of service-providers have found nifty ways to keep the Sunday crowd happy – young men with bike pumps offer to inflate tyres, older men with drinks carts offer thirst-quenching relief from the blazing sun, organic farmers sell fresh yoghurt and musicians belt out dangdut tunes that enhance the chilled-out vibe.

Indonesians have long shown themselves to be industrious and entrepreneurial, forever ferreting out opportunities to fill a commercial niche, not just in seeking out goods and services to provide, but finding inventive times and places to offer them. Across the vast archipelago of more than 17,000 islands, tens of millions of men and women with no training other than the wisdom inherited from past generations have established micro businesses. With minimal capital and a lot of sweat, these entrepreneurs are keeping turning the wheels of the economy of their family, community and country.

There are several theories on the origins of this entrepreneurial streak. Perhaps it's a legacy of Indonesia's place for centuries as a busy trading hub, with ships of all nationalities passing through the Malukus, also known as the Spice Islands, and across the archipelago. Or maybe it's a product of tight bonds of kinship in villages, with high levels of trust among families and neighbours allowing informal credit networks to flourish. Or maybe it's the result of the lack of a formal welfare safety net, leaving people with little choice but to rely on their wits for survival.

Whatever the reason, Indonesia's 240 million people have a commercial savvy that ought be the envy of many nations. Such a reflex shows that it is well positioned to compete in the global economy, if only it can unleash the creative power of its people and allow them to compete, cooperate and trade with the rest of the world.

But the nation's leaders seem to have their doubts. Many Indonesian opinion leaders, in both politics and business, seem determined to shield their people from the winds of the world economy, and in doing so cut them off from the benefits of globalisation. Through a combination of legislative edicts, ministerial utterances and dubious court rulings, Indonesia's elite has sought to demonstrate that the country is not open for business.

In demographic and economic terms, Indonesia is a highly desirable place to sell goods and services, manufacture products, extract natural resources and even just hold portfolio assets. A few stark facts make clear why Indonesia has investors, particularly those in stagnant economies, drooling.

The country is the world's fourth most populous, with more than half of its 240 million people living in urban areas and enjoying a doubling of their purchasing power over the past decade. It is the 16th biggest economy in the world, with its gross domestic product poised to break through the US$1 trillion barrier. Its middle class (those with capacity to spend between US$2 and US$20 a day) is projected to hit 170 million people by 2015. It has the world's largest geothermal power potential and is the world's largest palm oil exporter and second-largest coal exporter. It has successfully made the transition from autocracy to democracy and is located within reach of booming Asian markets.[1]

Plenty of investors have taken the plunge on Indonesia. Of the $28.6 billion of foreign investment in Indonesia in 2013, the largest share came from Japan, followed by Singapore and the United States. As to the industries in which they are investing, manufacturing represented a majority share, followed by the services sector and mining (the data excluded the oil and gas sector). The overwhelming majority of the funds were going into the densely packed island of Java. Such patterns reflect a trend going back a decade or more.[2]

High return, high risk

There is no question that Indonesia is an investment destination that offers high returns for companies that can achieve success there. But those rewards come with enormous risks.

There are myriad groups that have a vested interest in talking up the prospects of doing business in Indonesia. Apart from the national government through its Investment Coordinating Board (BKPM), powerful corporate lobbyists including the Indonesian Chamber of Commerce (Kadin) and the Indonesian Employers Association (Apindo) celebrate Indonesia as an investment destination. Foreign governments keen to reignite their stagnating economies and strengthen ties with an emerging global power pile on the froth.

But few talk publicly about the risks involved. To their credit, some corporate analysts and business journalists have done so (though many from the comparative safety of Singapore rather than Jakarta). And international chambers of commerce have struck a nuanced tone, talking enthusiastically of the returns while more quietly urging realism on the risks. It should come as no surprise that corporate risk consultancy, in which firms make big bucks advising foreign companies of where political and business land-mines lie in Indonesia, is big business. But most contributors to public debate have joined the Indonesian investment cheer squad.

The reality is that although the financial rewards on offer in the country are great, so are the risks faced in accessing them. Investment analysts talk about risk-adjusted return – the potential benefits of a particular investment multiplied by the probability of achieving that benefit. For any given investment return, the higher the risk the lower the risk-adjusted return. If the risk is high enough, the risk-adjusted return can be reduced to very little, regardless of how large the theoretical return may be. That is the position Indonesia finds itself in.

Such risks are hampering Indonesia's ability to achieve its potential, and allow the tens of millions of people still living on less than US$2 a day to join the tens of millions of their country folk who have already elevated themselves out of poverty.

Of course, Indonesia's leaders rarely say overtly that they are sceptical of globalisation and that they want to isolate their country. Indeed, they seem to compete with one another to declare that the nation welcomes foreign investment and that it is an attractive Southeast Asian base for international companies. Advertisements from the BKPM are beamed across the world with fantastical images of a diverse group of international businesspeople gliding through the Jakarta streets on their way to meetings to make multi-million-dollar deals.

But governments and businesspeople must be judged on their actions, not their words, and these create a vastly different impression. Time and time again, international investors have found that Indonesia is a complicated and at times downright hostile place to do business. These risks manifest themselves in several ways, some reflecting an overt hostility and others reflecting the benign neglect typical in developing countries.

Why discuss risks

This book is about those risks. It uses nine case studies to demonstrate the problems that can arise in seeking to do business in Indonesia, and draws out lessons from those case studies. It also looks in depth at two major policy debates of relevance to foreign investors – one on food self-sufficiency and another on the mining industry. It is hoped that by doing so future investors make decisions about Indonesia with their eyes wide open, and Indonesian institutions can reflect on their actions and the impact they have on investment decisions.

All case studies are from the five years to 2014. The accounts delve deep into the circumstances faced by investors, the way they reacted, the decisions made by government officials and the broader implications. The purpose of this book is not to judge the actions of individual actors in any given case study, but to look at the aggregate impact of the decisions made. Each study is broadly presented in chronological order, allowing the reader to understand the circumstances at the point of each of the key decisions. Information and perspectives from people at the time, rather than just in hindsight, help to explain their actions.

Focusing mostly on negative investment experiences might at first glance appear unfairly pessimistic about Indonesia. But the book is intended to be read alongside the myriad studies and reports (some independent, others government-backed) that rightly depict the country's rosy economic prospects but downplay the risks. Of course, there are many companies that are successfully investing in Indonesia, and although they may have faced some difficulties, are finding it a profitable enterprise.

The case studies cover companies from diverse countries of origin, industry and size, reflecting the broad international interest in the Indonesian economy. It looks at the experience of a telecommunications outfit from Qatar, cattle farmers from Australia, an oil and gas operator from France, a petroleum company from the United States and a bank from Singapore. All have chosen to invest significant amounts in Indonesia, and most continue to do so. But had their investment experience run smoothly, it is likely they would have invested a lot more. As Mike Elliot from Ernst & Young explained to *Reuters* in the context of the clouds hanging over Indonesia's mining industry: "Even though geologically it is quite an attractive place to produce, each of these risks essentially increases the cost of doing business, and the risk of sustaining the operations."[3]

The period being examined coincides with Susilo Bambang Yudhoyono's second term as president, but as will become clear, the rising economic nationalism appears to go well beyond his influence and so is unlikely to end when he leaves office in October 2014.

Were investment decisions to impact only on company shareholders, it would be a private problem rather than one of public policy. But the impact is much greater. At stake is the extent to which Indonesia can achieve the growth and development that is within its grasp. Without stable institutions, rule of law, a level playing field and predictable regulations Indonesia will struggle to attract the investment it needs to achieve the prosperity its people are seeking.

Indonesia has made giant strides in the past 15 years in advancing the quality of life of its people, with annual gross domestic product per capita rising rapidly to US$3,500 by 2012, and most other measures of people's welfare also jutting upward. But it risks falling into the middle-income trap, in which its people struggle to take the next step towards economic advancement, if it goes down a path of economic isolationism.

What's wrong with economic nationalism?

Given its status as a maritime trading thoroughfare, Indonesia has a rich history of international engagement in commerce. In discussing the environment in the 17th century, historian Anthony Reid notes: "Chinese technology, weights and coins, Indian financial methods, Islamic commercial laws, and European technology and capital all played a major part in creating the character of Southeast Asian urban and commercial life in this period."[4] Indeed, early rulers of what is now Indonesia saw great benefit in the free flow of goods across the seas, particularly as colonial rulers sought to dominate access. "God made the land and the sea; the land he divided among men and the sea he gave in common. It has never been heard that anyone should be forbidden to sail the seas," a 17th century Makassar ruler reproved the Dutch.[5]

But as Reid notes in his sweeping history of the four centuries to 1800, successive generations of sultans sought to squeeze whatever material advantages they could out of trade, and colonial rulers introduced monopolies that sought to curb the free-trading instincts of local people. From an initially high level of openness, a fortress-like mindset slowly enveloped the archipelago.

Today, it could be argued that economic isolationism is, to some extent at least, in Indonesia's self interest. It does, after all, have an abundance of natural resources and it would be better for the country's development for the wealth from those resources to stay in Indonesia. And who better to profit from the emergence of the middle class than local enterprises. This argument is superficially appealing, but ultimately flawed, for two main reasons.

Firstly, the natural resources wealth and emerging middle class are not assured if the country relies only on local expertise. Natural resource extraction is technically difficult and capital intensive, and the necessary capacity simply does not existing in Indonesia yet, nor at any time in the conceivable future.

Consider the supply of skilled labour. Indonesia had just 20,000 PhDs as of 2012, amounting to just 83 per million people, compared to 483 per million in Malaysia and 607 per million in China.[6] The QS World University Rankings for 2013 had the best Indonesian institution, the University of Indonesia, ranked at 309 in the world, while only one other, the Bandung Institute of Technology, was in the top 500.[7] Skills shortages are frequently cited by companies doing business in Indonesia as a major constraint on their expansion. Companies doing business in the country first seek to tap the local labour pool, but the reality is they must look further afield to meet demand. It is a similar experience in raising capital for major projects, with the local bond, equity and credit markets struggling to offer the volume of funds needed on adequate terms.

The state of natural resources fields exacerbate the constraints of labour and capital. In many cases, the cheaply and easily accessible resources have been tapped, and what remains are the resources that require deep mining or chemical extraction techniques, both of which are costly and technically challenging. In hydrocarbon extraction, for example, industry experts say outdated equipment means Indonesia lacks the capability to exploit reserves in more difficult locations. "In terms of technology advancement, we are 15 to 20 years behind," Indonesian Petroleum Association chairman Lukman Mahfoedz told the *Jakarta Globe*.[8] Were local companies to rely only on local capacity, many of these resources would go unextracted and the potential economic benefits unrealised. Foreign companies bring with them the experience, funds and technical know-how to carry out such major projects.

Secondly, policies that claim to benefit all Indonesians businesses in reality only help a handful of well-connected ones, and do so at the expense of ordinary people.

Indonesia's corporate sector is dominated by a handful of tightly controlled conglomerates whose operations stretch across a vast swathe of industries. For example, the Lippo Group, under the control of the Riady family, has interests spanning real estate, shopping malls, health care, retail and media. The Salim Group, started by Liem Sioe Liong as a young migrant from China in the 1930s, has control of a food producer, palm oil plantations and luxury real estate. Eka Tjipta Widjaja's Sinar Mas empire includes forestry, food production, banking, real estate, telecommunications and energy.

These companies operate on the classic Asian conglomerate business model, like the chaebol of South Korea or the keiretsu of Japan. Ownership is tightly held (few have any significant presence on the stock exchange), management tends to come from a small elite group, often members of the same family, and different parts of the group work in close cooperation with other parts. This last element is particularly evident in finance, where a bank within a conglomerate is often compelled to lend to other parts of the group on favourable terms regardless of the commercial merits of the decision. Such cooperation creates a barrier to entry, making it difficult for a smaller company to establish itself if it competes in just one of the sectors in which the conglomerate operates.

Many of the Indonesian conglomerates, almost all of them controlled by Indonesians of Chinese ancestry, enjoyed great opportunities for wealth during the three-decade reign of strongman president Suharto before his ignominious demise in 1998. After lying low in the early years of the Reformasi period, they have reasserted themselves as central to the nation's economy. "They had 30 years of cronyism and the Reformasi hasn't really made a dent in the legacy powers of those tycoons," Geoffrey Gold, an Australian consultant based in Jakarta, explained in an interview. "New players have been able to get involved in the expanding market, but those big areas that were held by the cronies are still held by the cronies."[9]

Government policies that seek to advantage local businesses are, therefore, in reality heavily benefiting powerful local conglomerates. The effect of protectionist policies has been to allow a handful of local conglomerates to carve up the local market among themselves, enjoying the benefits of being shielded from global competition. Consumers, on the other hand, are faced with higher prices and less innovation than would otherwise be the case. In instances where companies are bidding for mining licences and other government contracts, a lack of international competition means the government obtains less revenue than it otherwise would in a competitive market.

The power of the conglomerates can also stymie efforts to improve economic efficiency and the operations of major institutions. "When talking about the relationship between public and corporate governance, one cannot ignore the uncomfortable fact that politically powerful groups often dislike outcomes produced by institutions aiming to implement good governance," wrote corporate governance experts Peter Verhezen and Natalia Soebagjo. "Generally speaking, Indonesian politico-bureaucrats in league with domestic conglomerate owners have strongly opposed drastic reform of corporate governance practices because they benefit from the status quo."[10]

Consumers pay a big price too. Discussing the way economic nationalism seeks to privilege the interests of domestic producers, Indonesian economist Winarno Zain wrote in the *Jakarta Post* that: "The overall effect of these policies has been to deny consumers freedom to access cheaper and better-quality goods and services. The policies also rob the jobs and income of certain groups of people. Overall consumer spending could decline. This would not be good for the economy, since consumer spending has been the main driver for our economic growth, and would be the main driver of economic growth in the future."[11]

Unsurprisingly, these conglomerates – many of which own substantial media operations – tend to be politically influential. Bill Sullivan, a Jakarta-based lawyer with Christian Teo Purwono, sees baser motives in the emergence of a more hostile environment for foreign investors. "I think quite a number of local companies and entrepreneurs are probably licking their chops and saying, 'Well, actually, this is fantastic. If we force out these foreigners, and force them to sell at a song, and make life for some so unattractive in Indonesia that they leave, someone's going to pick up those assets and they'll be available at fire-sale prices,' " he said in an interview.[12]

Being shielded from global competition actually hurts all players in the domestic economy in the long run because it allows inefficiencies to become entrenched and productivity to stagnate. Without pressure from competitive markets and direct exposure to global trends, local companies can become risk-averse and complacent. Discussing economics in developing countries around the world, economist Paul Collier wrote: "High tariffs induced a high-cost, parasitic industry that realised its profits depended upon lobbying rather than on productive efficiency. Globally, we now know what produces productivity growth in manufacturing: it is competition. Firms hate competition because it forces them into painful changes, and painful change is what generates productivity growth."[13]

So economic nationalism has the effect of disadvantaging Indonesian consumers and taxpayers in the interests of an elite group of politically powerful local businesspeople. In doing so, it puts the development of an efficient and equitable economy at risk, channelling resources towards activities that can attract rents and easy returns. Ordinary people hoping that the wealth from a cashed-up local elite eventually flows down to them are likely to be sorely disappointed. Instead, those ordinary people would be far better off if they could enjoy better quality and lower priced goods and services, job opportunities from an expanding economy and greater transparency in the way their government allocates resources. These are unlikely to come in an economy that puts up walls between it and the rest of the world, operating as an autarky.

Foreign companies investing in Indonesia have, generally, proven themselves to be good corporate citizens who lead by example.

On measures such as the paying of tax, alleviation of impact on the environment, provision of workers' rights and implementation of corporate social responsibility programs, foreign investors often outpace their local counterparts. In the same way that many foreign companies bring with them technical know-how and capital from abroad, they also bring high standards of conduct. No doubt there are exceptions among foreign investors, but there are likely many more among local companies.

But within that pool of foreign investors, some are more desirable than others. Any country that provides a risky or corrupt environment in which to do business is likely to find that companies that set high standards will be reluctant to invest, while other more shady operators will flock in. "Not all companies are concerned about the risk to their reputation because not all companies have good reputations to protect," noted Paul Collier, the economist. "However, this gives rise to what is known technically as an 'adverse selection problem': the companies attracted to the risky environments are those that are not concerned about poor governance and so have no interest in helping to avoid the problems of the resource trap."[14] Policy-makers would be well advised to focus on the quality of investment, rather than just its quantity.

One charitable interpretation of the government's actions is that forms part of a broader plan for national development, helping local industries grow in a sheltered environment before exposing them to global competition. But no such strategy has been articulated by the government, and the local companies being protected have already been around long enough to stand on their own two feet. Even if protectionism was the goal of the policies, the economic foundations of such an approach are shaky. Operating separately from the global economy is likely to entrench inefficient and unproductive practices among local companies, and the transfer of skills to local businesses is likely to be choked back. The wealth of evidence instead suggests more pragmatic objectives are driving policy.

Looking back

To understand the risks faced by foreign investors in Indonesia it is essential to understand the historical context. A glance back reveals that the economic nationalism of the past five years has several historical precedents in the independence era – from anti-Dutch sentiment under Sukarno to anti-Japanese protests under Suharto – and provides some comfort that, like those past episodes, this too will pass.

During centuries of colonial rule, the Dutch, and for periods the British, the Portuguese and finally the Japanese, methodically exploited the natural resources and human capital of the archipelago. While the European masters brought with them many of the ideas of the Enlightenment age, the approach taken was often brutal and humiliating: farmers laboured under sufferance, natural resources were shipped off abroad and local people were denied a say in their own political affairs.

It was only when Japan was defeated in World War II that Indonesia could declare independence, and even then it faced a four-year struggle against the Dutch to have its claim recognised by the rest of the world. By 1949 Indonesia had achieved political sovereignty, but it had yet to achieve economic sovereignty.

Assuming the presidency was the debonair Sukarno, a socialist who nonetheless avoided Soviet overtures and put the newly independent Indonesia at the forefront of the Non-Aligned Movement. In the early years of Sukarno's presidency annual economic growth stood at a modest two percent following a more permissive economic approach. But by 1957, Sukarno was determined to give his young country control of its own resources and embarked on a fierce campaign of nationalist development that involved expropriation of Dutch property, discrimination against ethnic Chinese and major state investment in heavy industry. "To hell with your aid," Sukarno famously told Indonesia's American donors. The outcome of Sukarno's so-called Guided Democracy was disastrous: trade collapsed, industrial production nosedived and inflation reached beyond 2,000 percent a year by the mid-1960s. Even as the rest of the world was experiencing a post-war boom, gross national product per person in Indonesia declined between 1957 and 1965. Astonishingly, food consumption, in a country populated by many people who were already undernourished, fell backwards.[15]

The economic decline, and the fear that it represented a slide towards communism, prompted the military into action. General Suharto, a military commander, forced Sukarno from the presidency in a military takeover that began in response to the assassination of six senior generals in October 1965 and ended with Suharto's election to the presidency by acclimation in March 1968. During that period a brutal reign of terror was led by the military and their local thugs, who between then killed at least half a million people suspected of links to the Indonesian Communist Party (PKI). Many victims had little association with communism but were targeted because of their Chinese ethnicity, their links to organised labour or even to settle personal vendettas. The perpetrators of the violence were never brought to justice, and the spectre of their violence hangs over contemporary Indonesia.[16]

Suharto had been a mid-ranking military general with a history of opportunistic business dealings and friendly relations with the nation's Chinese entrepreneurs. While the early stages of his rule marked a period of political repression, it did come alongside greater economic openness. A phalanx of bright Indonesian economists, who came to be known as the "Berkeley Mafia" thanks to their shared American education, promoted a new model of development that sought to reopen the country to trade and manage growth in line with a series of five-year plans. The early results were encouraging. An emphasis on curbing inflation, promoting rice production and fostering import-replacing industries left annual growth per capita at 5 percent by the end of the 1960s.[17]

Economic development in Indonesia ebbed and flowed through Suharto's rule. An initial openness to economic activity beyond the control of the state was replaced in the 1970s by a more conditional one, where investment was reliant on favourable outcomes for the president and his cronies. Public anger against foreign investment was also brewing, prompting several days of vandalism of Japanese-linked businesses in 1974. A year later, a US government report for firms considering investing in Indonesia noted "the emergence of economic nationalism as perhaps the dominant force shaping government investment policies".[18] Following significant fluctuations, by the early 1990s Indonesia was consistently posting annual economic growth beyond 8 percent.

While Suharto's military bearing brought stability to the often fractious country, it also fostered an increasingly virulent streak of despotism. One of the most startling achievements of Suharto's New Order era was the president's ability to shape the entire government establishment in his image. The bureaucracy was filled with pliant apparatchiks who would tell the president and his ministers only what they wanted to hear. Government contracts and import and export monopolies were awarded exclusively to favourites of the president. The police and court system would turn a blind eye to the sprawling network of corruption that was later revealed to involve at least 500 companies with significant stakes held by the Suharto family. (By the end of Suharto's time in office, his family had accumulated at least US$15 billion in wealth, despite his presidential salary being only US$1,764 per month, according to a famous investigative report in *Time Asia* magazine.[19]) Legislative elections each five years, dubbed a "Festival of Democracy" by the softly spoken Javanese leader, would involve the ruling Golkar Party and just two others, with all candidates needing approval from the state. From among those legislators, Suharto would be elected president unopposed. Little happened in the country without the imprimatur of Bapak Presiden.

It was this very approach to governance that meant Suharto's Indonesia was especially vulnerable when the Asian Monetary Crisis, involving the exodus of foreign capital, emerged in Thailand in July 1997 and rapidly spread through the region. As political scientist Harold Crouch noted: "Tied to a maze of patronage networks, the Suharto regime had been much less able than other regional governments to take the firm measures necessary to avert the crisis or at least mitigate its consequences."[20] As a spiralling currency left scores of Indonesian banks on the brink of collapse and food and energy prices were forced sharply upwards, angry Indonesians took to the streets to demand change at the top.

When Suharto was forced out of office in 1998, those activists who were determined to bring genuine democracy to Indonesia faced enormous challenges. After decades of authoritarian rule, the country had endured a year of economic chaos, widespread rioting, communal conflict and fears of disintegration. An estimated 113 million Indonesians – 56 percent of the population – were living below the poverty line.[21]

For post-Suharto Indonesia to prosper, new institutions needed to be built from the ground up, and existing institutions needed to be so thoroughly reformed that they would be barely recognisable. And so, brick by brick over the first years of the Reformasi period, a new generation of technocrats sought to build a government that reflected the communitarian spirit of Indonesian decision-making and the rigours of democratic accountability. "Political reform was not inevitable but depended on a continuing struggle between those who saw benefit in further reform and those who felt disadvantaged by it," Crouch wrote.[22]

Come the end of the first decade of the new century, their achievement was impressive. Three rounds of genuinely competitive national elections had taken place, power had transferred between leading political figures without the spilling of blood, the army had been split from the police and driven from its privileged position in the parliament, a national corruption-busting law enforcement body had been established and a thriving civil society and media were taking part in dynamic debate on issues of substance. Indonesia had made real progress. In a 2013 speech to executives keen to understand how power is distributed in the country, prominent lawyer Todung Mulya Lubis explained: "Indonesia is not only about the president anymore; it is also the House of Representatives, the Corruption Eradication Commission and the Constitutional Court."[23]

Just how bad things could have been emerged when the Arab Spring revolutions rolled through the Middle East and North Africa in the early 2010s. Egypt and Libya both shared with Indonesia the characteristics of a Muslim-majority population that had thrown off the shackles of rule by a secular strongman leader. But where Indonesia had forged ahead peacefully, the African pair had descended into tribalism and upheaval, with rival factions seeking to reclaim the authoritarian mantle that had so recently been cast aside. The contrasting fortunes made clear what an achievement Indonesia's Reformasi era was.

But while a broad historical comparison casts Indonesia in a very favourable light, a closer inspection reveals many flaws that have persisted from Suharto's New Order. Venality and corruption remain endemic features of Indonesian public life. The pervasiveness of Suharto's values, if not his institutions, prompts an uncomfortable question: Did Suharto's fall represent the toppling of an autocratic system, or merely an individual autocrat? If officials continue to steal from the public purse, human rights activists continue to face harassment and legislators continue to treat their constituents with disdain, then the revolution can hardly be termed a success.

"The crisis failed to sweep away the very interests and forces incubated within the Suharto regime, which underpinned and defined it. These survived to re-establish the economic and political power relationships within new institutional arrangements," argued sociologists Richard Robison and Vedi Hadiz. The difference after 1998, they said, was only that "authority over the allocation of resources, contracts and monopolies had been shifted from a highly centralised system of state power to a more diffuse and chaotic environment of political parties, parliaments and provincial governments".[24]

In the immediate aftermath of Suharto's resignation, his deputy, B.J. Habibie assumed the presidency until free national elections the next year. From that ballot, Abdurrahman Wahid, a blind advocate of religious tolerance affectionately known as Gus Dur, assumed the presidency. But his ineffectual governing style led to an impeachment within two years, after which Sukarno's daughter, Megawati Sukarnoputri, took over national leadership. The rapid succession of leaders had left some Indonesians yearning for the stability of the decades that came before it rather than the chaotic uncertainties of democracy.

In that environment the country in 2004 elected Susilo Bambang Yudhoyono, a former military man, to Istana Negara. The president had a slew of challenges to confront: entrenching the newly established democratic institutions, quelling secessionist desires in Aceh and Papua and reinvigorating a stagnating economy.

Once in office, Yudhoyono pledged to raise annual economic growth to 6.6 percent, from the existing 4.5 percent. Top of his economic agenda was tackling corruption. In his first international interview after coming to office, Yudhoyono told *Time Asia* magazine:

> There needs to be some shock therapy so that the people know that this government is serious about corruption. We want to improve the investment climate, starting with political stability, improved security, good taxation and economic policies, and legal certainty – sanctity of contracts, and that all dispute-settlement systems are fair.[25]

The words were music to the ears of people who saw Indonesia's economic growth as coming through international engagement. And for much of his first term Yudhoyono was true to his word, giving anti-corruption agencies great latitude and hacking away at some of the intransigent rent-seekers who had clung to the state like barnacles since the fall of the New Order. The physical safety of investors and their facilities, identified by veteran Asia economist John Bresnan in 2005 as a major concern among foreign businesspeople scarred by daily acts of thievery, vandalism and intimidation by local gangs, would within a few years no longer be a source of headaches.[26]

But upon his re-election in 2009, Yudhoyono appeared drained of energy and reformist zeal, dodging many tough decisions and concerning himself with image rather than substance. On several major policy debates, the president appeared reluctant to confront powerful interests and instead sought comfort in broad populism.

Maria Monica Wihardja, a lecturer in economics at the University of Indonesia, laid blame for Indonesia's recent economic malaise at the feet of weak-willed politicians. "Indonesia's economy is exposed to the destabilising effects of populist domestic politics and a lack of leadership," she wrote in August 2013. "A bad economy is said to cause political instability. But Indonesia shows that causation goes both ways: bad politics can lead to economic instability."[27]

Economic nationalism clearly intensified during Yudhoyono's second term in office. But it is far from clear that he alone is responsible and that the trend will change when he leaves office in October 2014. Instead, there are broader social and institutional factors stoking hostility. Rather than being the cause of that mood, Yudhoyono seems to have been swept up in it. His reform-minded replacement, Jakarta Governor Joko "Jokowi" Widodo, will face a tough battle to institute change.

Ghosts of past mistakes

It is often said that one of the common errors made by military leaders is that they are busy fighting the previous battle rather than the current one. So it can be the case with regulators, who are so badly scarred by earlier problems that they orient their thinking and action to prevent them from reoccurring – only to inadvertently create a new set of problems. There are several previous investments whose spectre no doubt brings nightmares to government officials on warm Jakarta nights.

In the mid-1990s investors around the world poured huge amounts of money into Canada-listed miner Bre-X, which claimed to be sitting on 70 million ounces of gold in Busang in the forests of Kalimantan. Over more than a year the company offered up increasingly bullish estimates of its bounty, and the company's market capitalisation zoomed to a vertigo-inducing US$4.5 billion. Then, as the company sought to move to the exploitation phase in 1997, outside mining geologists did their own research into what lay in Bre-X's tenement. Not much, it found. Soon after, the company's Filipino deputy geologist mysteriously fell from a helicopter (theories of suicide, murder and a faked disappearance all proliferate) and the company's shares were worthless. Investors, it became clear, had fallen for an elaborate hoax. To some extent, Indonesia was merely the setting in which one group of foreigners had swindled another group out of vast sums of money. But the incident tarnished the reputation of the Indonesian mining industry, and left investors with the nagging suspicion that no matter how appealing the claims made about prospects in the country, the truth may be far more sobering.[28]

In 2002 the Indonesian government was keen to lock in supply contracts for the output from its Tangguh liquefied natural gas plant in West Papua. China, keen for a reliable energy supply to fuel its growth, saw an opportunity to turn things to its advantage. The upshot of negotiations was a deal that appeared gobsmackingly generous to the China National Offshore Oil Corporation (CNOOC). It was agreed that the price it paid for 2.6 million tons of gas a year would be linked to the oil price and capped at US$25 a barrel, leaving the Chinese paying US$2.40 per million British thermal unit (mmbtu) over 25 years. The amount was reasonable given global prices at first, but as demand picked up and the price skyrocketed, Indonesia was left receiving only a pittance for its resources. The Indonesians pleaded with CNOOC to renegotiate, and in 2006 it agreed to push the price up to US$38 a barrel, equating to US$3.35 per mmbtu. (By comparison, Indonesia was selling gas to Japan and South Korea for more than US$16 per mmbtu and to domestic buyers for US$10 per mmbtu). Another round of renegotiations was looming in 2013. But just how the original deal came about is shrouded in mystery – some say the Indonesian negotiators were fundamentally outplayed, but others suspect more sinister actions. Whatever the reason, the deal has deprived Indonesia of billions of dollars in export earnings.[29]

Casino Indonesia

On their own, each of the challenges identified would give pause for thought to investors considering doing business in Indonesia. In aggregate, they form a damning indictment.

In assessing a potential investment, every investor is thinking in relative rather than absolute terms, in essence comparing the potential returns from an array of different options. So in deciding whether to put their money in Indonesia, an investor is weighing up alternatives – perhaps putting it in the sluggish but stable economies of Europe, or the steadily growing behemoth of China or the enigmatic source of unrealised potential that is India. It is in these comparisons that Indonesia has set itself at such a disadvantage. Its rate of growth is solid but not spectacular when set against other countries at a similar state of development, but its level of risk appears much greater.

In discussing the investor response to the suite of changes to mining laws (discussed in Chapter 13), David Lennox, an analyst at Fat Prophets in Sydney, put it like this in an interview with *Bloomberg*: "This rule change won't make a company go away from Indonesia, but it will obviously mean they will look over their shoulders if an opportunity pops out somewhere else."[30]

The impact is starting to be felt. A PricewaterhouseCoopers study noted that in 2011 Indonesia's share of global spending on mining exploration fell to 1.8 percent, from 2.6 percent a year earlier. "Indonesia is still yet to capture a fair proportion of the global exploration spending despite its known geological potential," the 2013 report said. And things may only get worse – PwC's survey of existing investors found that 18 percent were considering pulling out of Indonesia altogether.[31]

Data on realised foreign investment prepared by the triumphalist Investment Coordinating Board (BKPM) does show a seemingly impressive 22 percent increase in 2013 compared to a year earlier, to $28.6 billion.[32] But several observers are doubtful of the integrity of the numbers (Bank Indonesia data seemingly measuring a similar thing recorded a four percent decline for the year[33]) and point out that the investment total would be higher if not for the decisions of companies that considered investing in the country but did not, or scaled back the size of their investment. Anecdotal evidence of investment foregone exists, but quantifying it is perilously difficult.

International bodies have expressed increasing concern with the direction Indonesia's policy-making is taking. The World Bank, in its Doing Business survey, ranked Indonesia at 120 in 2014, down four places on its position a year earlier and behind comparable countries including Brazil, Pakistan and the Philippines, with significant regression in the ease of dealing with construction permits and paying taxes.[34] Canada's Fraser Institute in its survey of mining companies found Indonesia to have the most hostile business environment of the 96 countries surveyed in 2013, compared to a ranking of 62 out of 72 countries four years earlier.[35] In Transparency International's Corruption Perceptions Index, the country has continued to hover at around 110 out of more than 170 countries surveyed, in 2013 finishing below Mexico, China and Turkey.[36] The World Trade Organization, in an April 2013 review of Indonesia, noted: "A number of measures ... have recently raised concerns about the direction of trade and investment policy-making."[37]

Indonesia's isolationism appears to be coinciding with a broader deterioration in the country's economy. The rupiah slid by more than 20 percent against the US dollar in 2013 amid investor worries over the current-account deficit. In 2012 the country sunk into a trade deficit for the first time in the modern era, and the deficit more than doubled to $4.06 billion a year later. Across 2013, exports fell 3.9 percent and imports 2.6 percent even as the global economy advanced its recovery. Inflation started 2013 at a tame 4.3 percent, close to the middle of the central bank's target zone, but ended the year at an alarming 8.4 percent. Economic growth in 2013 sunk below six percent for the first time in four years, leaving it well behind other Asian developing countries, including China. While the deteriorating position can be attributed in part to external factors such as the tapering of US government monetary stimulus, it demonstrates that Indonesia is ringing in the changes in an environment that is already vulnerable.

Certainly things could be worse – Sultan Iskandar Muda of Aceh in the early 1600s was fond of executing wealthy traders and confiscating their assets[38] – but they could also be vastly better.

There are signs that Indonesia has greeted past evidence of economic progress with complacency and self-satisfaction rather than a desire for further improvement. Take the sovereign debt ratings applied to the country by the big three big international ratings agencies. The downgrading of Indonesia into junk status during the Asian Financial Crisis was a stinging humiliation for President Suharto and for the country as a whole. President Yudhoyono set out to reclaim investment grade status, curbing the government's ratio of debt to gross domestic product, and accumulating foreign exchange reserves. In late 2011, the efforts yielded some results: Fitch Ratings pushed up its assessment of the country to investment grade, and Moody's Investors Service followed a few weeks later. Analysts speculated that Standard and Poor's was not far behind.

But then within months the mood turned – the budget deficit crept upwards, plans to rationalise state-owned enterprises stalled and the terms of the mining investment law were toughened. The earlier discipline appeared to subside, and S&P stuck to its junk assessment. Two years on, it remained that way. "Slow progress in improving critical infrastructure, along with legal and regulatory uncertainties and bureaucratic obstacles, detract from Indonesia's growth potential," S&P said in explaining why it was downgrading the company's outlook from positive to stable in 2013.[39]

A comment from Mahendra Siregar, the chairman of the Investment Coordinating Board (BKPM), was revealing in demonstrating the way that the magnetism resulting from Indonesia's sheer size can prompt complacency. "It must be noted that ultimately, people invest not only because of efficiency," he told *Tempo*. "If that is the case, no one would want to invest in BRIC [Brazil, Russia, India and China], which are far from efficient. But why do their investments continue to remain high? This is because of their markets. That is also why our investments are bigger than Malaysia. It's not because our infrastructure is better, but because of our economic growth, the domestic market and our middle class, which are all growing very fast."[40]

Ultimately, foreigners would be wise to treat investing in Indonesia as they would gambling in a casino – they should only put on the table money they are prepared to lose. Just as risking one's house on a hand of poker is a foolhardy endeavour, so is staking a company's future on an Indonesian play. In both cases, it might prove wildly successful. But it might also end in tears.

2

Breaking Down the Problems

So after centuries of colonial rule, a fiery socialist demagogue, a militaristic autocrat and a gaggle of democratic presidents, what is the state of the Indonesian government today? Understanding the way power is distributed between different arms of government provides a useful guide to the challenges that can emerge for investors that interact with them.

While a classic analysis of government looks at the three planks of the executive, the legislature and the judiciary, no study of Indonesian government is complete without also considering regulators, provincial and local governments and state-owned enterprises. Some problems – most notably corruption – stretch across all parts of government, but others reflect the particular circumstances of the arm of government in question. Only through a crash course in civics can we begin to understand where things go wrong.

Ministers and their ministries

Spend any length of time stuck in Jakarta's traffic, and you're likely to hear the bleep-bleep of a police motorcycle with its flashing blue light as it edges forward to carve a path for a tinted-window limousine bearing an "RI" number plate. Inside, a national government minister is being whisked to his or her next engagement, spared the tediousness of the congestion inflicted upon lesser citizens going about their business. Life is no doubt pretty good for those inside on the leather seats, assuming a role of power and responsibility in a country that pays great respect to those with grand formal titles. For many ministers the office serves as a reward after a life of political drudgery, while for others it is a chance to contribute to the nation following high achievement in business, the military or academia.

Among government ministers exists a hierarchy that is on display when they meet for regular cabinet meetings. While the president and deputy sit atop the hierarchy, enjoying a direct mandate from the people, beneath them is a trio of coordinating ministers (one for economics, another for political, legal and security affairs and a third for public welfare) who have broad scope to influence policy. Under them sit two dozen or so portfolio ministers, most of them drawn from the political parties in the ruling coalition. By all accounts, the cabinet under President Susilo Bambang Yudhoyono has acted largely by consensus, and given the Indonesian style of decision making this is likely to remain the case long after he has left office. Cabinet solidarity, in which ministers publicly advocate the government position even if they personally disagree, is patchy at best; it is not uncommon for representatives of different factions to make public their opposition to the prevailing view.

Each minister typically has a deputy, and the dynamic between the two can be intriguing. While ministers are usually political appointees and so often lack familiarity with the detail of their portfolio, their deputies are commonly drawn from the ranks of the senior civil servants and so are immersed in the intricacies of the policy area. Many of the deputies have developed a well-earned reputation for dependability, integrity and a keen appreciation of the practical impacts of the government's policy positions. The reputation of many ministers is far weaker.

The ministries they oversee are often chaotic to the point of being dysfunctional. The bureaucracy has some bright stars, particularly among those who joined after the fall of Suharto, but they are often thwarted in efforts to do good work by painfully complicated systems, colleagues who lack integrity and political masters keen to exploit their power. "Within the central government there are good bureaucrats, but they are simply destroyed by the political appointees at the top," lamented Farid Harianto, an economic advisor to the vice president, over ginger tea at a Jakarta hotel.[41]

For many people, a job in a government department is a chance to extract bribes from those people with whom they interact. Public expectations of civil servants are so low that users of government services have come to expect minor extortion as a part of the transaction. Initial recruitment and subsequent advancement in the civil service is often dependent on paying substantial bribes, and so once in a role a bureaucrat needs to make back the money they have paid. While the formal pay is usually modest, the potential windfalls are enormous. It is unsurprising that jobs that don't involve direct dealings with potential bribe-payers are far less appealing.

Given the extent to which bribes are embedded in government processes, there's an obvious vested interest among bureaucrats to keep systems opaque and complicated. There's simply no internal constituency for streamlining processes, improving transparency and otherwise boosting the quality of service received by the public. Political pressure for change, when it does come, is perceived to involve merely reallocating the spoils of formal rank rather than upending the system that creates such spoils. Economist Paul Collier has noted the way ineffective bureaucracies can act as a barrier to the wishes of reform-minded ministers in developing countries. "It is very difficult for them to implement change because they inherit a civil service that is an obstacle rather than an instrument," he wrote. "It is hostile to change because individual civil servants profit from the tangled mess of regulations and expenditures over which they preside."[42]

Problems often materialise when decisions involve multiple ministries, each of which are highly protective of their turf. Agung Wicaksono, a special assistant in the President's Delivery Unit for Development Monitoring and Oversight (UKP4), says an oil and gas project needs a dizzying 64 permits from 17 different government institutions and involves 600,000 pages of documents. "There will be little issue if a project is being handled by the same ministry or two ministries under the same coordinating minister, but when it goes through different coordinating ministers or even involves the regional governments, then things get more complicated," Wicaksono told the *Jakarta Globe*.[43]

The extent to which the sclerotic bureaucracy can slow progress is evident in an observation by Lukman Mahfoedz, the chairman of the Indonesian Petroleum Association, who noted that in the 1970s, the construction of the Badak liquefied natural gas plant in East Kalimantan took about three years from the project commencement to the first shipment of product, whereas today a similar process can take more than a decade. The more recent Tangguh LNG project in West Papua took 16 years, for example, while huge natural gas reserves found in the Masela block off Maluku in 2000 are not expected to move into production until 2018. "We are not without success stories but they are becoming increasingly rarer," a wistful Mahfoedz told the *Globe*.[44]

US oil and gas company ExxonMobil (Chapter 4) felt the consequences of falling foul of the bureaucracy when its leading executive in Indonesia had his visa renewal application denied, effectively sacking him from the role. The energy regulator acknowledged the decision was a payback for the company's slow progress on the development of the Cepu resources block in Java, but there are strong signs that intransigent local officials rather than the company ought shoulder much of the blame. The role of a separate decision by ExxonMobil to discontinue a sell-off of assets that companies linked to the government were keen to acquire is unclear.

Legislature

The design of Indonesia's democracy seeks to share power between the president and ministers on one hand, and the 550-member House of Representatives (DPR) on the other. Having witnessed the way the legislature under Suharto was stacked with cronies and cowered to the president's authority, the architects of Indonesia's democracy were keen to create a parliament with real power. Perhaps they went too far: the initial Reformasi structure involved the people directly electing the legislature, which then subsequently elected the president. Within a few years that system was changed so that the people directly elected their president as well as the House of Representatives, strengthening the mandate of the executive.

From that point onwards, the president and ministers have progressively gained more power. These days much of the legislation debated by the parliament is authored by ministers and passed with few changes. Even then, the legislation is typically little more than a broad document indicating general preferences, with detail to be filled in at a later stage by ministerial regulations. The House of Representatives has largely been reduced to an oversight function, having the power to call government officials before its committees for questioning. It has, however, retained some power over determining budget spending, giving it some leverage in its interactions with ministers, prompting widespread allegations of corruption. Members of the House of Representatives also sit with regional delegates in a body known as the People's Consultative Assembly (MPR), whose role is largely limited to considering constitutional amendments.

Law in Indonesia is often an expression of intentions and moral piety, rather than an achievable reality. Ministers and political parties will use a law to demonstrate their action, concerns and aspirations in a given policy area, often with the implicit understanding that the express terms of the law may long remain unenforced. Instead, the laws are used to affirm the virtue of the person or entity backing the law, and the powerful interest groups that they seek to please. This is how some laws can sit on the book with no serious attempts to enforce them.

Such unenforced laws are a source of headaches for people seeking to do business in Indonesia. For starters, a diligent investor (and the board they answer to) will expect to do business in the clear white of legality, rather than in the broad grey zone that haphazard laws create. Building confidence with investors and lenders is a whole lot harder when the legality of one's actions carry a shadow of doubt. Secondly, the risk that a long-ignored law will swiftly become enforced will put a chill up the spine of anyone operating a business on the premise that a given law was meant as a symbolic rather than practical measure. And thirdly, unenforced laws can create opportunities for sneaky (or indeed entrepreneurial) public officials to shake down people and companies for bribes with the threat that in the absence of such payments the laws will be enforced after all.

In many other cases, officials and legislators fail to consult with the people most affected by new laws, nor subject the proposals to a rigorous analysis. In cases where technicalities are significant and nuance in language vital to a law achieving its objective, a failure to consult can have widespread consequences. Andrew White, the managing director of the American Chamber of Commerce in Indonesia, points to a 2011 trade regulation that bans the import of used capital goods by manufacturers in an effort to protect local suppliers. However, the regulation inadvertently banned manufacturers from importing remanufactured equipment, an industry term for precision parts that have been extensively reworked and function as new. "The sad fact is that poorly drafted regulations, which lack sufficient stakeholder consultation, are each year causing thousands of people to lose their jobs while an untold number of jobs are not created," White wrote along with colleague Yvonne Chen. "The Indonesian government too often involves the private sector after decisions are already made, simply looking for rubber-stamp approval."[45]

The increasingly marginal role of the House of Representatives has led to a general decline in the quality of people aspiring to join it. The political parties who select candidates for the DPR fail to attract the best and brightest, with networks of patronage and fund-raising ability being vastly more important selection criteria than is legislative ability.

It should come as no surprise, therefore, than two of the most significant problems to afflict the legislature are absenteeism and court rejection of laws past. Frequently the House is found to be inquorate, leaving it unable to pass laws, while courts overturn laws that are found to be inconsistent with other laws or the nation's constitution. Since 2004, some 60 laws enacted by the parliament have been annulled by the Constitutional Court.[46] Diligence among lawmakers, or professional drafting skills among the legislature's staff, would likely catch such issues, but there is strong evidence that both are lacking.

The legislative process has yielded several vexing challenges for businesses operating in Indonesia.

The 2009 Mining Law (Chapter 13) was a vivid example of the failure of legislators and ministers to understand the impact of the decisions they make. The law introduced sweeping changes to the way mining companies do business in Indonesia, imposing rules on the processing of minerals, forcing foreign companies to divest assets and seeking to reopen long-settled contracts. Consultation ahead of the introduction of the law was minimal, and the haphazard way in which the details of the law were released led to acute uncertainty. With billions of dollars in investment on the line, the lackadaisical approach was troubling.

Another legislative project with painful unintended consequences has been the attempt to achieve agricultural self-sufficiency, particularly in several key foods (Chapter 10). In seeking to encourage the development of local agriculture by limiting imports, the government has created shortages of some foodstuffs, driving up prices for people already struggling to feed themselves. The use of quotas to regulate the flow of imports appears to have fueled corruption, with companies offering kickbacks to ministry officials or politicians in exchange for permits. For companies keen to sell agricultural products to Indonesia, long-term planning has become far more difficult.

Legal system

On paper, the Indonesian legal system offers high hopes to those seeking redress from injustice. A legacy of the Dutch colonial period, the courts use an adversarial approach to hear civil and criminal matters and are generally public in their operations. Courts are divided by areas of expertise (the Anti-Corruption Court and the Constitutional Court, for example, focus their efforts accordingly) and sit around the country, although unsurprisingly many are based in Jakarta.

Problems arise, however, in practice. Many judges are of dubious quality, their appointments based on political considerations rather than legal qualifications. Rather than sharpening their minds as practising lawyers before ascending to the bench, many have backgrounds in politics and have limited exposure to the law. They are also poorly paid relative to many of those who appear before them, leaving them particularly vulnerable to corruption.

One person in particular exemplifies these two problems. Akil Mochtar had served for 10 years as a Golkar Party legislator when he was appointed as the chief justice of the Constitutional Court in 2009. Four years later he was accused by the Corruption Eradication Commission (KPK) of taking bribes to rule in favour of certain candidates in regional election disputes being heard by his court. He later admitted to seeking a Rp 3 billion (US$250,000) bribe.[47]

The reasoning behind many rulings can leave observers scratching their head, given their idiosyncratic nature. The principle of precedent is only loosely applied in Indonesia, reducing the certainty and predictability of cases and making it difficult to apply the ruling in one case to the facts in another. Rulings themselves are often leaked to one side of a case, which may choose to share it in part or in whole with the public before it is released by the court, making a swift and reliable analysis by outsiders a difficult task.

The commercial legal system is frustratingly underdeveloped. In the World Bank's Doing Business index, Indonesia has consistently performed poorly in the categories of enforcing contracts, registering property, protecting investors and resolving bankruptcy.[48] As Asian business researcher Howard Dick notes in a 2013 paper: "These four indicators, all relating to grave weaknesses in commercial law, together show that private businesses remain acutely vulnerable to random shocks and have very little redress in the event that things go badly wrong."[49]

Foreign investors are often in a weak position to enforce their legal rights in the courtroom. "Local business interests have routinely used corrupt courts to extract concessions from foreign companies," Harvard Kennedy School's Ash Center noted in a 2010 report on the rule of law in Indonesia. It goes on to recommend that "the legal system — courts, prosecutors, police, lawyers – must uphold the law and the rights of citizens without bias."[50]

Considering the slew of legal cases in which foreign miners have had their claims on Indonesian assets undermined by court rulings, Australian mining analyst Peter Gray explained the broader impact. "The impression it gives to the wider investment community is that Indonesia is still a place you don't want to do business and you don't want to be investing capital there because you are never quite sure if your capital is being well invested or if you end up with nothing," the Hartleys analyst told *Reuters* in 2012.[51]

It can be difficult to gain a fair hearing in an Indonesian court when a local party is pitted against a foreign one. This was the experience of London-listed Churchill Mining (Chapter 5), which fought for years in Indonesian courts with little success to have its tenure over a mine site confirmed, and decided to instead seek justice through an international arbitration panel. Complicating matters was the fact that a big beneficiary of Churchill losing its mining rights was a powerful political figure.

In some legal cases, compelling evidence can often be overlooked. Telecommunications company Indosat (Chapter 9) relied on a letter from the Minister of Communications when it made its corporate arrangements to gain access to spectrum to provide internet services. But in 2013 a court ruled against it, dismissing the value of the ministerial letter, sentencing an executive to prison and leaving other players in the industry wondering if they would be next.

Individual executives can become the target of legal action even when their company, rather than them personally, would appear to be the more sensible target. Several executives and contractors linked to Chevron Pacific Indonesia (Chapter 6) have been imprisoned after being found to have misappropriated funds given to it as part of a contract to perform environmental remediation works. In that case, one executive's time in the relevant role barely overlapped with the supposedly illegal conduct, but the claim against her was nonetheless upheld. The ruling meant that contracts thought to be civil in nature could suddenly be the basis for criminal action.

Regulators

Like most countries around the world, Indonesia has opted to put responsibility for some politically contentious policy areas in the hands of authorities that act at arm's length from the government. Responsibility for monetary policy lies with the central bank, Bank Indonesia, which has filled its ranks with pragmatic economists keen to keep inflation under control while also achieving steady growth and a decent trade balance. It is a reflection of the esteem in which the body is held that Susilo Bambang Yudhoyono invited the bank's governor, Boediono, to serve as his deputy during the president's second term in office. Such reverence is a contrast to the Suharto era, when the body was stacked with figures from the banking industry. The situation meant it overlooked the terrible

governance of local lenders that acutely exacerbated the effects of the
Asian Financial Crisis.

While the influence of private bankers on Bank Indonesia appears to
have waned, executives at state-controlled banks still have the ability to
shape policy. For Singapore bank DBS (Chapter 11), the government's
confused policy objectives caused major headaches when the company
sought to take over another Singapore-controlled bank operating in
Indonesia, Bank Danamon. Even though the government had made clear
its desire to consolidate the highly fragmented banking sector through
mergers and acquisitions, the government stymied a corporate takeover
that would have done just that. Banking rivals, most of them owned by
the Indonesian government, lobbied hard on the issue and were relieved
at seeing off a potential competitor.

At the start of 2013, a new regulator was established to oversee
the financial sector. The Financial Services Authority (OJK) was
charged with keeping capital markets honest, a role that previously
rested with the Capital Market and Financial Institution Supervisory
Agency (Bapepam LK), and a year later it took over banking industry
regulation from Bank Indonesia. While the OJK is still new, its early
actions have given confidence that it is an honest and professional
regulator concerned with improving corporate governance among
companies operating in Indonesia. But corporate governance expert
Chris Leahy remains doubtful that the new body will improve the
state of regulation in Indonesia. "Nothing's changed. They're the
same people," Leahy, a researcher at the Asian Corporate Governance
Association, said in an interview. "They need to create a regulator with
proper laws and with teeth, they need to pursue people and there needs
to be consequences."[52]

Decentralisation

Since 2001, Indonesia has undergone a concerted campaign of shifting
power and authority from the central government in Jakarta to provincial

and sub-provincial governments across the country. This makes sense given the country's sprawling geography and the vastly differing circumstances that people in different regions face. It also minimises the risk of separatist movements gaining traction by diffusing anger towards Jakarta and the sense of disempowerment that inevitably comes with centralised decision-making. More pragmatically, it shifted the opportunities to benefit from corruption.

In large part, decentralisation has proven politically successful, encouraging economic growth in regions outside Jakarta and fostering a sense of local identity. But is has also led to myriad practical problems. In many cases, laws passed by legislatures at different levels of administration have left an area with a thicket of inconsistent laws. Trying to abide by such laws is clearly a fool's errand – compliance with the needs of one level of government will leave a person uncompliant with another, putting them in a Kafkaesque bind.

The competing desires of different regions have hindered efforts to improve the country's ramshackle infrastructure. "Efforts to draw up a master plan for port development have been hampered by the decentralised structure of government and the competing interests of provincial and district governments," the World Trade Organization noted in an April 2013 report.[53]

A lack of administrative capacity in smaller provinces and regions is also a major concern. Many simply lack the human resources they need to make the decisions that have been entrusted to them under decentralisation. This is particularly concerning in relation to natural resources projects, where about 400 district governments have authority to issue permits and have an ongoing oversight obligation. Without the ability to gather quality information on economic prospects, environmental impact and community safety, decision-makers face a difficult task. They are particularly vulnerable, therefore, to lobbying campaigns, be they from companies with a strong financial interest in a project's advancement or from local groups backing an alternative.

For districts and provinces keen to tap into new streams of wealth, the resources industry is a tempting target. While the potential revenue from such projects are clear, the costs involved are often hidden, creating unrealistic expectations among the public and officials about the extent to which benefits can be extracted from big projects. "The understanding of the industry is far from sufficient. There are excessive expectations from society," Marjolijn Wajong, president director of Santos Indonesia, told the *Jakarta Globe*. It takes years for investments by oil and gas firms to start generating real economic benefit, "and sometimes it does not materialise".[54]

That would seem to explain the actions of the regency administration in Tanjung Jabung in Sumatra's Jambi province, which in 2013 sealed 14 oil wells operated by PetroChina. The administration demanded the Chinese company pay a US$5,000 annual licence fee for each well – totalling US$700,000 – as well as boost its corporate social responsibility spending, even though the company held a production sharing contract with the national government that appeared to address those issues. Such disputes are far from unusual.[55]

Local administrations seem particularly vulnerable to corruption in the allocation of permits. Part of the reason is the expense of running for election, which, in the absence of public funding, requires candidates to aggressively seek out donations. That donors are looking for a return on their investment is undoubted. Home Affairs Ministry data shows that 390 regional heads were charged in criminal cases in the first 12 years of regional autonomy.[56] The National Police noted that there was a correlation between the issuance of overlapping mining permits in a given area and the approach of a local election. "We have found a great number of disproportionate permits that were mostly issued on the heels of local polls," National Police Criminal Investigation Directorate chief Comr. Gen. Sutarman told a House of Representatives hearing in December 2012.[57]

Suryo Bambang Sulisto, chairman of the Indonesian Chamber

of Commerce and Industry (Kadin), identifies decentralisation as a
major source of the country's investment headaches, but argues it is a
necessary stage the country's administration must pass through. After
the concentration of so much power in Jakarta during the New Order
period, the sharing of power is essential. "The regions want to have their
voices heard," he said at an interview at his Jakarta office. "They want to
show independence in decision and regulations."[58]

Local administrations have been a source of angst for Hong Kong-
listed miner G-Resources in its Martabe mine in North Sumatra (Chapter
3), where conflicting and competing permit arrangements contributed
to violent confrontation. The company has also faced challenging issues
involving its social licence to operate, with the gaining of trust and
support from some local groups prompting others to raise their fists in
anger and seek to stymie the process.

One possible solution to overcoming dysfunctional provincial and
district resource industry regulators might be to have strong overnight
from a professionally staffed national regulator. But in recent years such
plans have fallen onto disarray.

Performing that role with mixed results had been upstream oil and
gas regulator BP Migas, but in November 2012 its work came a cropper.
A Constitutional Court ruling annulled several aspects of the 2001 Oil
and Gas Law under which it was established, and the organisation was
disbanded. In essence, the court found that putting commercial and
regulatory responsibilities in the hands of BP Migas contravened the
clause in the constitution that declares the state, and not an executive
agency, has responsibility for the nation's natural resources. In its place
a temporary regulator, SK Migas, was established, and this was later
entrenched as a permanent body under the name SKK Migas.

But just as this new regulator was seeking to assert its authority, it
encountered another difficulty. Rudi Rubiandini, the veteran bureaucrat
appointed to lead the regulator, was in mid-2013 arrested and accused
of receiving more than US$1 million in kickbacks from a Singapore

company seeking import contracts from the regulator. With such problems dominating its attention, the regulator was in a weak position to make decisions on contracts, nor to pull errant lower-level government bodies into line. For investors in the oil and gas sector, recent years have been a period of considerable uncertainty.

Even laws under national jurisdiction are significantly impeded by the nation's sprawling geography, where effectively communicating the law and consistently enforcing it is tough. Were the 5,000-kilometre distance from east to west the only barrier, modern communications would overcome the problem. But the issue is broader than that. A wide range of educational backgrounds mean that basic literacy and numeracy cannot be assumed, while the country's cultural diversity means that edicts from Jakarta are often coolly received in other parts of the country.

State-controlled companies

State-owned firms account for 40 percent of Indonesia's gross domestic product,[59] and there are few sectors in the economy in which they do not compete. In the earliest days of colonial administration the state-controlled Dutch East India Company (VOC) was the major driver of economic activity, forcing most cities into monopolistic arrangements for products ranging from Perak tin to Ambonese cloves. The legacy of the VOC, and the developmental approach that put the state front and centre of economic activity, persists today. After taking on the role of developing the fledgling independent nation in the 1950s, state-owned companies have undergone a mission creep of sorts, moving into new areas of the economy in competition with privately owned rivals.

The nation's first president, Sukarno, was a socialist dreamer with big ideas and a need for methods to execute them, so he was sympathetic towards these business-oriented extensions of the state. In discussing this period across the region, historian Norman G. Owen wrote: "The state also came to be an interest group in its own right, growing in response to its own imperatives as well as the perceived needs of the country. The absence or weakness of competing interests had made it possible to erect state enterprises in the first place. As there was no strong indigenous bourgeoisie, Southeast Asian governments did not have to placate the private commercial sector by promises of non-interference, and there was no popular insistence on the sanctity of market forces. Once established in business, the bureaucracy tended to expand."[60]

When Suharto rose to the presidency, despite his avowed anti-socialist political philosophy, state-owned companies remained integral to the economy, though for more pragmatic reasons: they were a powerful means of distributing patronage, as well as delivering projects to placate a sometimes-restless population. One consequence of the Asian Financial Crisis that brought down the strongman was that many of the banks and companies previously owned by either ethnic Chinese entrepreneurs or members of the Suharto family were nationalised to prevent their collapse. As economic historian John Bresnan noted, "these new acquisitions gave Indonesia one of the most highly nationalised economies in the world".[61]

Fifteen years on, there are more than 120 state-owned companies, despite the efforts of several ministers to prune them. Some compete in sectors in which a role for the state is understandable – such as the Indonesia Port Corporation and toll road operator Jasa Marga – but others have a more dubious claim on national development, such as the state-owned steel producer, aircraft manufacturer and rubber plantation manager.

In Suharto's time, each enterprise was overseen by a minister in the relevant portfolio, but one Reformasi era-creation was the Ministry of State Enterprises, which took over responsibility for all of them. That has failed to foster substantial improvements in efficiency. When former media executive Dahlan Iskan was appointed as State Enterprises Minister in 2011 he had grand plans of shutting down loss-making enterprises, merging others and corporatising or even privatising some. The fact that two years into his tenure there were few results to show for his efforts is telling of their entrenched place in Indonesian business and politics.

State-owned enterprises are convenient tools for politicians. Those that make a profit often deliver a dividend to the state, providing a source of revenue to complement the porous taxation system. Many appointments to boards and executive positions are politically motivated, providing a handy way to reward allies and exercise control. Allegations have also surfaced that state companies are used as vehicles to channel funds to political parties, capitalising on partisan appointments and opaque finances. They also give governments a method of advancing projects of dubious financial merit, but great political significance. "As long as the state owns a large portion of the productive forces in the economy, leaders and others in high places will look for ways to tap this state sector for their own purposes," John Bresnan wrote.[62]

Given their exalted status, and as a trade-off for their loss-making nation-building projects, state-owned companies are often at an advantage over their private-sector rivals in dealing with the government. Sometimes this is overt but more often it is underhanded and difficult to identify unequivocally. State companies have a remarkable success rate in bidding for government contracts, for example, and court cases between state companies and their private competitors, whether foreign or locally owned, often seem stacked towards the former.

State-controlled companies have also proven a handy way for the government to increase its leverage in contract negotiations with private companies, using the threat that the state company will take over an asset to extract better terms. In some cases, that threat is acted upon, with private companies being pushed aside from long-standing projects, particularly those involving natural resources, to make way for state companies.

Jakarta's Tanjung Priok port (Chapter 8) has long had far more traffic than it was designed to handle, leading to wait times of more than a week for the clearance of containers, one of the world's longest. The national government in the late 2000s decided to expand its capacity, issuing a tender for companies keen to take on the work of a massive new development. Months later, the tender was abandoned, but not before millions of dollars had been spent by some of the world's leading port operators to prepare their bid. Soon afterwards, the government announced that the initial project had been scrapped and a more moderate expansion would take its place. The contract was granted to the state-controlled Indonesia Port Corporation.

French energy giant Total (Chapter 7) has a long history in Indonesia, including operating the Mahakam oil and gas block in East Kalimantan. With the contract on the project due for renewal in 2017, the company and the government entered discussions on the project's future in 2007. Six years later, however, the discussions were stalled with little sign of progress. State-controlled energy company Pertamina is angling to take over the project, though some observers doubt that it has the capital or the technical know-how to do the job. The consequence has been a high degree of uncertainty for Total and stakeholders dependant on the resource block's output, and a choking back of investment on a project whose future is in doubt.

State of corruption

The extent of the challenges of doing business in Indonesia extend far and wide, but it is the problem of corruption that has proven most pernicious and grabbed most attention. Indonesia has long occupied a lowly rung on Transparency International's Corruption Perceptions Index, lagging its Asian rivals and showing few signs of improvement. Of the major economies that make up the G20, only Russia trails Indonesia on the list.[63]

Keen to root out the corruption that had become a feature of Suharto's time in power, lawmakers in 2002 established a body to lead the fight against graft – the Corruption Eradication Commission (KPK). Its brief was to pursue cases that involve law enforcement or government officials, attract significant public concern, or are thought to have resulted in at least Rp 1 billion ($833,000) in losses to the state.[64] Since then it has embraced its task with zeal, achieving prosecution of government officials at all ranks, up to and including members of the legislature and cabinet. In 2013, the KPK had 560 cases under investigation, charged or arrested 1,271 people, including 62 from legislative bodies, and identified Rp 7.3 trillion ($608 million) in state losses.[65]

In the dedicated Anti-Corruption Court, the KPK has achieved a near-perfect prosecution record and in doing so has built a popular constituency for efforts to attack corruption. When the government denied it a funding increase to expand its building facilities, members of the public donated more than Rp 400 million ($33,000) as part of a "Coins for the KPK" campaign led by activists.[66]

While the KPK has had great success in pursuing individual cases of corruption, it has had less success in instilling systemic change across government agencies to combat it. Drilling down into the Transparency International data gives some indication of corruption's pervasiveness. Each year the integrity organisation compiles a Global Corruption Barometer, in which it looks at the perceived degree of corruption in major institutions in each country.

For Indonesia, it found that police performed the worst, with a 91 percent corruption perception, followed by the parliament on 89 percent, political parties and the judiciary each on 86 percent, and the civil service on 79 percent. This demonstrates a sense that corruption spreads from institutions near the apex of government. It also shows that bodies designed to keep each other healthy are afflicted with the same disease, and that anyone who feels they are a victim of injustice at the hands of one institution can have little confidence that another institution will offer redress.[67]

Howard Dick, the Australian academic specialising in the business environment in Asia, has written about "the state as a market" in contemporary Indonesia. "By this I mean that the Indonesian state has monetised many of its most important internal transactions," he wrote.

"Even in the DPR [House of Representatives] itself, ministers and public servants must bargain with and pay the chairs of committees (komisi) to bring forward and pass legislation, to ask (or not ask) questions, and so on. These funds are distributed by the chairs among the members of their committee for the benefit of their respective parties and their own personal needs.

"Likewise, court judgments are often subject to 'commercial' negotiation instead of being decided on their merits. The same applies to whether matters are investigated and how they are prosecuted, which helps to explain why it is not infrequently the 'whistle blower' who is prosecuted. The system works, after a fashion, but very much to the benefit of insiders with power and money. It is not 'rule of law' as usually understood; 'rule of money' might be a more appropriate term."[68]

Other problems

Many of the largest companies and conglomerates in Indonesia are owned and administered by a small group of cashed-up elites, who are willing to use their assets to advance personal as well as commercial interests. So long as they have plenty of cash available, the companies have found little need to diversify their ownership base and so remain tightly held, sometimes with most shares remaining in the hands of members of a single family. But as they have sought to grow at a rate faster than their finances will allow, some companies have sought to attract outside investors, either through an initial public offering or the private placement of shares.

Such moves have proven difficult for all parties. Rather than being seen as legitimate partners in the business, minority shareholders are sometimes kept on the outer as the original shareholders seek to continue business as usual, including the making of decisions guided by personal rather than commercial considerations. Acquisitions and loans, for example, that have no good commercial justification might proceed because the company feels a sense of obligation to the beneficiaries. (In perhaps the most notorious example, when Bank Central Asia was bailed out by the state in the late 1990s, government auditors found 70 percent of its loans had gone to other companies in the Salim Group that had owned it.[69]) Minority shareholders can do little but watch or impotently whisper frustrations.

The push for greater corporate governance standards that has taken place in other countries has gained limited traction in Indonesia. Independent board members, rights for minority shareholders and shareholder activism are rarities in companies that operate at the behest of a powerful majority owner. "Indonesia still lags behind its neighbours in terms of applying best governance practices within government and the private sector, potentially undermining its future political status and competitive advantage," academics Peter Verhezen and Natalia Soebagjo explained in a 2013 essay.[70]

This difference in expectations on corporate governance came to the fore in recent years in the failed attempt at an alliance between Indonesia's Bakrie Group and British investor Nathaniel Rothschild (Chapter 12). The plan – to roll some of the Bakrie Group's coal assets into a company listed on the London Stock Exchange – fell apart within months as the gulf in business cultures became apparent. As attractive as the Indonesian assets were to Rothschild, the corporate governance concerns were so great that he sought to end the partnership and extricate himself from the financial tie-up. The episode put into the spotlight the question of whether companies used to operating in a cosseted environment like that of Indonesia can achieve the level of transparency and accountability needed to take on shareholders from other parts of the world and list on stock exchanges in developed countries. The evidence is not encouraging.

On paper, Indonesia should be a ideal choice for manufacturers keen to establish a base in Southeast Asia: the country has an abundance of land and cheap labour, two of the key inputs in production. But such benefits are eroded by the abysmal state of the nation's infrastructure, particularly with regard to transportation and logistics. A dilapidated road network means getting goods to sea from a plant can be slow and unreliable, and the nation's ports are often antiquated and overwhelmed by the volume of throughput they are expected to handle.

"The level and quality of infrastructure spending remains a key determinant of long-term trade and growth performance," the World Bank explained in a quarterly report in October 2013.[71] In that regard, the numbers are damning: in the 2013 budget, 25 percent of expenditure was committed to fuel subsidies, while just 16 percent was dedicated to capital expenditure, including infrastucture.[72]

To some extent, the underinvestment in infrastructure is not surprising given the long time horizons until projects prove beneficial and the impatience of people and politicians in a young democracy. This is all the more than case when natural resources have helped fill government coffers with money that was rather politically painless to extract. Paul Collier, a former senior researcher at the World Bank, has noted this as a theme in many parts of the world. "Resource-rich democracies not only underinvest but invest badly, with too many white elephant projects," he wrote in his development treatise *The Bottom Billion*.[73]

One of the reasons for the poor state of infrastructure is the difficulty in gaining access to privately owned land for construction. This state of affairs was in part an effort to avoid some of the excesses of the New Order era, when the government would force poor people off their land with minimal compensation in order to build big projects like dams and highways. The Reformasi response was to entrench property rights in law to the point that the government essentially gave up the right to compulsory acquisition of land. This approach, however, made new infrastructure far more difficult and time-consuming to construct. The effort to strike a new balance on the issue came in the form of 2011 legislation that gave the state the right to claim land, but set in place strict rules about the circumstances in which it could be invoked and the compensation owed to those who gave up their land. The dust is yet to settle on the new law and its effectiveness.

To develop infrastructure, one approach in vogue in Indonesia has been public-private partnerships, in which the financing and delivery burden is shared between the government and private investors. Given the government's balance sheet is already strained, there's a compelling logic to seeking private finance. But the administration of PPP projects has been lacklustre. Economics advisor Farid Harianto has identified a string a failures: toll road concessions running into difficulty, foreign water utility providers in Jakarta walking away after consumer price hikes stated in the contract were ignored, and two oil refinery projects in Java being aborted by the government amid questionable economic analysis. "Our track record in this area is disappointing, so we need a change in mindset," Harianto wrote in the *Jakarta Globe*.[74]

Another solution has been proposed by the Indonesian Chamber of Commerce and Industry (Kadin): an infrastructure development bank operated by the government and pooling local and international funds to offer cheap, long-term finance for big projects. So far, at least, the idea has failed to take hold among legislators and ministers.

One of Indonesia's selling points to international investors has been cheap labour, brought about by a large population and low cost of living. But cheap labour is of little benefit to a manufacturer if the end product is difficult to get to buyers in an economical and reliable way. Many companies have opted to develop their own infrastructure, particularly electricity generation, to overcome the problem, but such a move is difficult and costly and only viable for large operations.

It should come as no surprise, therefore, that companies are looking elsewhere in Southeast Asia, including places with higher labour costs, to establish manufacturing bases. Most stark are the cases of companies that have found it cheaper to manufacture outside Indonesia and then transport goods to end-users in Indonesia than to manufacture in one part of the country and transport it to another. The World Trade Organization estimated shipping costs in Indonesia at between 50 percent and 80 percent higher than elsewhere in Southeast Asia.[75]

Some economists have raised fears that Indonesia's notional economic growth is in fact a bubble, with the large waves of easy credit washing through the economy creating artificial demand. Economics writer Jesse Colombo mapped out the extent of the bubble in a jarring article for *Forbes*. Consumer credit (excluding mortgages) nearly tripled in the six years to 2013, while the number of credit cards has surged 60 percent, he pointed out. The credit surge has underpinned rapid growth in retail spending, which has risen by more than 10 percent annually in recent years, and helped drive up Jakarta condominium prices by more than 50 percent in the four years to late 2012. All that happened as the benchmark interest rate set by Bank Indonesia followed global trends, dipping from 12.75 percent in April 2006 to 5.75 percent in February 2012.

Already Bank Indonesia has taken some measures to deflate the bubble – minimum down payments on automotive and second home purchases have been sharply increased, and interest rates are again heading northwards. But if that easy credit dries up too quickly, Indonesia could be in for a nasty shock. "Record low interest rates have fueled an epic credit and consumption boom in Indonesia, which is no small matter given the fact that domestic consumer spending accounts for nearly 60 percent" of the country's economy, Colombo wrote.[76]

Changed with helping foreign investors navigate their way through government decision-making is the Investment Coordinating Board (BKPM). Reports on its performance vary, with some investors encountering a sympathetic ear and others finding the body unwilling to stand up to other government bodies impeding investment. Tamba Hutapea, BKPM's deputy chairman for investment planning, explained that the body is seeking to encourage officials at all levels of government to embrace high standards and procedures in a bid to attract investment. "We admit that some local government do not fully follow all good governance practices," he said in an interview in his Jakarta office, adding that some foreign investors seek to cut corners as well.[77]

One major policy administered by the BKPM is the negative investment list – a list of industries that are reserved for local companies. Notionally the list is designed to support local companies in strategically significant sectors, and includes agriculture, forestry and fisheries, energy-related activities, communications, financial services and health services. But the inclusion of sectors such as advertising casts doubt as to its genuine purpose and fuels suspicions it is a tool to enforce unwarranted protectionism. Hutapea noted that lobbying for the inclusion of items on the list is common, including by existing foreign investors keen to block access from new foreign rivals, knowing the list does not apply to existing investments.

The collection of problems identified here means that intrinsically, the state lacks credibility. People and investors have little faith that the government decision-making process will be fair, and so do all they can to avoid it. Appeals to the collective interest carry little weight in the face of particular winners and losers willing to press their case forcefully. Regulations are created by ministers and legislation passed by the parliament without subsequent follow-up, leaving those people affected reluctant to act until they are convinced that the shift will materialise. Government struggles to gain "traction" in implementing its reforms and must go to considerable lengths to demonstrate that it is committed to their introduction.

Given these myriad structural barriers to success, it's little wonder that many foreign companies have encountered difficulties. Studying their experiences in detail reveals just how these challenges manifest themselves in practice.

3

A Riot at the Gates

The damage toll was significant: two burnt cars, one of them a police vehicle; a local government office left a charred wreck; several people, including a police officer, taken to hospital for medical care. Police and military officers with machine guns and knives were trying to keep the peace. Thankfully there were no fatalities. The protest against the construction of a pipeline to remove wastewater from a North Sumatra mine site followed several months of simmering anger in late 2012 and threatened to leave work on the mine suspended for a prolonged period. For the mine's developer, Hong Kong-based G-Resources, the stakes were high.

G-Resources had taken a textbook approach to getting its mine up and running. Its executive ranks were filled with old hands in developing-world mining operations, as well as some savvy and well-connected locals, and the company had developed good relations with governments at all levels, including offering up equity stakes to those close to the mine site. It had miscalculated, however, in assuming that those levels of government genuinely stood for the people they claimed to represent.

Appealing prospect
Martabe was the sort of asset that had miners licking their lips. The site, nestled in the steeply sloping jungle terrain of North Sumatra's Batang

Toru area, contained about 8 million ounces of gold and 80 million ounces of silver, most of it packed into a dense 30 square kilometres. The bounty was remarkably easy to get to, with the gold sitting close to the surface, allowing for easy – and cheap – extraction through open-pit mining. The "strip ratio" – a measure of the ease of accessing a resource that shows the units of waste material for each unit of ore – stood at 1.3:1, one of the lowest in the world. The grade of the ore, which indicates its concentration, was also high, with gold averaging 2.1 grams per metric ton.[78]

For miners weighing up their options, Martabe had some other selling points. The site had much of the infrastructure needed to extract and move the resources nearby: it was adjacent to the Trans-Sumatra highway and could access airport and port facilities at the town of Sibolga, about 40 kilometres away. Utility services were also within reach: on-site streams could be tapped for water, while a 230-megawatt coal-fired power station operating just eight kilometres from the site gave confidence that power could be reliably accessed.[79]

All this makes it surprising that it took so long for the deposit to be found and exploited. Despite intensive copper and gold exploration efforts across Indonesia in the 1980s and 1990s, it was only in 1997 that the deposit was found at the site, close to the Trans-Sumatra highway. Normandy Anglo Asian Indonesia, an offshoot of an Australian miner, inked a 30-year contract of work over the site in 1997, giving it clear title and leaving it with the right to extract resources.

But work on the site was slow to start. Control of the undeveloped mining concession passed through so many pairs of hands that it was the resources equivalent of a tattered 2,000-rupiah note, reflecting the broader consolidation that was taking place in the global mining industry. US company Newmont Mining took over Martabe through its takeover of Normandy, but its interests in Indonesia were focused elsewhere so it sat on the asset for some time before selling it to Australian miner Agincourt Resources in 2006. Before Agincourt advanced the project far the company was taken over by fellow Australian miner Oxiana, which then merged with Zinifex to form OZ Minerals.

But as the Global Financial Crisis parched the reservoir of easy borrowings, OZ Minerals found itself desperate for cash, and sold Martabe to G-Resources Group in mid-2009 for US$220 million. In getting its hands on Martabe, G-Resources, backed in the transaction by investment firms Mount Kellett Capital and BlackRock, edged out Aneka Tambang, the Indonesian state-owned miner keen to diversify beyond its core specialty of nickel.

Along the way plans were afoot to establish the Martabe mine but they never materialised. Signs of local resistance emerged in 2006. That year, North Sumatra's then-governor Rudolf Pardede paid a visit to the Agincourt Resources headquarters in Perth to plead the case for the project to go ahead, but respected green activist group Indonesian Forum for Environment (Walhi) raised objections. The group's Medan executive director Job Rachmat Purba said at the time there was local opposition to the project because mining in the area would involve deforestation in what was supposed to be a protected area. "Whatever the results of the visit by the governor to Australia, we will be determined to oppose any operation of a mining company in the national park," Purba warned.[80] Whatever the reason, Agincourt did not push ahead with the project at the time, and a pledge two years later by Oxiana to spend US$310 million on the mine never materialised either.

(A quick aside. The name Martabe is a clever Indonesian pun of sorts. Officially it is said to be a portmanteau of "marsipature hutana be", a phrase in the local Batak language meaning "Let's build our homeland". But to many North Sumatrans, the name evokes "Martebe", a short form in Indonesian for "markisa-terong belanda", a juice combining passion fruit and tamarillo that is a popular local pick-me-up.)

Preparing the ground

Come 2009, Martabe rested with G-Resources, a Hong Kong-based company that hoped to parlay success in North Sumatra into a plan to get hold of a pan-Asian array of lucrative gold mines stretching from Papua New Guinea to Mongolia. The North Sumatra mine, therefore, was essentially a bet-the-company play in which nothing short of a functioning mine would give the company the momentum it needed to take on other projects. That undivided attention, along with a rising global gold price as investors stepped away from riskier investments, meant that Martabe was finally making progress. Taking on senior roles in G-Resources were some of the veterans of Oxiana who had seen the possibilities of the Martabe site several years earlier but lacked the finances to pursue it at the time.

Oxiana founder Owen Hegarty, a veteran of the Australian mining industry, came out of semi-retirement to become an executive director of G-Resources. Hegarty was something of a heroic maverick in the industry, learning the trade for more than two decades at established mining house Rio Tinto before using his nous and contacts to start Oxiana. Under Hegarty's direction, the small exploration company, dubbed by its backers "The Mighty Ox", accumulated some serious capital and bought up a string of precious metals mining assets in Australia and Asia that were off the radar for the major players but were just right for an emerging star.

Peter Albert, Hegarty's former Asia lieutenant at Oxiana who stuck around for a little while after the company was rolled into OZ Minerals, came on board as the G-Resources chief executive. Albert, a metallurgist by training with an MBA in his back pocket, brought to the table more than 30 years of experience in project and operations management in mining and minerals processing in Australia, Africa and Asia.

Within months of grabbing hold of Martabe, G-Resources swung into action to develop it. The company sketched out a plan in which it would achieve annual production of 250,000 ounces of gold and between 2 million and 3 million ounces of silver for at least 10 years. The company opted for a mining process known as carbon-in-leach, in which the gold ore is dissolved with cyanide and absorbed by granules of carbon. For the time being, G-Resources aimed to invest US$900 million to develop the project.

To help get it there, the company raised US$600 million through a new share placement, appointed global engineering firm Ausenco Services as the main contractor and inked a nine-year electricity deal with state-owned power company Perusahaan Listrik Negara. Continued exploration activity reinforced the company's bullish attitude towards Martabe's bounty: in July 2010 the company announced that 62 out of 84 drill holes at the site returned significant gold intersections. Three months later, the company signed a refining contract for Martabe's silver and gold with Aneka Tambang, the state-controlled miner it beat to the punch in acquiring the mine.

An agreement on royalty payments was also reached, under which the national government received 20 percent and the remaining 80 percent was split between the North Sumatra provincial government, the South Tapanuli regency government that hosts the mine, and other nearby regency administrations.

In line with the terms of the Contract of Work struck several years earlier, G-Resources transferred a 5 percent share in the Martabe project to the governments of North Sumatra province (1.5 percent) and South Tapanuli regency (3.5 percent) in July 2012, to be funded through future dividend payments. At a more local level, the company established a community consultation committee comprising representatives of 11 local villages directly affected by the project.

It also embarked on a corporate social responsibility program, putting funds towards basic education, job skills, local infrastructure and emergency relief in the event of natural disasters. Initiatives like a reading garden for children and an infant nutrition program, in which mine staff played a hands-on role, were used to demonstrate the miner's commitment to the area. A database of local resident seeking employment opportunities and training was developed, which the miner and its contractors would draw upon.

As the mine moved closer to reality, enthusiasm was growing among local officials. In early 2012, with some 860 local people employed by the miner, Syahrul M. Pasaribu, the South Tapanuli regency leader known as a bupati, said the massive spending by the company over the preceding three years had benefited the local economy. "I have seen it myself. Women in our villages can now operate those big mining trucks," Pasaribu told the *Jakarta Globe*.[81]

Several mining projects in Indonesia had recently faced local resistance that often manifested itself in violent protest. Two people died when villagers and students rioted in Bima on Sumbawa Island in early 2012, prompting the government to curtail an exploration permit for Arc Exploration, a small Australian company. And just 75 kilometres south of Martabe, hundreds of protesters had razed buildings at a project run by Sihayo Gold, another Australian company. The theme uniting these disparate stories was a sense among some local people that others were getting rich off the resources right under their feet while they were missing out on a fair share.[82]

Bump in the road

As mines go, Martabe was a reasonably straight-forward operation, but there were still plenty of facilities needed to keep things moving. As well as the mine itself, Martabe had a conventional processing plant with 4.5-million-metric-tons-per-annum capacity, accommodation facilities for mine workers, haulage roads, a high-voltage switch yard, an onsite workshop and warehouse, and a tailings storage facility with associated water catchment and diversion systems. Scale and the easy access to the resources meant Martabe would be one of the cheapest mines to establish and operate. G-Resources estimated that the "life of mine" costs were less than those for at least three-quarters of gold mines around the globe.[83]

In July 2012, Martabe's first commercial gold production took place, at the Pernama pit. Indonesia's biggest mining investment in more than a decade was six months behind schedule, but given the history of false starts at the mine, the tardiness was not significant.

The water required by the mine and the heavy downpours of the wet season meant the mine operator needed to find a way to discharge excess water from the site. To achieve that, a 2.7-kilometre pipe would run one metre underground through a plantation from the plant to a discharge point on the nearby Batang Toru River. The Batang Toru is significant to the livelihoods of people living in the area, providing a place to bathe and wash clothes, as well as fish, cook and water crops. Any threat to its safety is a threat to the community itself.[84]

The company and regulators, therefore, were at pains to ensure the discharge of the water was safe. In early July, the company launched an information campaign to inform local residents that construction on the water pipe would start within months.

The water from the pipeline, G-Resources said, was clean and no hazard to health because it was passing through a water treatment facility on the mine site. The pipe was consistent with the formal environmental impact analysis, known as an AMDAL, issued by the regency government in 2008. It also met Indonesian environmental laws and regulations. Reducing the impact was the fact the Batang Toru is a big body of water, and its natural rate of flow would dwarf that coming from the pipe. According to company data, the flow of water from the pipe would typically stand at 0.1 to 0.2 cubic metres per second, peaking at 0.83 cubic metres per second. The river itself, however, flows at 50 cubic metres per second in the dry season, and at a torrent ranging from 200 to 700 cubic metres per second when the rains come.[85]

But in the realpolitik of community concern over a major project, those assurances counted for little. As construction on the pipeline was about half complete, trouble struck. Local residents gathered to make their displeasure felt. Demonstrators argued that the company should discharge the water directly into the sea rather than into the Batang Toru River.

One great development of the Reformasi era is that ordinary people have found their voice, and are willing to take to the streets to defend their rights. The student-led protests that brought down Suharto in 1998 made clear the power of mass action in the face of a seemingly powerful foe. As sociologist Yatun Sastramidjaja noted in the mid-2000s, "through the past six to seven years of so of continuous, intense political action, the student movement has gained more political experience and expertise than it could ever accumulate before, and also it has grown more mature in terms of organisation, strategy, ideology and public relations than it probably has ever been."[86] But this embrace of protest politics has also created a class of opportunists who seek to create the impression of mass opposition when none exists. Add to this a large pool of poor people willing to don T-shirts, wield placards and chant slogans for Rp 50,000 (US$4), and the environment is ripe for synthetic dissent to supplant the grassroots variety.

On September 9, soon after the protests started, the company halted the installation of the pipe and met with local residents in an effort to quell objections. "There is misinformation being spread, relating to poisoning of waters and other issues relating to the river," G-Resources chief executive Peter Albert later told *Reuters*.[87] The response of one resident of the embankment along the river, Arifin Siregar, showed the extent to which fear and misinformation about the water pipe had spread. "We worry about possible pollution from the company's waste. We are afraid that if the river becomes polluted, we would no longer be able to use its water anymore," he told the *Jakarta Post*.[88]

G-Resources knew it had a battle on its hands to win hearts and minds locally: formal permits and backing from government officials had not been matched with grassroots community support, it became apparent.

The company also had to reassure nervous investors that it could push through difficult times and would not become another developing-world corporate mining casualty.

On September 20 the company informed the stock market of its troubles, attributing them to "community concerns and misunderstandings", but then added a warning: if construction of the water pipe did not resume by the end of the month, "the company will need to take further action to suspend fully the mine and plant".[89]

Digging in

The national government, realising the potential broader implications of a big mining operation being disrupted by a gaggle of protesters, got involved. The Energy and Mineral Resources Ministry dispatched a team to the area to help the company convince local people on the merits of the mine. "They [the local community] feel that they did not get anything beneficial from it [the gold mine] and thus they reject the plan from the company. Therefore, the company must improve its approach to the community," Energy and Mineral Resources Minister Jero Wacik told reporters.[90] The provincial government also recognised the dangers of the issue remaining unresolved. "I fear that many foreign investors would be afraid to invest in North Sumatra if PT Agincourt Resources [the G-Resources subsidiary operating the mine] ceases operations. This is a serious challenge for the investment climate in North Sumatra," provincial mining office head Untungta Kaban told the *Jakarta Post*.[91]

Despite these sentiments, little progress was made in negotiations by the end of the month. A few days later, G-Resources put out a statement conceding that it had been unable to reach a satisfactory resolution and so was following through on its threat: it would be begin cutting back on all operations, activities and programs. Company chief executive Peter Albert fronted a media briefing in Medan, the North Sumatra capital, to explain the decision. "After we officially ceased our operations ... we had practically no income to pay our employees or fund our operations," he said.[92]

With protest organisers able to muster considerable opposition, the company knew it needed to encourage some grassroots advocates of its own. With G-Resources a major employer in the area, its several thousand staff, most of them locals, were the perfect candidates. Even if the economic imperative was the company's primary driver, the decision to stand down staff also strengthened its negotiating hand and made clear to employees and contractors the extent to which their welfare was entwined with that of the gold and silver mine.

It was not the first time such a tactic had been used, and the national government was wise to it. Minister Jero Wacik warned that mining companies that sacked workers to slash costs without liaising with the government would face "tough measures", noting that mining companies sometimes sought to publicly exploit layoffs as a means of lobbying the government and gaining public support when they faced troubles. "We have our own ways to take tough measures if mining firms suddenly fire their workers without consulting us first, but I cannot tell you what ways," he told the *Jakarta Post* cryptically. For its part, G-Resources said it had informed all levels of government of the standing down of workers in advance.[93]

As public interest in the dispute intensified, the company mapped out its case. While it was conscious that it had to stand its ground on the overtly stated concerns of demonstrators (the water pipe complied with environmental regulations and "the excess clean water will not harm anybody or any thing", the company said), it was keen to make clear the broader economic implications of a prolonged stoppage. The mine directly employed about 2,000 people, it said. Nearly US$900 million had been spent on investment, capital expenditure and working capital so far, with ongoing operating, capital and exploration expenditure estimated at more than US$200 million per year. Export revenue from Martabe's gold and silver at current prices would reach more than US$500 million a year.[94]

The company undertook a charm offensive, seeking to win over locals while also assuaging the concerns of uppity investors.

"It's really only a question of time, we're talking days. We are fully permitted. It is not as if we're waiting for a piece of paper from anybody," executive director Owen Hegarty told *Bloomberg* in an interview in early October. "People came to the front gate and were sort of querulous about what's going on. What we couldn't do was to keep going against that. That's not a good start to things at the early stages of operation. Our focus is on getting Martabe right."[95]

His chief executive took a more bullish approach. "Inevitably this will put gold miners off. Investors are going to look at this and ask if this is the right environment, that's a fact," Peter Albert thundered in an interview with *Reuters*.[96]

The impact of the stoppage started to hit local businesses, who had come to rely on the Martabe mine and its contractors as a major source of revenue. A local garage operator complained he was no longer getting vehicles from the mine to repair, and a labour hire company experienced a sudden slackening in demand.[97]

A week after they were stood-down, 300 mine workers took to the streets to call for the pipeline dispute to be resolved and the mine to resume operations. Keen to avoid a clash with their neighbours, the miners instead directed their anger at the national government, which they said should have done more to settle the dispute. By this stage, October 10, about 900 of the company's 2,700 workers had been stood down, according to company figures, and workers feared the painful impact of the dispute dragging on. "The government has to act as quickly as possible to save the ailing mining company, on which many workers rely," Martabe workers union secretary Puja Kesuma said. The focus on the national government to help broker a compromise was shared by the North Sumatra government, with Untungta Kaban, the provincial mining chief, saying, "We're waiting for the central government's decision."[98]

Breakthrough

Nearly two months after the protests started, the company's discussions with the demonstrators yielded a result. The company struck a deal that was symbolically significant but had little material impact beyond its existing commitments. The company agreed to guarantee that water channelled to the river met the standards set in a 2004 Environment Ministry decree, build clean water facilities for residents, extend the geographic scope of its corporate social responsibility program and prioritise the employment of local people.[99]

On October 30, a relieved G-Resources informed the stock market that construction of the water pipe had recommenced, and ore was once again flowing through the processing plant. All up an estimated 2,700 workers had been stood down during the stoppage, and 1,200 workers were swiftly reinstated with the others expected to follow soon.

But for some protesters, the issue wasn't over just yet. A day after the deal was struck, thousands of people joined a protest against security officers involved in the installation of the pipeline. "The people are disappointed that the local government was siding with the company," Ali Sumurung, a legal representative for Batang Toru residents, told national news outlet Merdeka. Vandalised in the protest were a pair of district administrative offices, a police station and cars belonging to the local government. Several people – demonstrators and police officers – were injured in the scuffles.[100] "We cannot work today because our office is badly damaged. The mob smashed the windows and burned the office's facilities," Hotma Harahap, the Batang Toru district head, told *Tribun News*.[101]

Local officials, concerned the violence could escalate, called in backups from the police and military to restore order. Security was also intensified around the mine site, with soldiers and police at the ready with machine guns and knives, although the restoration of activity was able to continue unabated.

There were some suspicions that this latest wave of protests was not just a spontaneous uprising from local people concerned about their welfare. Senior Comr. Heru Prakoso, a spokesman for the North Sumatra police, was quoted afterwards as saying that the arrival of residents from far away, and the fact police offices were damaged, indicated the action was premeditated. But with the deal struck, the protests soon dissipated, and work on the pipeline was able to continue.

Lessons learned

The debate over the safety of the pipeline was a stark example of the gulf between reality and the perceptions of that reality. In reality, the pipeline was of exactingly high standards, complying with government environmental requirements. But communicating that level of safety, and overcoming anxieties, was a great challenge. With good reason, many Indonesian people are deeply sceptical of the claims made by the government and private companies. Such is the history of charlatanism and deception that the words of officials carry little weight, and people are inclined to trust their own intuition over the advice of experts. Allaying these concerns requires more than just the words of officialdom.

A few weeks after the pipeline was completed, G-Resources held a public event to celebrate. At it, senior company officials were joined by representatives of provincial and local governments. All filled bottles with water from the river in which the pipe was depositing its load – and took a gulp. All the formal documents and official reports counted for little compared to the sight of senior people filling their mouths when it came to persuading people of the safety of the flowing water. "There's no need to worry because the water has been processed at the lab before being dumped in the river," exclaimed South Tapanuli deputy bupati Aldinz Rapolo Siregar.[103]

Independent safety tests were commissioned and two months later, the results came back. At another ceremony, the results of the tests confirmed that the water met the legal requirements for acidity, arsenic, cadmium, chromium, copper, cyanide, lead, mercury, nickel and zinc. "For us in Martabe, today becomes an important milestone to demonstrate and reaffirm our commitment as a transparent and credible foreign investor in conducting our business in Indonesia," Peter Albert told the assembled dignitaries.[104]

Of course, efforts like these to demonstrate the safety of the mine will only be effective in warding off future protests if the cause for the unrest is genuine. Theories abounded that dark forces were at work in instigating the protests, with the finger pointed at community leaders seeking to extort easy benefits from mining companies beyond those already on offer through royalties and social responsibility programs.

Arif Siregar, the former Indonesian Mining Association chief taken on by G-Resources as an advisor, pointed out that the local community had known for some time the pipe was coming but had not previously expressed dissatisfaction. "Those who are against the pipe installation are outside parties [upset over] the unequal division of funds," Siregar told the *Jakarta Post*, adding that government and security personnel had declined to get tough on trouble-makers.[105]

Speaking more broadly about local unrest against big resources projects, industry veteran John Towner said the protests amounted to an attempt at extortion. "In reality, these people are paid by someone to cause a disturbance," he told the *Sydney Morning Herald*. "I've been there longer than most, I've seen it all ... someone thinks we're making an absolute fortune and they think they can come in and take it over until it runs out."[106]

Many people felt that they were missing out on the benefits of the mine. The fear was not just that the profits from the mine would flow overseas; it was also that even within North Sumatra the pool of beneficiaries would only be small. Many people felt that the local government did not represent them, but instead only represented itself and an elite group of allies. Persuading local people of the merits of the project, therefore, required G-Resources to reach beyond official government channels, and instead undertake a project of mass engagement.

That explanation was endorsed by senior energy regulator Rudi Rubiandini in his analysis of the Martabe dispute. "I think it resulted from the euphoria of regional autonomy," he told *Globe Asia* in a November 2012 profile. "The regional officials forget that they need approval from the people as well. Don't worry, the regents [bupatis] have already been told to sort the problem out. But on the flip side, foreign investors are also required to understand the local culture." He added that the mining permit, known as an *izin usaha pertambangan*, was issued by the bupati before local people were briefed about the mine, a requirement for the issuance of an IUP.[107]

Later, antigraft czar Abraham Samad noted that half of all mining companies operating in Indonesia do not pay royalties or taxes, leaving local administrations unable – or unwilling – to provide basic services to their citizens. "It's ironic. When I visited areas with many mining companies, the further I went into the rural areas, the poorer the people. However, when I visited the homes of local district heads, they had luxurious cars parked in their garages," the chairman of the Corruption Eradication Commission noted in May 2013.[108]

It's a theme picked up by Bill Sullivan, the Australian lawyer with more than a decade of experience advising foreign mining companies in Indonesia. He says the payment of obligatory royalties and benefits is not enough to keep local communities on side.

"Why doesn't that translate into benefits for the local community? Because of the huge leakage of funds at all levels of government," Sullivan said in an interview. "I have no difficulty accepting that the central government does rebate to the provinces and regencies the required percentage of royalties collected. But merely because a particular regency receives X dollars in terms of royalty payments, that doesn't mean that X dollars is actually going to be spent on local community projects."[109]

Regardless of whether the principled or the pragmatic explanation for the protest is accepted, the lesson for G-Resources was a similar one. Engagement needs to happen with communities directly rather than through intermediaries, including the government.

In recent decades corporate governance experts have emphasised the principle of a social licence to operate, especially for companies in extractive industries. A major project must go beyond fulfilling the legal requirements, the theory goes, and must also ensure its social acceptance in the community in which it takes place in order to achieve legitimacy. Gaining that social licence involves a company demonstrating that it is willing to be a part of the community and not seek to operate separately from it. To that end, it needs to employ local people, undertake corporate social responsibility programs and take a restorative approach to its impact on the environment. There are less tangible approaches to gaining a social licence, too: having a local representative who is open and willing to advocate for the project with conviction can go a long way towards bridging the divide between locals and an outside entity.

During the New Order era of President Suharto, the state had little shame in silencing activists through intimidation, even accusing demonstrators of being communists and arresting their leaders. But today such an approach would thankfully fail, with a suite of environmental organisations, academics and media outlets shining a spotlight on abuses of power and attempts to stifle debate about mining projects and other forms of economic development. Long-term and consistent public advocacy, rather than secretive deals with powerful figures behind the scenes, is how social acceptance is achieved in contemporary Indonesia.

A year on from the demonstrations that paralysed it, the Martabe mine is progressing at a rapid pace. In August 2013, the company bumped up its Martabe gold output target for the year by 12 percent to 280,000 ounces, citing improved mining operations. Claims of low operating costs were being proven correct – the company's costs amounted to US$596 per ounce, compared to an industry average of US$750 per ounce.[110]

A more systemic approach has been put in place to check on the safety of the discharged water and maintain public confidence. In October 2013, the North Sumatra provincial government formed a 51-person monitoring team made up of environmentalists, academics and governmental officials to take river water samples to a laboratory for examination. Among those volunteers on the team are people who were part of the protests against the pipe a year earlier, like Parsaulian Lubis, the Wek Ampat village head. "We are tired of staging protests because on many occasions we had to deal with the police. Now, I am a member of the team that monitors the water in the Batang Toru. This is a more effective strategy [for protecting the river]," he told the *Jakarta Post*.[111]

Local officials are keen to emphasise that North Sumatra is open for business, but the experience of Martabe has served as a reminder that the economic growth brought about by big mining projects is not enough on its own to foster social acceptance. "We urge the mining companies to not only seek profits, but to also have a commitment to empower the community and carry out sustainable development programs in the regency," South Tapanuli regency secretary Aswin Effendi told a public forum.[112]

It's a message mining companies that want to avoid operating in a fortress would be wise to heed.

4

Time to Pack Your Bags

As the first anniversary of his appointment as the Indonesian head of US oil giant ExxonMobil approached, Richard Owen's staff lodged the paperwork with the Ministry of Energy and Mineral Resources to renew his tenure in the role. It's standard practice in Indonesia, and while the wheels of bureaucracy inevitably turn slowly, the process usually proceeds without a hitch. But not this time.

In the dying days of 2012, Owen learned that his work permit renewal had been denied, an act unprecedented for the head of a major oil and gas company in Indonesia. He would not be allowed to continue in the role, and within weeks would need to leave the country. ExxonMobil had operated for decades for Indonesia and had grappled with its share of tough encounters with the government. But the denial of the permit escalated tensions, and was a sign the government was willing to use whatever means were at its disposal to wield influence over foreign companies operating in its midst.

While the denial of the visa itself was a shock, what followed offered great insight into the way decisions are made at the top levels of government. Rather than communicate the reasoning directly to the company and offer a more anodyne and face-saving explanation in public, government officials spelt out in a fair degree of detail just why the permit had been denied. Those official explanations, coupled with a few well-sourced news reports on what was going on behind closed doors, shows how companies can pay a big price for failing to deliver outcomes that are favourable to the government.

Decades of activity

ExxonMobil dates its presence in Indonesia to 1898, when its forerunner opened its first marketing office in the country, but the 1968 commencement of its contract in Aceh marks the start of its status as a significant player in the country's oil and gas business. Three years later it came across large reserves of gas in Aceh's Arun and over the subsequent decades expanded across the breadth of the archipelago, sniffing out resources in the East Natuna field in the Riau Islands, Cepu block in East and Central Java, several sites in the Makassar Strait to the west of Sulawesi, and Cendrawasih in Papua. Come 2012, the company employed about 850 people in Indonesia, about 90 percent of them locals, and its total in-country spending had reached US$19 billion.

The company had traditionally appointed someone with international experience to run the Indonesian operation. Australian Richard Owen was given the nod to take up the role in January 2012, succeeding Terry McPhail. Owen, a chemical engineer by training, had spent nearly three decades across the company, most recently as managing director of the company's production operations in Germany.

News that Jero Wacik, the Energy and Mineral Resources Minister, had declined to renew Owen's work permit emerged in the first days of 2013. The minister's deputy, Rudi Rubiandini, was blunt in his public assessment of the executive: "His performance was not in the best interest of the nation. So he should be replaced."[113]

Hadi Prasetyo, a spokesman for interim upstream oil and gas regulatory task force SK Migas, an agency under the control of the minister, said Owen's application had been denied because he was "uncooperative" and "inconsistent". Prasetyo later said the decision was an example of the government reasserting its sovereignty over oil and gas after the recent court ruling that invalidated the previous regulator, BP Migas, for being too distant from the government. "The regulation regarding working tenure has been widely understood by oil companies for a very long time," he told the *Jakarta Globe*.[114]

The decision appeared to catch the company unawares. "We have always been engaged in dialogues with the government in relation to this issue and thus we are taken by surprise," ExxonMobil Indonesia spokesman Erwin Maryoto said when news emerged of the work permit rejection.[115]

Over the days that followed, more details emerged on the reasoning for the decision. In essence, the work permit was denied as a form of punishment for the company's actions with regard to two of its Indonesian projects: the slower-than-expected development of the Cepu oil and gas project in East and Central Java, and the halting of efforts to sell the company's Sumatra assets to local interests.

A closer examination of the circumstances of these two cases reveals much about the willingness of the government to lay blame for the problems of local government intransigence at the foot of companies (in the case of Cepu) and protect politically connected local companies (in the case of the Sumatra assets).

Challenges in Cepu

The first strand of the government's explanation was that the company had been too slow in developing the Banyu Urip oil field that sits in the heart of Cepu, straddling the border of Central and East Java. The government has long had high hopes for the field, which is estimated to hold a massive 450 million barrels of oil, in helping the country return above the threshold of one million barrels per day of oil production it slipped below in 2007. But Banyu Urip's development has been chaotic and delayed by conflict between the developer and the local district administration. T

ExxonMobil first started exploring for oil and gas in Cepu in 1999. Two years later it found Banyu Urip, whose hefty bounty made it the largest untapped oil reserve in the country. While the company went on to find another oil reserve and four other gas fields in Cepu, Banyu Urip remained the jewel in the crown. In 2005, the company agreed to partner up with state-owned oil and gas company Pertamina to develop the project, with each of them taking a 45 percent share, and a company owned by the administration of the local district, Bojonegoro, taking the remaining 10 percent. ExxonMobil took the role of lead operator.

The planned scale of the US$1.3 billion Banyu Urip field was enormous: it involved the construction of 49 oil wells, a 95-kilometre pipe to deliver the oil to depots, a floating storage facility and an off-loading facility with capacity for 1.7 million barrels. At its peak, the field would be capable of producing 165,000 barrels of oil per day. The company indicated that such a level of production was achievable by 2012 if work were to commence in 2008. But progress was anything but smooth.

Under the decentralisation policy introduced early in the Reformasi period, district administrations have considerable power to grant – and deny – permits for big resources projects. Early in Banyu Urip's development, the perception emerged in Bojonegoro that locals were missing out on the benefits of the project; the job opportunities are going to outsiders, went the argument expressed at a 2008 protest, and the project was putting local agriculture at risk.

Given this sentiment, the Bojonegoro administration decided to use the leverage it had available to it. The district chose to push a hard bargain for the permits needed for construction and demanded that the company invest in local facilities and accommodation for employees, using a new regulation it had introduced to strengthen its claim. The company had already previously committed some of its corporate social responsibility budget towards several public health clinics and a program to pump water from the Bengawan Solo river to help irrigate farmland, but the district administration was seeking much more. It had plenty of patience and saw little urgency in developing the project.[116]

Another major barrier to progress at Banyu Urip was the difficulty of land acquisition. After the capricious approach of the Suharto government to claiming privately owned land for big projects, Reformasi Indonesia had taken an approach that valued property rights highly, making it almost impossible for the state to forcefully acquire land. For the Banyu Urip developer, it was therefore tricky to get the land needed for pipelines transporting oil to the refinery and off-shore storage facility. Speculators had grabbed hold of great tracts of land around Banyu Urip and were seeking extortionately high prices to make it available to the project operator.[117]

And so delay after delay hit the project as the impasse between the company on one hand and the district administration and land owners on the other rolled on. The time by which peak output would be achieved drifted back to mid-2014, and under Richard Owen's watch, to the end of that year.[118]

Figures in the national government grew restless with the problems, and directed their ire at ExxonMobil as lead operator. Following an official visit by a parliamentary delegation to Cepu in 2009, lawmaker Tjatur Sapto Edy let fly. "Costs [at Cepu] have been skyrocketing," said the member of the House of Representatives commission overseeing energy issues. "It shows that Exxon is incapable of fulfilling its commitment to develop the block. We recommend that Pertamina take the lead."[119] The refrain that Pertamina should take over was repeated frequently, sometimes encouraged by the state-backed company. Given this mood, regulator BP Migas felt a need to keep a close eye on ExxonMobil.

Even the small progress that was achieved was mired in controversy. In August 2009 the company commenced early extraction of oil from the site, but the rate at which that oil should be processed was in dispute. The government, keen to meet the ambitious oil output targets it had set itself, leaned on the company to squeeze the oil field to produce 15,000 T barrels per day, but the company pushed back, expressing doubts that the early-stage facilities were capable of upping their output beyond 5,000 barrels per day. The company's resistance prompted a threat from BP Migas that foreshadowed Richard Owen's eventual fate. "ExxonMobil's credibility will be questioned if it fails to meet the production target," BP Migas head Raden Priyono said,[120] later adding that he had prepared a list of ExxonMobil executives for whom he was considering denying work permits.[121]

The difference between the two output figures would barely make a dent in the government's aim for one million barrels per day within a few years, but the symbolism was important. Disputes over output between the company and the national government became a running sore.

In 2011, a breakthrough of sorts was achieved. After securing many of the permits it required, ExxonMobil signed five engineering, procurement and construction contracts with companies, most of them Indonesian, to construct the supporting infrastructure needed to develop Banyu Urip and process and transport oil. Late in the year a ground-breaking ceremony was held, attended by Jero Wacik, just weeks after he was appointed as Energy and Mineral Resources Minister. Wacik, the man who would ultimately make the call on the work permit, is a seasoned politician in President Susilo Bambang Yudhoyono's Democratic Party. A mechanical engineer by training, he served as Tourism and Culture Minister in Yudhoyono's first term, before taking charge of energy and mineral resources.

Early in 2012 another dispute over early-stage output at Banyu Urip emerged, this time with the government urging the company to increase flow to 25,000 barrels per day, from the existing 20,000 barrels per day. The government had been stung by a failure to achieve the national output target the year before, and was desperate to do all it could to meet it in 2012. "They have the technology. All they have to do now is to execute it," Rudi Rubiandini, the deputy minister, said of ExxonMobil at the time, again adding that the future tenure of company executives could be at risk if it failed to deliver. ExxonMobil was a little less certain that such an increase was possible in the short-term, noting concerns about the project's "security and integrity".[122]

Soon after Richard Owen took the reins as the head of ExxonMobil's Indonesian operation, the Bojonegoro administration returned to its earlier approach of obstinacy in the issuance of permits. This time around the district government produced a list of six demands for the company, including a land swap that would have required the company to acquire new land it could then transfer to the administration in exchange for the land it was using for the oil project.[123]

Discussions ground on for months, all the while eroding the prospects that the project might meet its latest mid-2014 target for completion. The national government laid the blame at the feet of the project developers, arguing they had failed to properly communicate with local people. After being pressured by a new presidential regulation requiring government agencies to maximise oil and gas production, regulator BP Migas eventually intervened. In August the agency brokered talks between the company and the local administration, and a deal was reached. The oil field developer could get the construction permits it needed if it agreed to build public health and sport facilities.[124]

In the dying days of 2012, the government made its decision on Richard Owen's work permit. It is not clear whether the company knew his fate when it updated the media on the progress of Cepu on 26 December. The development of Banyu Urip, the company said, was already 35 percent done. Completion, however, would not occur until the end of 2014, seven months later than previously discussed.[125]

Just days later, the news that Owen had been given his marching orders was made public, with sluggishness at Cepu identified as a key factor. "The clock is ticking and those expatriates continue to receive paychecks while the project continues to be delayed. Perhaps this is not entirely Owen's faults but since he is the leader, we decided not to grant T an extension of his contract," Gde Pradnyana, operations deputy at the regulator known at this point as SK Migas, told the *Jakarta Post*.[126]

The fairness of the government using delays over Cepu to justify expelling Owen depends on the extent to which the company as lead operator of the project is responsible for the delays. There are signs that the Bojonegoro administration had no real interest in advancing the project and was willing to use it to extract all the assistance it could from the developer. The administration suffered few adverse consequences for its approach.

As for delays linked to land acquisition, the issue is one that the government had long acknowledged as a factor inhibiting the development of infrastructure and other major projects. The fact that the government introduced sweeping changes to national land acquisition rules in 2012 seems to reflect its view of the breadth of the problem. There appears to have been little within the law that ExxonMobil could have done to access the land it needed to build its pipeline, short of giving in to the demands of land speculators.

If the government was upset at the slowness of the development of Cepu, there are other places it ought point its finger.

Arun around

The other factor cited in the work permit decision was the aborted sale of shares in gas and liquefied natural gas assets in northern Sumatra.

ExxonMobil's first resource development project in Indonesia was in Aceh, the province at the northern tip of Sumatra that for decades was riven with conflict between locals seeking autonomy from Jakarta and a national government keen to stop the archipelago from splintering. Since the discovery of abundant gas at Arun in 1971, four field clusters were developed around the site under a production sharing contract held by ExxonMobil, with the gas extracted consumed domestically and also exported to Japan and South Korea.

Come August 2011, ExxonMobil decided that its capital was better committed elsewhere and so moved to sell down its stake in the three companies that held its interests around Arun: Mobil Exploration Indonesia, ExxonMobil Oil Indonesia and Mobil LNG Indonesia. The assets included a 100 percent stake in Arun Block B, 100 percent of the North Sumatra offshore gas field, and 30 percent in the Arun natural gas liquefaction plant, which was majority owned by Pertamina. Between them, the assets produced about 215 million standard cubic feet of gas per day in 2010, so local firms salivated at the prospect of getting access to ExxonMobil's holding.

In total 27 companies expressed interest in purchasing the shares, including MedcoEnergi, Indonesia's largest listed oil and gas company, and Perusahaan Gas Negara, the state-owned gas distributor. Over the next year the list was whittled down to 12 companies, who were invited to prepare bids; that list was further pared back to three.

And then the company decided to nix the plan to sell the assets. Instead, it would maintain control over the three subsidiaries, a right it had reserved for itself in the terms of the tender documents. The company said the decision was made after consultations with relevant stakeholders, and that the assets would perform better under ExxonMobil management. The bidding companies, and the government, were dismayed at the decision.

ExxonMobil's decision was cited by SK Migas spokesman Hadi Prasetyo in explaining the work permit decision that followed a few months later. "They have announced their plans for Arun … and then abruptly cancelled although some local firms had expressed interest in purchasing the shares. The government lost face due to the incident," he told the *Jakarta Post*.[127]

But the full story seems a little more knotty. Reports surfaced in the *Jakarta Globe*[128] and *Tempo*,[129] attributed to an unnamed source with knowledge of the Arun negotiations, that offered some insight into what went on behind the scenes.T

According to the *Tempo* account, the final three bidders in the running for the Arun assets were Energi Mega Persada, Mandiri Oil, and a consortium made up of Intera Arun Energi and Ratu Prabu Energi. ExxonMobil appeared to be leaning towards the Intera Arun-Ratu Prabu bid because of its size (the *Globe* source put the bid at US$1.1 billion) and the consortium's oil and gas experience.

Mandiri Oil's bid (which the *Globe* put at US$600 million) was foundering. But then, according to the *Tempo* account, the company was given a boost by Gatot Suwondo, the president director of state-owned Bank Negara Indonesia who is also the brother-in-law of President Susilo Bambang Yudhoyono. The nature of the assistance, which was reportedly backed by Energy and Mineral Resources Minister Jero Wacik, was not clear. Suwondo denied the story, saying he was "not familiar" with ExxonMobil.

And who was Mandiri Oil? The *Globe* identified the company as part of the Indoland Group, a luxury property company whose interests include the Pacific Place mall in South Jakarta, and said that its move into oil and gas had only come about in the previous two years. Heading up Mandiri Oil was president director Yanuar Arsyad, who denied having received support by state officials in the bid for ExxonMobil's assets.[130]

By late 2012, ExxonMobil had come close to deciding to sell the assets to the Intera Arun-Ratu Prabu consortium and met with Wacik. According to a *Globe* account of the meeting, the minister was upset with the decision and urged the company to "pick another winner", presumably Mandiri Oil. Given the circumstances, ExxonMobil decided to shelve the asset sales plan altogether.

If the sources are correct, it appears that in denying the work permit the minister may have been taking revenge against a company in part because it refused to sign off on a deal that would have involved it selling an asset for little more than half of the highest bid to a company with powerful advocates within the government. For his part, Wacik denied the allegations of interference in the sale process, but did confirm that Owen had his permit denied because he was not cooperating with the government.[131]

Aftermath

Conscious of the need to stay on good terms with the government, the company chose to not vent its frustrations over the work permit decision in public, opted to not appeal, and stated that the decision would not prompt it to reduce its investment in Indonesia.[132]

Risk analyst Keith Loveard described the work permit decision as a case of "scapegoating". "The government had to find someone to blame for not meeting its output targets," he said in an interview.[133]

The decision sent shivers up the spines of executives at other companies operating under production sharing contracts. After all, if falling short of production targets was grounds for having a work permit application rejected, few were safe. In May 2012, regulator BP Migas revealed that just five of the 56 company operating on production sharing contracts had met their targets.[134] The targets, set by the government in consultation with the contract-holders, often reflect aspirational thinking rather than hard realities, and given the figures are used to estimate revenue in the national budget, there's a strong political motivation to increase the expected output.

Petroleum engineer Jon Gibbs was appointed to succeed Richard Owen in Indonesia, and Owen himself was appointed to lead the company's operations in his home country, Australia. On Gibbs' appointment in June 2013, he was delivered a blunt warning by Gde Pradnyana, the secretary of oil and gas regulator SKK Migas, to be "more supple and reliable" than his predecessor. "We hope Gibbs can deliver on all the deals we have previously made with ExxonMobil. In addition, we want him to be more flexible and down-to-earth in dealing with officials as well as other Indonesians," he said.[135]T

In the wake of the decision and the factors that led to it, it seems inevitable that Owen's successor, and every other foreign executive who works in Indonesia at the whim of the government, will be influenced in their actions not only by commercial reasoning and the need to be a good corporate citizen, but also the fear of upsetting powerful people in government. The presence of such a spectre is unlikely to contribute to sound decisions.

5

Legal Tangles

One day, Perth-based Churchill Mining hopes to get back to doing what its name suggests it should be doing. For several years, though, it has been little more than a participant in a legal battle of existential proportions, its mining-focused managing director replaced with a lawyer, legal costs being its single biggest expense and its updates to shareholders reading like the minutes of court hearings. Its objective is to reclaim the 2.73 billion metric tons of high-grade coal it discovered in the grounds of inland East Kalimantan, valued at US$1.8 billion. In the struggle to stake its claim, Churchill has become a cautionary tale demonstrating the difficulty of achieving legal certainty on Indonesian resources projects.

Most likely, the company's fate will be decided in a Washington arbitration hearing some time near the middle of this decade. While the facts of the case remain hotly contested, it seems apparent that Churchill's quandary has arisen through the combination of two of the unavoidable realities of business life in Indonesia. The first is the chaos of overlapping mining permits issued by district governments empowered by a decade of decentralisation but lacking the expertise to wield that power diligently. The second is the way that powerful figures from the political and business elite can cloud the judgement of public officials in their thrall. Churchill's decision to seek international arbitration after exhausting its legal options in Indonesia suggests it sees a third factor at play – the difficulty of receiving a fair and impartial hearing in an Indonesian courtroom.

Borneo looms

Churchill's entry into Indonesia started uneventfully. The mining exploration minnow had scored a listing on the Alternative Investment Market of London's stock exchange in 2005, and with a bit of cash to its name started hunting for assets to develop. Its first instinct was to head to the resource-rich Pilbara area of Western Australia, in the country from which its core of senior executives hailed. It set its sights on some manganese it believed was sitting beneath the soil in South Woodie Woodie, and found a modest supply. As that project was meandering along, it turned to Indonesia and the West Kutai regency of East Kalimantan province. It sought out coal-bed methane at a site called Sendawar, sending out rigs to drill down and test the soil. But the bounty was modest and unlikely to yield success any time soon.

Chairing the company was David Quinlivan, a three-decade veteran of the mining industry with a particular enthusiasm for speculative projects who also served as chief executive of Australian mid-tier iron ore producer Mt Gibson Iron. Managing director of the emerging company was Paul Mazak, an old Asia hand whose crowning achievement was spearheading a successful bid for the world-class Madhya Pradesh diamond property in India.

Come late 2006, a rival explorer struck success searching for coal in Pakar, a field in the East Kutai regency of East Kalimantan. The discovery caught the attention of several coal explorers, who suspected the find was unlikely to be a one off, and that the seams of coal may open far and wide into neighbouring fields. Churchill was among those who headed to East Kutai to try their luck; local company the Ridlatama Group was another.

Ridlatama in 2007 grabbed hold of four exploration permits (two in May and another two in November) in East Kutai from the regency administration. The permits had been allowed to lapse more than a year earlier by a rival local coal company, Nusantara Group, after it failed to undertake exploration. A civil servant in the East Kutai regency administration, Djaja Putra, in February 2007 prepared a report in which he confirmed that Nusantara had let its licence lapse. The area was "open to other companies", the document declared, because Nusantara had not applied to renew its licences a month before they expired, as required by law. [136]

Ridlatama had got its hands on permits over about 35,000 hectares, but lacked the capital to do a lot with them. Sensing an opportunity, Churchill stepped forward and sought out a partnership. Under the arrangement they struck in late 2007, the London-listed company would take a 75 percent stake in Ridlatama and bankroll the exploration, a sum that came to top US$40 million. [137]

When company geologists headed into the field to test out the resource, the company expected to find perhaps 100 million metric tons of coal. Instead, when the reports came back from the laboratory in May 2008, the field was found to hold at least 150 million metric tons, with an expectation that there was still far more to be found. The discovery sent ripples of excitement through Churchill and Ridlatama; the high-grade coal they had found was in hot demand to fuel the growing economies and China and India.

But the announcement left ringing in the ears of executives at Nusantara Group, who appeared to have let a fortune slip through their fingers. Desperate to deal themselves into play, Nusantara Group representatives within weeks quietly approached Awang Faroek Ishak, the leader of East Kutai regency known as a bupati, and sought extensions to the exploration licences they had allowed to lapse in 2006. Despite these licences appearing to overlap with ones already issued to Churchill, Ishak acquiesced, issuing licences running from July 2008. Djaja Putra, the civil servant who had in early 2007 declared the area "open to other companies", issued a completely contradictory assessment, smoothing the way to Nusantara having its licence renewed. Ridlatama, at this point, was unaware of the decision. [138]

Powerful connections

Just who was behind Nusantara Group, an entity that seemed to hold such sway over the regency administration?

Nusantara appeared to have a complex legal structure, but Prabowo Subianto, a former military leader who had found success in business and politics, held a significant share. According to a Churchill presentation, a half-dozen key companies in the Nusantara Group were clustered almost entirely under the name Nusantara Energindo Coal, which was 40 percent owned by Subianto (who also, intriguingly, held a direct 0.1 percent stake in the six companies). Of the remaining 60 percent, the major two individual shareholders – via no less than three holding companies – were identified as Husein Susilo Tjioe and Karel Budiman.[139]

Subianto is a hugely divisive figure in Indonesia. The son of a leading economist and former husband of a daughter of President Suharto, Subianto rose through the military ranks under the strongman president before his career came to a shuddering halt with the ousting of the New Order regime in 1998. Accused of involvement in human rights abuses in East Timor during his time as a commander of the military's notorious Kopassus special forces division, Subianto retreated to Jordan, which was led by King Abdullah, a close friend. When the dust settled in the early 2000s, he returned to Indonesia and started up the Great Indonesia Movement Party (Gerindra), which he hoped would be his vehicle to the presidency.

It is unclear just how actively involved Subianto was in the running of Nusantara, given the former general already had his hands full with Gerindra. But he has accumulated considerable wealth over the years (it was estimated at US$160 million in a 2009 report by the Corruption Eradication Commission[140]), much of it through ventures like Nusantara, giving him tremendous cachet in the money politics of Indonesia.

Media reports suggest some other high-profile people stood alongside Prabowo and Nusantara. One shareholder was Anthoni Salim, third on Indonesia's rich list and a scion of the Salim Group, a vast conglomerate.

The company's legal representative was Hotman Paris Hutapea, a smooth-talking Jakarta lawyer famous for cruising around town in his Ferrari.[141]

Churchill went searching for local supporters it could bring on board. The company established an Indonesian Advisory Council, enlisting the help of former government heavy hitters it claimed "guarantee[d] access to government and industry". Chairing the Advisory Council was Alwi Shihab, the Foreign Minister under the presidency of Abdurrahman Wahid who had gone on to be President Susilo Bambang Yudhoyono's point-man on the Middle East, while serving under him was Faroek Basrewan, a former special aide to Wahid. Basrewan was also named as a director of Churchill.[142]

By the time Awang Faroek Ishak took on the position of East Kalimantan governor in December 2008, the impact of the overlapping exploration licences he had signed off on were starting to be felt. But his successor as bupati of East Kutai, Isran Noor, took on the issue with enthusiasm and sensed a way forward that might prove advantageous to Subianto, a man he later described in a *Sydney Morning Herald* interview as a "friend", though not one from whom he had received material benefits.[143]

Keen to strengthen its case that it was the rightful holder of the exploration licences, Nusantara in January 2009 approached the East Kutai police accusing Churchill's Ridlatama of criminal acts in obtaining the licences. As that investigation was underway, the State Financial Audit Agency (BPK) was chasing down similar allegations. By this stage, alarm bells were ringing for Ridlatama. The control of the mine they believed the licences conveyed on them was not nearly as clear as they thought.

The two bodies reached conflicting results. The BPK in a February report found that the licences held by Ridlatama were in fact counterfeit. The police, however, in their May report found that there was "no case to answer".[144]

The East Kutai regency picked up on the BPK finding and launched its own investigation into the confusion over the licences. In March 2010, a study carried out by local government auditor Achmad Surya delivered a result favourable to Ridlatama: it found that the company's licences were "legitimate and accountable" and that Nusantara's licences had expired at the time the Ridlatama licences were issued. Surya also urged punishment for two civil servants for their conduct in the issuing on the apparently overlapping licences.

"All the [Ridlatama] documents were original. They were all legal," Surya told the *Sydney Morning Herald* in an interview later, adding that the Nusantara licences, which the company insisted were genuine despite others' assumption that they had lapsed, could not be produced by anyone while he was conducting his investigation. "Somehow, Nusantara's licences on the area were extended. How come? It's such a wrong practice." Infuriated that the audit was unfavourable to Nusantara, bupati Isran Noor swiftly sacked the auditor, claiming his report was the product of corruption. "I'm sure it was Ridlatama people who produced the document and he signed it," he said. "I don't know if he received money."[145]

As the local administration weighed up how to deal with the overlapping permits over the lucrative coal field, a mysterious development emerged. In April 2010, a complaint letter was received by the national Forestry Ministry purporting to be from representatives of the Dayak tribe, the indigenous people of East Kutai, accusing Ridlatama of illegally cutting down trees. Two days later, the Forestry Minister wrote to bupati Isran Noor instructing him to cancel Ridlatama's mining licence for alleged forestry crimes. Ridlatama said it remained oblivious to the developments as they occurred.[146]

The East Kutai administration sensed a path out of the muddle, and so sought to strengthen the claims of wrongdoing against Ridlatama. Within a week of the letter from the Forestry Ministry being received, the chief mining bureaucrat in East Kutai produced a new report backing the claim that Ridlatama's April 2008 licence had in fact been forged. In early May 2010, bupati Isran Noor revoked Ridlatama's four exploration licences, using the twin justifications that they had been fraudulently obtained and that the concessions overlapped with a forest conservation area. The licences held by Prabowo Subianto's Nusantara Group would stand.[147]

Legal options

Aghast that the control it believed it had over the field was crumbling, Churchill in August 2010 launched legal action to re-establish its claim. It took the local administration to the Samarinda Administrative Tribunal in the East Kalimantan provincial capital, arguing that the revoking of its exploration licence was invalid and asking that it be expunged from the record. For his part, bupati Isran Noor argued that he did not technically revoke the permits but instead they had been improperly obtained in the first place since the would-be mining sites overlapped with forest conservation areas.[148]

Given the significance of the stakes, both Ridlatama and Nusantara desperately sought to strengthen their case. Ridlatama approached local Dayak leaders and received an assurance that they had not penned the letter sent to the Forestry Ministry in April that alleged illegal tree cutting. What had happened, it later emerged, was that Dayak people themselves had cut down trees to construct a communal building and church, as they are permitted to. Ridlatama had simply helped to transport the logs as part of an effort to build better relations with the local community. The chief of the Dayak tribe then wrote to the Forestry Ministry seeking to clarify events.[149]

Nusantara, which had formally joined the Administrative Tribunal proceedings in October, sought to reinforce its position by seeking forestry licences from the Forestry Ministry, similar to those obtained by the Churchill-controlled company a year earlier. Even though the court ruling was still pending, Nusantara's application received the endorsement of the national Ministry of Energy and Mineral Resources. The Forestry Ministry had the good sense to at least wait for the court ruling before deciding on the application.[150]

Even as uncertainty swirled around the project in late 2010, Churchill continued to talk up its investment plans for the mine. It proposed building a massive 20-million-metric-ton-per-annum conveyer to carry the coal to port, a piece of infrastructure that would take two years to build and rely on overland high-voltage transmission lines for power. It mapped out a fast-track schedule that involved three years of construction before the project began production in 2014.[151]

For East Kutai, the discovery and development of a major coal field should be the catalyst for an economic boom. With limited existing transportation infrastructure in the part of East Kalimantan where East Kutai lay, much work would be needed to bring the coal to market. But such a boom would only materialise if investors had certainty over their control of the resources block. Significant doubts ran the risk of sending them scampering.

In early March 2011, the Administrative Tribunal delivered its finding – the revocation of Ridlatama's licence by the bupati was administratively correct and would stand. Not long after, Ridlatama announced its intention to appeal to the Administrative High Court in Jakarta. The Forestry Ministry, with some legal certainty granted by the tribunal ruling, gave the green light to Nusantara's forestry licence application.[152]

It had become clear to Ridlatama that even with its Indonesian Advisory Board, the company was falling short in establishing local connections and opening the doors it desperately needed to access. To overcome that deficit, it issued shares worth £7.7 million (US$12.9 million) to what it described as "new strategic Indonesian shareholders". Joining the board as non-executive directors were Rachmat Gobel, a well-connected Indonesian business figure serving on President Susilo Bambang Yudhoyono's National Innovation Committee, and Fara

Luwia, a businesswoman who had amassed a fortune in the agricultural sector.[153]

The legal dispute with the East Kutai administration had brought to the surface other tensions within Ridlatama. As Ridlatama and Churchill's corporate arrangements went under the legal microscope, claims emerged that the deal had been improperly administered and sought to gain for Churchill opportunities only legally available to local companies. The East Kutai administration claimed that Ridlatama failed to notify local authorities about the change in corporate structure when Churchill purchased the 75 percent stake in Ridlatama.[154]

Fearing that its local partner Ridlatama had been sloppy in establishing the investor agreement when they joined forces, Churchill decided to pursue its legal options. Churchill lodged an unlawful act claim against company official Andreas Rinaldi in the Tangerang District Court, and on the same mid-August day commenced arbitration proceedings in Singapore against other members of the Ridlatama group for alleged breaches of the investor agreement. Churchill's David Quinlivan told the *Straits Times* a little later: "As a foreign investor in Indonesian mining, you can't get anything done without a powerful local partner, and once you get a powerful local partner, they turn that power against you."[155]

Later that month, the Administrative High Court in Jakarta ruled on the appeal against the verdict of the Samarinda tribunal. Ridlatama, now at war with itself, lost the appeal. The partnership and exploration plan that had appeared so promising three years earlier was now looking decidedly tattered.

Battered but not beaten, Ridlatama in September 2011 again appealed the case, this time to the Supreme Court, the highest legal authority in Indonesia authorised to hear such proceedings. Quinlivan expressed his frustration with the sequence of rulings and indicated the extent to which the company had been blindsided by the initial East Kutai decision. "It's disappointing where we are. Indonesia's a great place for natural resources. But we never expected the government to reissue licences, that never entered our heads," he told *Agence France-Presse* later. "If land title isn't fixed, that's a real problem for Indonesia. Investors need security."[156]

As the legal battles raged, Ridlatama continued the exploration of the East Kutai field. Its estimates of the coal contained there steadily rose, up to a 2011 estimate of an eye-watering 2.73 billion metric tons, making it the second-largest undeveloped coal mine in Indonesia and the world's seventh-largest. Churchill put the value of the site at around US$1.8 billion, and argued it could produce coal for at least 25 years.[157]

Come November, the investor partners with which Churchill was doing battle hit back. Two Ridlatama Group companies claimed that Churchill had failed to make the initial purchase payments provided for in the investor agreement each of the companies had signed. Given this, the Ridlatama Group companies wanted to terminate the investor agreement. Whatever the motivation, Ridlatama seemed keen to head for the exits. Churchill was furious, and rejected the claims that it had baulked on its investor agreement obligations. "Churchill's solicitors also believe that the ... letters have no legal merit and are ineffective," the company told its shareholders.[158]

Keen to regain momentum in its substantive case and show that it hadn't been sidetracked by the fight with fellow investors, Churchill sought to escalate the dispute over the mining exploration licences. The company's solicitors wrote to President Susilo Bambang Yudhoyono and other senior officials, asking the government in a 10-page letter to enter into discussions to amicably resolve the dispute. "If an amicable resolution cannot be achieved, we regret that Churchill will have no other choice than to initiate international arbitration against the Republic of Indonesia, thus putting Indonesia's reputation as a reliable country for foreign investment at risk," the letter said.[159] Even before the Supreme Court ruling had been delivered, the company had decided that formal legal channels were unlikely to deliver it the result it was seeking.

Desperate to keep faith with investors as their patience was tested,

Churchill mapped out its strategy to get its way in East Kutai. In a presentation to its annual general meeting in late 2011, company officials reassured investors that "Churchill is well funded to continue to protect shareholders interests" and added that an "active lobbying and media campaign [is] underway to all levels of government/media in relation to the injustice to Churchill and further implications for foreign investment into Indonesia".[160]

With the East Kutai dispute one of several that were eroding faith in the administration of the mining sector, the Energy and Mineral Resources Ministry in December 2011 launched a project to map all the coal mines across the country. The aim? "To provide more legal certainty to businesses," the ministry's director-general for coal and minerals, Thamrin Sihite, was quoted as saying.[161]

In January 2012, Churchill's fear about the outcome in the Indonesian judicial system was confirmed. The Supreme Court refused to overturn the decisions of the earlier courts, meaning the bupati's revocation of Ridlatama's licence remained.

Global escalation

Seeing itself with little alternative if it was to hold onto its prized Kalimantan asset, Churchill in May 2012 turned to the International Centre for Settlement of Investment Disputes, a body backed by the World Bank that is charged with arbitrating in commercial disputes between a company and a national government.

The Washington-based court has been a controversial one over the years, with critics arguing that it undermines the right of sovereign states to make and enforce their own laws. But accepting the court as a valid forum for hearing intractable disputes has been an important step for some developing countries to show to potential investors that they offer a safe legal environment in which to do business. "International arbitration is not an affront to sovereignty," argued former World Bank researcher Paul Collier in his book on boosting development. "The governments that would find such a facility most useful are those that have severe problems of reputation and are trying to live them down."[162] Some 140 states have signed up as members of the court.

The court is intended only as a forum of last resort. Because rulings can take so long – sometimes up to three years – and hearings can be painfully expensive, few parties turn to it, with many seeking to reach an out-of-court settlement instead. Critics, such as British legal academic Mahnaz Malik, have described it as "the legal monster that lets companies sue countries",[163] but circumstances like that in which Churchill found itself underline its importance. Use of the court as an avenue to resolve commercial disputes has surged in recent years. After hearing just 69 cases in the period from 1972 to 1999, the number shot up to 103 cases in 2004-2005, 134 cases in 2005-2009 and 74 cases in the two-year period of 2010-2011.[164]

Indonesia has developed a distrustful attitude toward international forums like the ICSID after a couple of stinging high-profile defeats. Among them was the 2000 case in which state oil and gas company Pertamina was ordered by the International Arbitration Institute in Switzerland to pay around US$300 million to US-based power company Karaha Bodas after the government annulled a contract due to the Asian Financial Crisis in 1997. A shoddy adherence to due process was blamed for many observers for Indonesia's embarrassing defeat.

Churchill argued it had a right to appeal to the court under the terms of a 1976 bilateral investment treaty between the United Kingdom and Indonesia; in June 2012 the court agreed and said it would take on the case. Churchill's claim was for US$1.054 billion, plus interest, from the national government in compensation for the seizure of assets without compensation.

The prolonged legal battle meant the fundamental nature of Churchill's business had changed. It was, in the medium-term at least, a company whose fortunes depended almost entirely on its ability to navigate its way through the deep sea of global legal battles, and possibly high-stakes negotiations. To that end, the company changed its managing director: out was mining industry warhorse Paul Mazak, and coming into the job was Nicholas Smith, an experienced lawyer. Smith, like Quinlivan a part of the West Australian mining establishment, previously spent more than a decade as group general counsel for Normandy Mining and gained experience making the most of bilateral investment treaties, the legal instrument central to Churchill's future.

Also brought in to bolster its discussions with the government was Robert Gelbard, a former US ambassador to Indonesia now offering his services as a corporate consultant. Gelbard's take on the sequence of events was that a regional power play was at work.[165]

The fact that such a significant case was to be heard in an international forum like the ICSID sent a shudder through the Indonesian establishment. Listed as a defendant in the case was President Susilo Bambang Yudhoyono, meaning it had to be taken seriously at the highest levels of government.

Indonesia was confident that the East Kutai administration was right in revoking Ridlatama's permit in 2010. It argued that the mining licence was issued to Ridlatama Group at a point when it was locally owned, and that the licence was invalidated when a majority stake in the company was taken by a foreign entity, Churchill. Furthermore, the government also claimed that Churchill had failed to obtain the appropriate Forestry Ministry permit to mine in a natural forest before it commenced exploring.

The national government made clear it would defend itself vigorously at the forum and believed it would be vindicated. For President Yudhoyono, the implications were profound.

"We must defend our honour, truth and justice. This is a matter of principle," the president told the media in June 2012. "I do not want such a multinational corporation to oppress a developing country like Indonesia." But he also offered a begrudging acknowledgement that some of the chaos of a decentralised decision-making system had increased the risk of confusion. "Just imagine, we have hundreds of districts [like this]. If we are the one wrong, the implications would be extraordinary."[166]

Some analysts argued that Churchill's real beef was with Ridlatama rather than the Indonesian government, saying the two companies had between them failed to take adequate protection to ensure that their licences were in full compliance with the law. "Not all mining disputes were caused by the local government because there are also many fraudulent companies," Jeffrey Mulyono, a former chairman of the Indonesian Mining Association, told the *Jakarta Globe*.[167]

In a flight of bravado, East Kutai bupati Isran Noor sought to make the most of his time in the spotlight. "I am certain that we have a 100 percent chance of winning," he said soon after the international escalation was announced. "This is a non-issue for us, but it's being made into a big issue."

He went on to add to the pile of accusations against Churchill and Ridlatama. While reiterating his claim that his administration was never informed of Churchill's purchase of a 75 percent stake in Ridlatama and that its 2008 exploration permit was forged, he added that the miner had falsified the size of the estimated reserves in the concession area in order to boost its share price. All of the claims were rejected by Churchill.

Perhaps Noor's greatest flourish came when he said he had considered prosecuting Churchill and Ridlatama officials for the supposed forgery of their licence. He stopped, he said, because the penalty would have been too harsh. "The perpetrators could have gotten the death sentence, and I didn't have the heart to go through with it," he said, apparently ignorant of the fact that forgery is not a capital offence in Indonesia.[168]

In October 2012, the case started its slow progress through the tribunal. Three arbitrator were appointed – one selected from each side and another selected by the tribunal administrators – and preliminary hearings proceeded. As of early 2014, the case was still in its early stages and an outcome was not expected for at least a year.[169]

Despite the suggestion that the real source of Churchill's woes was Ridlatama's conduct, relations between the two parties appeared to be warming. The Singapore courtroom showdown between the two never materialised, with the companies agreeing to withdraw from the proceedings in which Churchill had accused Ridlatama of a breach of their investor agreement. In a related dispute, in which Ridlatama took action against Churchill in an Indonesian court for alleged "unlawful acts", a ruling in favour of the Indonesian company in the South Jakarta District Court was followed by an appeal to the Jakarta High Court. While the appeal had not been ruled upon as of early 2014, Churchill indicated in its 2012-13 results that the outcome was not crucial to the future of the company. The rift, it appeared, had largely been resolved.

The drawn out legal saga has testing the patience of the company's shareholders. After peaking at £1.45 in mid-2010, as the early details of the legal troubles were emerging, the shares had fallen to below 20 pence for much of 2013. Investors remain doubtful of the company's prospects for success.

Problems exposed

More than decade of decentralisation has left many local governments with considerable authority to administer the resources in their domains, but there is mounting evidence that they are inadequately equipped to exercise that power. A thicket of overlapping claims has made it difficult for companies to obtain clear title over valuable lands, and left them vulnerable to legal challenges. Complex sets of rules surrounding mining projects that necessitate multiple licences only add to the confusion – and the opportunities for wrongdoing. National Minerals and Energy Ministry data from 2012 revealed that only 40 percent of 10,235 mining permits had been given "clean and clear" status, indicating that the permits were properly issued and their mining activities were in line with the government's environmental policies.[170] President Yudhoyono himself acknowledged the way decentralisation had allowed local political operators to cause chaos through issuing overlapping permits. "Often, new regents issue new permits [at the same location], which can be a time bomb," he said in commenting on the Churchill case.[171]

Experts differ on the question of whether decentralisation has failed to the point that authority over mining permits should be returned to Jakarta. Komaidi Notonegoro, vice director of research body ReforMiner Institute, argued that poorly managed regional administrations were responsible for disputes involving overlapping concession areas and unregistered mining activities. "Judging from past experience, several regional administrations cannot be trusted. The right to issue mining permits has to be given back to the central government," Notonegoro told the *Jakarta Post*.[172]

But with local officials unlikely to give up their power without a struggle, more creative policy solutions may be required to avert the confusion of overlapping and inconsistent mining licences. One proposal, put by Noke Kiroyan, a former mining executive now working as a consultant, is for the central government to allow licences to be decided on by district heads, but verified by the central authority to give it more certainty.[173] A half-hearted version of such a model was trialled by President Yudhoyono in 2012, when he decided to give provincial governors oversight over bupatis and mayors in the issuance of new mining permits.[174] (In the case of Churchill, it is unlikely to have made much difference: the East Kutai regent who sowed the seeds of chaos, Awang Faroek Ishak, went on to become the East Kalimantan governor.)

Failing to rectify problems of overlapping and inconsistent mining permits, whatever the approach chosen, will likely prove to be expensive. As business commentator Hendarsyah Tarmizi noted in an essay, "the government's arrogance in revoking permits and other forms of mining contracts will not only result in damaging the overall investment climate in the country but could also result in the loss of millions of dollars of taxpayers' money to pay compensation awarded to plaintiffs".[175]

Resource nationalists, long keen to gain a leg up for local businesses over their foreign rivals, get extra succour in industries like coal mining, where the resource is relatively simple to extract and does not require the more sophisticated technologies and deep pockets needed to exploit oil and gas fields. "Indonesian businesspeople have seen the huge amount of money foreign owners of mining projects have made and stand to make in the future, and they'd like to take it away from them," Australian lawyer Bill Sullivan told *The New York Times*. "I think that's exactly what happened in Churchill's case."[176]

A thorough due diligence process, scrutinising potential partners as well as regulatory institutions and legal agreements, can go some way towards overcoming the risk. But as Churchill's David Quinlivan admitted, that doesn't necessarily provide adequate comfort. "My advice would be, be wary and make sure you've done extensive — and I mean extensive — due diligence," he told *Reuters* in late 2011. "Even though, whilst you may have done all this due diligence, and we certainly believe we had, things can turn around that are very unexpected. If there is a loophole there, somebody will use it."[177]

Two years later, with the case still grinding its way through the international arbitration process, Quinlivan remained irate at what he termed the "illegal expropriation" of Churchill's coal property rights. "We would be unlikely to consider further investments in Indonesia until such time as the bone fide property rights of foreign investors are recognised, supported and protected by the Republic of Indonesia," he said in an interview.[178]

Powerful people seem to hold exceptional sway over key decision-making institutions. While investors have long been wary of overt attempts to corrupt legal processes through money, perhaps more pernicious is the way those processes can be corrupted through the fear induced by certain people. Parties to a legal case staring across the table

at powerful local interests have few options available to them – other
than to perhaps enlist some powerful interests of their own. Such an
approach, however, does little to pave the way for legal certainty.

6

Zealous Prosecution

With so many moving parts to big oil and gas projects, uncertainty is inherent – for the government that controls the field and the contractor keen to access its riches. No one knows for sure whether the resources that are expected to be there actually materialise, whether the technology will work as planned and whether financial projections will come to fruition.

To share the burden of risk, oil and gas projects in Indonesia operate under a production sharing contract, a legal agreement a private operator signs with the resources industry regulator that maps out key terms. From time to time disagreements pop up, and most are resolved amicably in line with the dispute resolution mechanisms built into the contract. But in the case of Chevron Pacific Indonesia, the local arm of the American energy giant, the civil nature of the production sharing contract counted for little when possible irregularities emerged.

Since 2011, the company, Indonesia's biggest crude oil producer, has been in the sights of the Attorney General's Office, which is convinced the company has behaved improperly in carrying out bioremediation, a method of cleaning oil-contaminated soil that involves the use of micro-organisms. The AGO has aggressively pursued the case, accusing the company of fraudulently claiming reimbursements for the work from the government, despite assurances from the company and the regulator with which it shares a production sharing contract that the bioremediation arrangements are above board.

97

The AGO's campaign has yielded some success in court: by early 2014 four Indonesian employees of Chevron Pacific were given prison terms for their involvement in the case, as were two contractors. The escalation of the matter from a civil one to a criminal one has sent jitters through an industry reliant on production sharing contracts. If the AGO can intervene and lay charges whenever a dispute arises, the personal risk for those involved in commercial arrangements multiplies. Money is not the only thing at stake.

Long heritage

In one form or another, Chevron Pacific has a history in Indonesia dating back nearly a century. In 1924, the Standard Oil Company of California (Socal) and Texas Fuel Company (Texaco) set up a joint venture under the name Nederlandsche Pacific Petroleum Maatschappij to go hunting for potential oil fields in Sumatra. After two decades of searching they came across Minas, which was to become the largest oil field in Southeast Asia. In the 1950s, the company changed its name to Caltex Pacific Oil Company, and began exporting oil from Minas while also discovering new oil wells in Duri, Bengkalis and Petapahan, all of which were located in the resource-rich Sumatran province of Riau.

For several decades Caltex continued its extraction activities in Sumatra, maintaining good working relations with presidents Sukarno and Suharto. The lawlessness of the 1950s in Sumatra had some effect on Caltex and its staff, with threats of a "scorched earth" action from anti-government militias prompting the United States to prepare to send in protective troops in 1958, a move that ultimately proved unnecessary as Jakarta asserted its control.[179] By the mid-1980s, the company shifted its focus from Minas to the Duri field, where it introduced the world's largest steam injection system to boost oil production and reach otherwise hard-to-access deposits.

In the first half of the 2000s, California-based Chevron went on a global acquisition spree, buying up Caltex and Unocal, another oil company with a big footprint in Asia. Come 2005, all the company's Indonesian assets were grouped under the banner Chevron Pacific Indonesia. As its oil fields approached their mature phase and output dwindled, the company broadened its activities to tap into Indonesia's rich reserves of hydrocarbon energy.

Come 2013, the company was Indonesia's leading oil major, producing about 342,000 barrels of oil per day, accounting for 40 percent of the country's crude oil production. Its projects, spread from Riau to West Papua, employed about 6,400 staff, all but 200 of whom were Indonesian. In its 2013 work plan submitted to the government, the company committed to invest nearly US$4 billion in Indonesia, bringing its cumulative total over the previous decade to more than US$30 billion. Chevron Pacific was crucial to Indonesia's oil industry, and to the development of the country as a whole.

Chevron Pacific operates 90 fields in Sumatra, most of which are in the Rokan and Siak blocks of Riau. From the wells, the oil is transported to the coastal town of Dumai through a pipeline system extending some 550 kilometres, reaching a tank farm with a storage capacity of 5.1 million barrels. From there, oil is pumped to a Pertamina refinery and oil tankers at the wharf, from where it is transported across Indonesia.[180]

BP Migas, the one-time upstream oil and gas regulator for whom output was a fundamental measure of performance, was well aware of Chevron Pacific's significance. The company was the "backbone" of the nation's energy production, Lambok Hutauruk, deputy of evaluation and legal affairs at BP Migas, told the *Jakarta Globe* in early 2012. "If Chevron coughs, even a little, it will hurt national production," he added.[181]

Crude oil production in Indonesia has been steadily sliding for two decades. Once a net exporter of oil, and hence a member of the Organization of the Petroleum Exporting Countries (OPEC), Indonesia has become a net importer as its wells have reached maturity. From a peak of 1.6 million barrels of crude oil production per day in 1995, production sank below one million barrels in 2006 and to 900,000 in

2013. The government has high hopes of arresting the slide – the Energy Minister in mid-2012 put the 2015 target above one million barrels per day, using technology to boost output from existing fields, as well as a handful of new projects. But attracting the capital needed to achieve this goal requires a stable investment environment.[182]

Greening projects

Though technology has made oil extraction a lot cleaner than it used to be, the lands surrounding oil wells can often become contaminated. A combination of environmental regulations and the desire to preserve a social licence to operate has meant that oil companies have become increasingly concerned about cleaning up after themselves. To that end, Chevron Pacific's forerunner in 1994 launched a pilot project with the Environment Ministry to experiment with different techniques in Riau to normalise contaminated soil. Three years later the company began a field project using bioremediation.

Bioremediation involves clusters of micro-organisms being set loose to work their magic on earth contaminated with oil. Over the course of several months the oil compounds are consumed by the microbes, whose digestive processes turn the compounds into water and inert gases, thereby returning the soil to its natural state. The contamination of oil in soil is typically measured in total petroleum hydrocarbons concentration. Soils that have concentrations of TPH as high as 15 percent are suitable for bioremediation, which seeks to reduce that to below one percent, a safe level in which new plant life can grow.[183]

In recent decades, bioremediation has been used to clean the earth around many sites that have the potential to damage the environment, including petrochemical facilities, munitions factories and shipping and rail yards. Traditionally, bioremediation is conducted where soils are initially situated. Around some infrastructure such an approach works well, but in densely packed areas there is simply not enough space to carry out bioremediation on site. This was the challenged faced by Chevron Pacific in Riau.

The solution it developed was to excavate the soil and move it to a more convenient location away from the oil well that initially contaminated it, a technique known as land farming. At the new site, the soil is spread out at a thickness of up to 50 centimetres, regularly mixed with water and fertiliser, and tilled for aeration. The process takes three to six months, after which the soil is deposited elsewhere for use as topsoil in regreening projects.

By the early 2010s, the bioremediation project was in full swing. Nine bioremediation facilities in Riau had the combined capacity to remediate 42,000 cubic metres of soil per cycle. As the company explains, in the project's first decade it successfully treated more than half a million cubic metres of soil, the equivalent in volume to 200 Olympic-sized swimming pools. The treated soil has been used for the regreening of 60 hectares of land in Riau.

But 15 years earlier, that success was far from assured. At that point the company was conducting field tests of the technology. As promising results filtered in, the company sought formal approval to scale it up. By 2003, after several years of patient persuasion of bureaucrats, the company was able to launch its off-site bioremediation project and included it in its formal work plan lodged with the government. Given it had developed the technology itself, Chevron Pacific opted to keep the project in-house, using its own staff to evaluate, excavate and treat the soil.

Three years later, the company decided it would be more efficient to outsource the bioremediation to other companies so that Chevron Pacific could focus on its core activities. After sizing up some potential partners to help manage field operations, including providing, operating and maintaining heavy equipment, Chevron Pacific chose two to carry out the work: Green Planet Indonesia and Sumigita Jaya.[184]

Legal framework

Chevron Pacific's right to extract oil from Duri came via a production sharing contract it had signed with oil and gas industry regulator BP Migas. Given about 30 percent of state revenue comes from the oil and gas sector, amounting to US$36 billion in 2012, the industry is tightly regulated through contracts like this.

These decades-long agreements spell out that the government is entitled to the lion's share of revenue from the project, usually 85 percent in the case of oil and 70 percent for gas. They also stipulate that the contractor is able to claim back reimbursements from the government for some of the expenses associated with exploration, development and operations, a process known as cost recovery. The reimbursements are intended as an incentive for resources companies to invest in projects rather than let output dwindle. Among the expenses for which reimbursement can be sought are environmental restoration projects, such as bioremediation.[185]

The range of expenses for which cost recovery is sought has come under scrutiny in the past, such as in 2009 when a Supreme Audit Agency (BPK) investigation found Rp 14.6 trillion ($1.2 billion) in losses to the state through dubious expenses such as the cost of educating the children of expatriate employees and corporate social responsibility programs. Keen to uphold the legitimacy of the reimbursement system, companies have since become more cautious in lodging their claims. In cases where resources companies were paid more in reimbursement than they were entitled to, BP Migas (or its successors SK Migas and later SKK Migas) typically recoups the loss by withholding the contractor's oil or gas production share.[186]

Production sharing contracts also explicitly spell out that the approval and auditing of oil and gas projects is the responsibility of BP Migas or its successors and the audit process is governed by civil law. Disputes are resolved between parties through an established arbitration process rather than through a court. For Chevron Pacific, the sanctity of the contracts was fundamental to its confidence in doing business. "Consistency in production sharing contact rules is needed. Otherwise, the oil and gas investment in Indonesia will not be very attractive," president director Abdul Hamid Batubara told the *Jakarta Globe* in late 2010, warning that his and other companies' exploration activity depended on it.[187]

Trouble looms

For five years, Chevron Pacific continued its arrangement with its bioremediation contractors. Then in October 2011, the Attorney General's Office came sniffing, apparently acting on a tip-off from a member of the public that not all was as it seemed in the bioremediation project for the Duri oil wells in the Rokan block.

After its initial investigation, the AGO laid out its claims: the bioremediation work had not been carried out but Chevron Pacific had still been reimbursed from regulator BP Migas under the production sharing contract; the soil on which bioremediation took place was not contaminated in the first place; and Green Planet Indonesia and Sumigita Jaya, the two contractors, lacked the technical expertise to do the work. The AGO claimed Chevron Pacific had been paid US$23.4 million in reimbursements for bioremediation costs from 2006 to 2011, meaning BP Migas was also under scrutiny for its actions.[188]

The prosecuting body said it was working with the Corruption Eradication Commission (KPK), the respected national graft-busting agency, which promised that if it found any evidence on the Chevron Pacific case it would present it to the AGO.[189]

Chevron Pacific and BP Migas fiercely denied the accusations. Chevron Pacific said it paid for the cleanup itself and had not yet sought reimbursement. It also argued that the bioremediation project had been cleared by the Environment Ministry and BP Migas. In a bid to clear its name, the company agreed to cooperate with the AGO investigation.

For its part, BP Migas agreed that no money had been handed over to Chevron Pacific from the government because the project was not yet complete. And any payments that are made are already subject to oversight by government watchdogs the Finance and Development Supervisory Agency (BPKP) and the Supreme Audit Agency (BPK), which check the documentation and do field checks. "We are ready to be investigated, anytime," BP Migas spokesman Gde Pradnyana told the *Jakarta Post*.[190] The subtext was clear – BP Migas believed the AGO was barking up the wrong tree.

The investigation centred on five Chevron Pacific employees and the president director of each of the two bioremediation contractors. In March 2012, the seven were named suspects in breaches of the 2001 Anti-Corruption Law, offences that carried potential jail sentences of 20 years, and an overseas travel ban was sought for each of them. The seven were initially identified in public only by their initials, as is common practice during Indonesian investigations, but to the people and companies involved, the identities were no secret. Four Chevron Pacific employees being investigated over the project were Bachtiar Abdul Fatah (the general manager of the company's Sumatra operations), Kukuh Kertasafari (the head of the environmental cleanup department), Endah Rumbiyanti (an environment manager) and Widodo (a local Duri waste management team leader), while the contractors named suspects were Sumigita Jaya chief Herland bin Ompo and Green Planet Indonesia leader Ricksy Prematuri. The pursuit of a fifth Chevron Pacific employee, identified as Alexiat Tirtawidjaja, the company's general manager, appeared to stall when the suspect headed to the United States.[191]

Come May, Chevron Pacific realised that the courtroom was not the only forum for its battle; it also had to explain its position to a public, both in Indonesia and abroad, quick to latch onto accusations against a major company. In an interview with the *Jakarta Post*, Abdul Hamid Batubara, the company chief, explained that its bioremediation program was completely legitimate and included in the annual work plans and budgets presented to the government. "Our audit from 2003 to 2011 found no violations or misconduct in the implementation of the bioremediation project," he said.[192]

As its investigation continued in August, the AGO found a thorny piece of evidence that appeared to undermine its claim that the soil was not contaminated by oil in the first place. Testing of samples from the supposedly bioremediated soil found that the soil did in fact have indications of oil contamination. Desperate to keep its case alive, it reframed the accusation: now the AGO was claiming that the bioremediation had been carried out, but was done inadequately.[193] As the case rolled on, it switched between the two accounts of events, seemingly drawing on whichever suited the circumstances.

Arrest

On September 26, 2012, the Attorney General's Office swooped, arresting four of the Chevron Pacific employees earlier named as suspects (Bachtiar Abdul Fatah, Kukuh Kertasafari, Endah Rumbiyanti and Widodo), as well as Sumigita Jaya's Herland bin Ompo and Green Planet Indonesia's Ricksy Prematuri. Legally, the AGO now had 30 days (with a potential 30-day extension) to continue its investigation and either lay charges against those it arrested, or set them free. Lawyers for the Chevron Pacific staff were outraged, arguing that the AGO had not done the basic legwork, such as formally calculating the size of state losses, to arrest them as suspects.[194]

The arrests also raised the hackles of the Indonesian Petroleum Association (of which Chevron Pacific was a member), which was fearful about the implications for production sharing contracts. "The possibility of criminalising the cooperation contract would set a bad precedent carrying wide implications on the future of the oil and gas industry in Indonesia," the organisation said in a statement. "All disputes arising from the implementation of a cooperation-contract project should have been settled based on civic law principles and not criminal laws as stated in the contract."[195]

Johannes Simbolon, the editor of the energy monthly OGE Asia, explained what was at stake in stark terms. "Following the detention of the [Chevron Pacific] workers, oil and gas players now feel they are being watched over not only by BP Migas but also by the AGO or police. Any accounting mistake they are likely to make in their operation may not only result in reprimands or fines from BP Migas but also bring their workers into jail on charges of corruption," he wrote in an opinion piece in the *Jakarta Post*. "No oil company, particularly highly reputable multinational firms such as Chevron, is willing to see their workers in jail on charges of stealing state money. Indonesia is no longer considered an attractive destination for oil and gas investors due to the massive depletion of its resources. The criminalisation of [Chevron Pacific] has made Indonesia less alluring."[196]

Desperate to get the upper hand in the case, the AGO used its power to the fullest. The investigation involved 80 witnesses and ran for the full two months, during which time the AGO declared the case involved US$9.9 million in state losses, citing an audit from the Finance and Development Supervisory Agency (BPKP).[197] The cases of the four arrested Chevron Pacific employees came to the South Jakarta District Court in November 2012.

The hearing into their conduct did not get far. In the pre-trial stage, when an outline of the evidence is presented, the court found the case against the four was insubstantial and that in naming them as suspects on such flimsy evidence the AGO had itself violated the Anti-Corruption Law (the very law under which the AGO hoped to try the suspects). It ordered the AGO to drop the case, declare the four to no longer be suspects and let them go. Under the rules of Indonesian criminal procedure, a pre-trial ruling is final and binding. After the presiding judge knocked his gavel three times to close the hearing, the crowd – mostly Chevron Pacific staff and the families of the accused – stood and jubilantly cheered. Late that evening, November 27, two months after they were arrested, three were freed, with the fourth coming out the next morning.[198]

(It wasn't all good news for the newly released Chevron Pacific staff: a request for Rp 4 billion (US\$333,000) between them in compensation from the AGO for "embarrassment" was rejected by the court, which said the compensation limit for arbitrary arrest and unlawful charges stood at just Rp 1 million.[199])

Undaunted by the apparent absoluteness of the ruling, the AGO in December 2012 tried to appeal the release of the Chevron Pacific employees to the Jakarta High Court. The District Court refused to refer the case for appeal to the High Court, arguing the latter did not have the authority to hear the case. The AGO then referred the spat to the Supreme Court for a ruling. Lawyers rejoiced.[200]

From the AGO's perspective, the case was far from over. It had hit dead ends through the conventional court system, but still had another path to pursue. Since it was established early in the Reformasi period, the Anti-Corruption Court has heard cases on the problem often identified as the country's largest barrier to development. Setting up a separate court was a controversial decision, but it was taken because of a wish to introduce a court staffed by people of heightened integrity. While judges in many other courts have been accused and convicted of acting improperly, so far the Anti-Corruption Court has stayed clean. Prosecutors in the court have something of a home-ground advantage: defendants in cases have almost never won a case in the Jakarta branch of the Anti-Corruption Court, and fared little better in other provinces. For the AGO in its pursuit of the Chevron Pacific case, a high success rate sounded like an attractive proposition.

Pushing ahead, for now

Come the start of the new year, Chevron Pacific lodged its 2013 work plan and budget with the national government. Total investment would stand at nearly US\$4 billion, the highest in 25 years, the company said. Some of that investment was going towards the Duri oil field at the centre of the bioremediation controversy. A US$500 million expansion sought to add an additional 17,000 barrels of oil per day to its output at peak production, using 539 wells to breath new life into an oil field in decline. But the submission came with a sting in the tail: the legal tangles, the company said, may force it to lower its investment in Indonesia.[201]

The gung-ho handling of the case by the Attorney General's Office attracted the interest of the National Commission on Human Rights (Komnas HAM). In May, Komnas HAM presented a 400-page report to the president, the parliament and the Judicial Commission accusing the AGO of violating the human rights of the Chevron Pacific employees and contractors when they were arrested on flimsy grounds, and then pursued even after the ruling of the District Court. Komnas HAM commissioner Natalius Pigai explained that the organisation had found four violations of the rights of the accused: the rights to justice; a fair, honest and balanced legal process; certainty; and fair legal treatment.[202]

Just as momentum in the court of public opinion seemed to be swinging the way of Chevron Pacific and its contractors, the progress of the legal case went the other way. The Jakarta Anti-Corruption Court trial of the contractors – Green Planet Indonesia's Ricksy Prematuri and Sumigita Jaya's Herland bin Ompo – came to a climax. The panel of judges convicted the pair, finding their companies lacked appropriate qualifications to carry out the bioremediation work.

Prematuri was sentenced to five years in prison and ordered to pay a Rp 200 million (US$16,700) fine, while bin Ompo was sentenced to six years in prison and given a Rp 250 million fine. Their companies were fined the funds they had received from Chevron Pacific that were thought to have been reimbursed by the government: for Sumigita Jaya it amounted to US$6.9 million, while for Green Planet the figure stood at US$3.1 million.[203] (The punishments meted out to the two executives were the subject of a successful appeal to the High Court, which cut the jail time, a ruling that itself was appealed by the AGO to the Supreme

Court. As bin Ompo said after the initial trial, "We will continue to fight this to the end of the earth."[204])

The convictions strengthened the will of the AGO. Already cases against three of the Chevron Pacific employees were being prepared for the Anti-Corruption Court, and now the AGO decided to pursue the case against the fourth, Bachtian Abdul Fatah. But while the others had been allowed to prepare for their trials without detention following their November release, Abdul Fatah was arrested, in defiance of the District Court ruling and the damning Komnas HAM human rights report. An AGO spokesman argued that the earlier instruction to curtail proceedings related only to the investigation stage, but the case had now reached the prosecution stage. Chevron was outraged, saying the latest detention was a violation of the court order and of Abdul Fatah's legal and human rights. "The courts must step in and protect the rights of our people against this kind of action," Chevron Pacific said in a statement.[205]

By this stage the AGO was acting largely on its own. The initial close cooperation the agency claimed it was having with the Corruption Eradication Commission (KPK) had seemingly dissipated. Given that the KPK takes the lead in most corruption cases and is a body renowned for its high integrity, its absence in this case was noteworthy. Also, the scrutiny the AGO claimed it was applying to regulator BP Migas and its successors yielded no formal suspects or arrests, an unusual outcome given the nature of the allegations. The case had instead become the AGO versus Chevron Pacific and its contractors.

Even if its staff were not the subject of investigation, the oil and gas regulator knew it was under fire. The body, which by this stage was known as SKK Migas, had repeatedly insisted that payments for the bioremediation had not been made to Chevon Pacific, that payments are subject to audits and that no criminal conduct had taken place. But its assurances seemed to count for little to the AGO, and it fretted that the prosecutor's activities would rattle the energy industry. "This issue will definitely disrupt exploration operations and the exploitation of oil and

gas," Elan Biantoro, a spokesman for the regulator, told *Reuters* upon
Bachtiar Abdul Fatah's rearrest. "Upstream oil and gas workers fear they
may some day be hit by a similar situation if they are criminalised when
a civil case becomes a criminal case."[206]

Developments in the Jakarta Anti-Corruption Court formally
revealed the charges levelled against three of Chevron Pacific's
Indonesian staff. The heaviest accusation was levelled against Widodo,
a staff member at Chevron Pacific's environmental division, who was
charged with abusing his authority by signing a document estimating
the cost of the bioremediation project without proper consultation.
Two of his supervisors, Kukuh Kertasafari, the head of Chevron
Pacific's environmental cleanup department, and Endah Rumbiyanti, an
environmental manager at the company, were both accused of negligence
in failing to detect wrongdoing in the selection of the 28 bioremediation
sites that were allegedly already uncontaminated.[207] (The charge against
Rumbiyanti was particularly extraordinary given she was working for
Chevron in the United States for much of the period when the alleged
offences were said to have taken place, only returning to Indonesia in
mid-2010.[208])

The sentences sought by prosecutors for each of the participants
in the case gives clues as to where they believed responsibility lay. The
heaviest sentence demands fell on the shoulders of the two contractors:
15 years in the case of Sumigita Jaya's Herland bin Ompo and 12 years
in the case of Green Planet Indonesia's Ricksy Prematuri. Among the
Chevron Pacific staff, a seven-year sentence was sought for Widodo, six
years for Bachtiar Abdul Fatah, five years for Kukuh Kertasafari and four
years for Endah Rumbiyanti, indicating that prosecutors believed they
were respondents to, rather than initiators of, wrongdoing.

Just how the AGO decided who to pursue was unclear. Only Chevron
Pacific's Indonesian staff were targeted by the AGO, while their foreign
colleagues were spared. Were American staff to have been prosecuted,
the ripples caused would have been much greater: under Washington's

Foreign Corrupt Practices Act, those staff could have also faced prosecution in their home country. "Chevron is a foreign company, but the suspects are all Indonesians," Taslim Chaniago, a legislator from the National Mandate Party (PAN), noted during the proceedings. "The foreigners should be the suspects, but instead it is our people that they have named suspects. This is strange."[209]

Fallout

The Attorney General's Office crusade was causing increasing angst among investors both foreign and local, and this in turn was causing a split at the highest levels of government. Energy and Mineral Resources Minister Jero Wacik hit out. "As it's a civil case, it should be pursued under civil law, not criminal law; otherwise, it will hurt the investment climate," he said.[210]

Djoko Suyanto, the Coordinating Minister for Political, Legal and Security Affairs, in June 2013 chose to launch *Fighting for Justice*, a book penned by Kukuh Kertasafari in which the accused Chevron Pacific employee declares his innocence. In his speech at the event, the coordinating minister said that Attorney General Basrief Arief was acting in defiance of the wishes of President Susilo Bambang Yudhoyono. "The president called in the attorney general. This Chevron case is not right. Instructions given by the president were clear, but apparently the system ignored instructions and went against them," Suyanto said. (Arief later denied that interpretation of his meeting with the president.)[211]

About eight months after a District Court ruled there were no cases to answer, the Jakarta Anti-Corruption Court trial into the three Chevron Pacific employee got underway. Prosecutors from the Attorney General's Office presented similar evidence to that presented in the earlier hearing, alleging both reimbursement payments amounting to US$9.9 million in state losses heading to Chevron Pacific and also inadequate qualifications being held by the two contractors, Sumigita Jaya and Green

Planet Indonesia. Chevron Pacific refuted both claims, reiterating that no payment had been made, that the two contractors were selected for their expertise as part of a diligent tendering process and that the Environment Ministry had monitored the project.[212]

Prosecutors then added a new plank to their case. They brought to the court the results of testing of soil samples, which purported to show that none of the sites on which Sumigita Jaya had been asked to perform bioremediation had been contaminated by oil in the first place, indicating they had received payments for nothing. For the research, prosecutors commissioned environmental expert Edison Effendi. But as the court heard, Effendi was far from independent: he previously worked as a consultant at Putra Riau Kemari, a company that bid for Chevron Pacific's bioremediation tender but was beaten by Sumigita Jaya and Green Planet.[213]

The panel of judges retired to consider the evidence, and in July returned with the verdicts. Widodo, the Chevron Pacific employee accused of abusing his authority, was given a two-year sentence and a Rp 500 million (US$42,000) fine. His supervisors, Kukuh Kertasafari and Endah Rumbiyanti, were also each sentenced to two years behind bars and ordered to pay Rp 200 million in fines.

Defence lawyer Maqdir Ismail was fuming, saying the decision "defie[d] logic" and the trial was intended "to punish, not find justice". "There's something wrong with the mindset of the judges trying this case," he told the media afterwards. Fellow Chevron Pacific legal counsel Todung Mulya Lubis said the company was considering taking the case to an international arbitration court because of Indonesia's poor legal environment.[214]

Broad implications

The convictions sparked howls of outrage among oil and gas companies, with calls for the government to act to reaffirm the sanctity of production sharing contracts. "The industry is undoubtedly shocked as Chevron has followed every rule of law before executing its projects," said Lukman Mahfoedz, chairman of industry lobby group the Indonesian Petroleum Association. "The government should do something about it as the situation will raise questions from foreign investors."[215]

Elisabeth Proust, president director of French oil company Total E&P, told *Agence France-Presse*: "Under the PSC and so on, people can be criminalised and go to jail, so this is a very big concern to the industry. … The only thing that we expect is more certainty from the government, more certainty from the legal and judicial system."[216]

The regulator, too, was well aware of the impact the convictions would have. "The case could upset the investment climate in the upstream sector, and ultimately delay the government's campaign to increase production and find new hydrocarbon reserves," said SKK Migas spokesman Elan Biantoro.[217]

The aggressive prosecution has put into the spotlight the approach taken by the AGO. When the Chevron Pacific case is joined with two other prosecutions – of an Indosat executive (discussed in chapter 9) and of state electricity company Perusahaan Listrik Negara – it becomes clear that the AGO is willing to pursue cases even when evidence is slim and experts doubtful. "In all three cases, AGO prosecutors are focusing on technical, convoluted or abstruse details in making their allegations of wrongdoing, rather than producing clear-cut evidence of graft or bribery," noted veteran Indonesia watcher Kevin O'Rourke in his *Reformasi Weekly* bulletin. "This serves to complicate the ability of the media and public to assess the truth."[218]

For its part, the AGO rejected criticism of the way it had pursued the case. "The prosecutor is just doing its job in line with the law," a spokesman told the *Financial Times*. "We hope all parties honour the ongoing judicial process, which aims to save the state's money."[219]

But perhaps part of the problem lies with the poorly drafted laws the AGO is seeking to enforce. "If the logic of the laws is wrong, law enforcement will lack logic," Investment Coordinating Board deputy chairman Tamba Hutapea said over coffee. "We have to improve the logic of our regulations."[220]

In October 2013, the verdict was returned in the final Anti-Corruption Court case against Bachtiar Abdul Fatah, the general manager of Chevron Pacific's Sumatra operations; perhaps predictably given the outcome of the earlier trials, he was convicted and sentenced to two years in prison.[221] In his case and that of the other staff convicted, Chevron has appealed, with the cases set to go back to court in 2014.

Throughout the cases, Chevron Pacific Indonesia stood by its staff, both in the courtroom and in the battle for public sympathy. After the first batch of convictions, the company's staff were so outraged by the verdicts that they went on strike. While they returned to work soon after making clear their frustration, a longer-term question remained unanswered: would talented Indonesian staff be reluctant to work for a foreign oil company if it could leave them vulnerable to the sort of ordeal their jailed colleagues had faced?

With disputes over production-sharing contracts no longer necessarily a commercial dispute between two parties but instead potentially a criminal matter, reliance on the contracts has taken on an extra element of risk. Given its long history in Indonesia and established projects, Chevron Pacific is unlikely to be scared off altogether by the bioremediation case. But it remains to be seen whether it scales back its investment in the country, a prospect alluded to when it lodged its 2013 work plan with the government. And other companies that keenly watched the case also need to decide the level of funds they wish to commit to future investments in Indonesia. The success of government plans to return crude oil output beyond one million barrels per day by 2015 may hinge on the decisions they make.

7

The Battle for Mahakam

When executives at Total E&P Indonesie started discussions with the Indonesian government over the Mahakam offshore oil and gas block in 2007, they knew the decision would take a while. But the French company's contract to operate the giant natural resources block in East Kalimantan still had a decade to run, so they figured that time was on their side. What they couldn't have imagined, however, was that more than six years later the future of the project would remain unresolved, be the subject of an international diplomatic spat and a row within the cabinet room, and a frustrating example of the quagmire of government decision-making when large projects and state-owned companies are involved.

The saga of the contract discussions over Mahakam has a tragicomedic quality, where firm progress is suddenly undermined by unanticipated shocks – say, the death of a key participant or a bombshell court ruling. Time and time again decision-makers would acknowledge the need for a prompt decision, sometimes even indicating that one was looming, but the decision would not materialise.

Oil and gas is a major part of the economy of Kalimantan, the vast Indonesian southern portion of the heavily forested island of Borneo, and Mahakam is the biggest project. Sitting beneath the waters of the Makassar Strait, to the east of Borneo, lie vast reserves of energy requiring complex engineering to extract. The scale of the block is enormous – it stretches across 3,339 square kilometres, and yielded 2.2 billion standard cubic feet of natural gas and 82,000 barrels of oil and condensate per day in 2011. The gas alone accounts for one-third of Indonesia's total gas production, making the block's output vital to national development. Activity in the block centers on several fields – Tambora, Tunu, Peciko, Sisi and Nubi – while much of the administration takes place in the nearest big city, Balikpapan in East Kalimantan, or in Jakarta. The workforce of several thousand people is overwhelmingly Indonesian.

Most of the natural gas extracted at Mahakam is delivered to the Bontang liquefied natural gas plant operated by state-run energy company Pertamina, accounting for 80 percent of the gas received by the plant. From there, the LNG is distributed domestically, as well as being exported to countries including Japan, South Korea and Taiwan.

Suharto era

Exploiting the abundance of natural resources in the seas east of Kalimantan was part of President Suharto's plan to power the nation's development. In March 1967 Indonesia commenced a 30-year deal with Japanese energy company Inpex to tap into Mahakam.

Within a few years Inpex realised it had bitten off more than it could chew in taking on 100 percent of the production sharing contract for Mahakam, and in 1970 off-loaded a 50 percent stake to Total, the French company known at the time as CFP. With its considerable experience around the world and deep pockets, Total was considered well placed to drive forward development of Mahakam, and went on to become the lead operator. By 1974, output started flowing from Mahakam.

Total has long been an industry giant, with oil and gas exploration and production operations in more than 50 countries. As one of the six "supermajor" oil companies in the world, its scale and experience means it is adept at playing the long game, developing relations with countries and partner companies that may take decades to pay off, if at all.

Mahakam is the biggest project for Total E&P Indonesie, the French company's local offshoot, but the outfit has started to diversify in recent years, buying up exploration permits for other parts of the country: in East Kalimantan, West Papua, the Arafura Sea and elsewhere in the Makassar Strait. By 2012, the company was the largest gas producer and the number four oil producer in Indonesia, with output reaching 382,000 barrels of oil equivalent per day.

For decades from the 1970s onwards, Mahakam proved a boon for Inpex, Total E&P and the Indonesian government, which collected significant royalties for the bounty beneath its waters. As the 1997 end of the 30-year contract approached, Suharto remained in power, ageing but seemingly entrenched. Satisfied with the progress of Inpex and Total in extracting the resources of Mahakam, Suharto's government offered them a production sharing contract for a further 20 years.

Indonesia had established itself as a low-risk market up to 2001, with straightforward oil and gas regulations that imposed a high tax rate but enabled steady profits. In essence, on an oil exploration project, the government would receive 85 percent of the proceeds with the rest going to investors, while for gas exploration about 70 percent went to the government. But those rules, and the stability that came with them, started to break down through the first decade of the new century, as a policy of decentralisation shifted decision-making power from Jakarta to provincial and regional governments.[222]

As the operator of Mahakam, Total E&P acted as a representative for itself and Inpex in discussions with the government over the project's future.

Discussions begin

In 2007, discussions started on Mahakam's future beyond March 31, 2017. The block was approaching its mature stage, which meant that the period of easy access to resources was coming to a close and future extraction would be more difficult, and more costly. Total E&P knew that the dynamics had changed since its last contract started a decade earlier. Pertamina, the state-controlled energy behemoth, had developed its expertise in resource extraction and was keen to get access to Mahakam given its intensive search for oil and gas to meet domestic demand.

Total E&P and Inpex had two objectives in their discussions with government – to retain their joint majority stake in the field, and for the decision to be made promptly. The case for the first objective relied on explaining how their expertise and capital were necessary to the complex process of extracting resources out of Mahakam as it aged. Implicit in this case was the claim that no local company, including Pertamina, possessed the necessary capabilities on its own.

The second objective involved persuading the government that a lack of certainty would put the output of Mahakam at risk. Projects to extract oil and gas have a long lead time, all the more so in the case of a maturing block, and returns on investment are often not achieved for a decade or more. Without knowing whether they will have control of Mahakam beyond 2017, the existing controlling parties would have little choice but to pull back on investment. With one-third of Indonesia's gas coming from Mahakam, a drop in output could have disastrous consequences for a rapidly growing economy already grappling with energy shortages.

The task of Total E&P and Inpex was made more complex by the fact that pursuing the goal of a swift decision could put at risk their joint majority stake. After all, if forced into a quick decision, regulators would most likely opt to give the contract to Pertamina, given that patriotism meant it was the least politically risky outcome, in the short term at least. Strategically, the two foreign companies could not afford to push too hard for an urgent decision, but still needed to make clear that one was needed.

After its formation following the expulsion of the Dutch in 1957, Pertamina was pushed by the government to expand both in the upstream extraction of oil and gas from within Indonesia and abroad, and also the downstream delivery to consumers. Over time, however, it became a cash-cow for the Suharto regime, allowing cronies of the president to siphon off for their own use benefit the spoils of a rising oil price. With a board stacked with government supporters and few probity checks in place, Pertamina between April 1996 and March 1998 managed to clock up US$6.1 billion in direct losses and potential savings due to inefficiencies and collusive business practices, according to a later PricewaterhouseCoopers audit.[223] But with the fall of the New Order, things changed significantly. In 2001, a new law meant that Pertamina no longer gained priority access to contracts and had to compete on market terms with its rivals. A decade later, the company was rapidly gaining international respect and was keen to establish itself as a major player in Asia's oil industry.

Talks over Mahakam moved slowly. Both the government and the contractors knew that the decision was still likely several years away, and would be made after national elections scheduled for 2009. A change in the occupancy of Istana Negara might have a significant impact on the decision over Mahakam, making early discussions little more than preliminary.

Leading Total E&P through the difficult process of negotiations was Elisabeth Proust, the Frenchwoman who assumed the top role at the company in December 2008. A 30-year veteran of the oil and gas industry, Proust has worked much of her career in the sorts of rugged places in which the sector does business; Cameroon and Angola in West Africa, as well as Brazil, the North Sea and Russia, all feature in her resume.

When she took on the Total E&P job, Proust opted to pursue an exploration-focused strategy, seeking to exhaust all exploration possibilities in existing blocks, running the ruler over potential reserves that were little developed and rethinking areas previously considered off-limited because of high exploration costs.

Her counterpart at Pertamina was Karen Agustiawan, a trailblazer who in 2009 became the first woman to lead the revenue-rich state-owned company. Agustiawan, a graduate of the Bandung Institute of Technology, started her career at Mobil Oil (now ExxonMobil) in the mid-1980s before going on to work for local company Landmark Concurrent Solusi Indonesia and the local arm of US energy industry services giant Halliburton.

Agustiawan has established for herself a reputation as a shrewd operator able to satisfy the demands of her shareholders – the government – while also showing to the corporate world that the company is a capable business partner. Placating demanding voices on both sides while keeping the company focused on growth is a delicate balancing act that she has performed with aplomb. In June 2013 she was given the nod by the government to serve for a second five-year term, such is the esteem in which she is held. The achievement was all the more remarkable given several lawmakers publicly questioned her ability to run the company when she was first appointed.[224]

During her time in the role, Agustiawan has made it her mission to reconceptualise the company – from an oil and gas operator to an energy company, one that is open to alternative sources of fuel such as geothermal and has a considerable research and development capacity.[225]

Plenty of goodwill

Once President Susilo Bambang Yudhoyono secured a second term in power in July 2009, talks on the future of Mahakam stepped up a gear. The decision on Mahakam notionally rested with the oil and gas regulator, BP Migas, but given its significance it would be made at the highest levels of the government. As his Minister of Energy and Mineral Resources, Yudhoyono appointed Darwin Zahedy Saleh, an academic with a background in finance.

The existing developers showed signs that they were confident of retaining the Mahakam contract. In 2008, Total E&P and Inpex signed a 20-year contract to supply gas to the planned Senipah plant, also in

East Kalimantan. Total E&P had also recently inked a memorandum of understanding with a consortium of state firms — Pertamina, as well as retail gas and electricity suppliers — to deliver 1.5 million tons of liquefied natural gas each year to a floating storage terminal in Jakarta Bay starting in 2012. Meeting the commitments required having access to the flow from Mahakam.

Total E&P and Inpex recognised early that if they were to succeed in renewing the contract, they needed to demonstrate their commitment to Indonesia's development.

Like a politician on the stump, Total E&P's Elisabeth Proust approached her constituents, in this case members of the legislature, and offered a campaign promise: if our contract is renewed, we will supply 33 percent of the gas from the Mahakam block to the domestic market in 2020, up from 25 percent in 2012. "Although there is no obligation to allocate [more] gas, we have committed to supply the domestic market," Proust told House of Representatives Commission VII, which oversees energy issues, in December 2009.[226]

Nudged on by the government, Total E&P reached out to Pertamina. There was much goodwill between the companies, and an acceptance by both parties that if Pertamina was to play a greater role in Mahakam the transition would need to be gradual with steady transfer of technology and know-how.

After an August 2009 visit by Pertamina's Karen Agustiawan to Total E&P headquarters in Paris, a preliminary agreement was struck that involved the transfer of a 15 percent stake from the existing Mahakam stakeholders to Pertamina, in exchange for a share in the state oil and gas company's other assets. As part of the deal, Total E&P sought to capitalise on its global footprint. According to Agustiawan's account to reporters after the meeting, Total E&P offered Pertamina the right to participate in its exploration activities in Australia, Angola and Vietnam.[227]

But once Agustiawan returned to Jakarta, the deal appeared far from settled and discussions rolled on. Come the new year, Pertamina sought to bump up the size of the stake it would receive to 25 percent. Despite the apparent amity between the parties, the deal did not go ahead. Pertamina, it seems, was not satisfied with holding only a sliver of Mahakam.

Understanding just what Pertamina's position was as talks advanced is difficult to know. The company does not seek the communications discipline that is common in big business and politics around the world. Instead, company representatives speak their mind, often confusing rather than clarifying the company's position.

In March 2011, for example, Pertamina spokesman Mochamad Harun said the company planned to acquire a 10 percent Mahakam stake from Total E&P in 2012 and a further 5 percent stake in 2013. He then pointed to Total E&P's predicament, noting that operators with production sharing contracts are often hesitant about boosting production without an assurance its contract will be extended, and added: "In that case, we will take over the investment … Just trust us and we will develop the block."[228]

A few months later, Pertamina offered a further glimpse into the boldness of its plan with the statement of Salis Aprilian, a senior company official, that the state enterprise was ready to take over oil and gas blocks from foreign companies whose contracts would expire over the following decade.

"What we want is for the government to offer those expiring oil and gas blocks to us because we are the state company," Aprilian was quoted as saying. "The government still does not give us a 100 percent controlling stake, but what we want is to control 100 percent." He added: "We have experience and competency from more than 50 years in both offshore and onshore exploration."[229]

Pertamina was just one of several state-owned energy companies around the world getting more assertive in claiming energy assets. Amid a looming scarcity of energy and the maturing of many major resource fields, state-owned companies like Brazil's Petrobras and Malaysia's Petronas sought to expand into new terrain, often beyond their own country's borders, to ensure energy security. Their increasing technical sophistication and deep wells of capital meant these state-owned companies were no longer reliant on private partners to do the heavy lifting.[230]

Seeking certainty

Big resource projects require certainty. They can be extremely capital-intensive, meaning lots of money needs to be spent upfront for a return that can take a decade to materialise. No company will make a major commitment of funds if it believes it won't be the operator of the project for a significant share of its lifespan, and may not get compensation for the funds it has sunk if circumstances change. Too much uncertainty for too long means investments won't be made, and the flow of resources will dry up.

Such fears materialised in 2011 in the case of the West Madura offshore oil and gas block, in the seas north of Java. South Korea's Kodeco Energy had for 30 years been the block's operator, but a government decision on its future was left to the last minute, making the operator hesitant to expand it with fresh investment. Regulator BP Migas calculated that the uncertainty resulted in a 5,500 barrel-per-day reduction in oil output. In the end, Pertamina snared 80 percent control of the West Madura block, and became its operator.[231]

The case for certainty in the case of Mahakam was backed by the influential ReforMiner Institute, an energy industry think tank. "The clarity is important because it is related to the continuation of investments in the block. Whoever operates [the block] or gets involved [by having shares in the block] has to be committed and ready to invest," ReforMiner's Pri Agung Rakhmanto told the *Jakarta Post*. He added that without clarity production activity and exploration to discover new reserves at Mahakam would likely continue to decline.[232]

As the decline in Mahakam's output advanced, Total E&P and Inpex in 2011 embarked on a strategy to squeeze more from the block, deploying costly additional rigs and advanced technology. All up, the two companies pledged to spend US$16.5 billion by 2017, including developing 297 new and existing wells and embarking on drilling projects for 41 offshore wells. "To keep maximum production after 2017, the gas block will need an additional US$6.75 billion in investment, which requires long-term preparation, recent technology, competent and well-trained human resources and strong financial capacity," Total E&P's Proust said.[233]

Total E&P and Inpex appeared to be getting a good hearing from the government as the discussions stepped up a notch in early 2011. Speaking in March, Energy Minister Darwin Zahedy Saleh hinted that the government was inclined to extend Total E&P's contract for the block. "I believe, with its positive contribution to this nation, we will still be together after 2017," he was quoted as saying.[234]

His view was backed by Raden Priyono, the chairman of energy regulator BP Migas, who added that Total E&P's investment in Indonesia was crucial to meeting national gas production targets over the decade ahead.[235] (The largely policy-focused Saleh only went on to serve another seven months in the cabinet, being replaced in an October reshuffle by Jero Wacik, a veteran in President Susilo Bambang Yudhoyono's Democratic Party who had served for seven years as Minister of Culture and Tourism.)

Economic nationalism

By 2011, as the world economy slowed and Indonesians became increasingly anxious about protecting their recently acquired prosperity, the winds of economic nationalism blew a zephyr across the archipelago. More pragmatically, a deteriorating budget position had left the government searching for ways to plug the gap without resorting to unpopular measures like increasing the subsidised fuel price.

President Susilo Bambang Yudhoyono said in late May that the government would review resources contracts with foreign companies to seek better terms, claiming that the country's robust economy put it in a stronger bargaining position. The industry sought to push back. "I think the contracts are a very sensitive problem. A bad contract or a one-sided change will scare investors away," said Sammy Hamzah, the vice chairman of the Indonesian Petroleum Association, an industry group. "Please be careful when talking about the contracts. It should be fair for investors."[236]

In July, legislators called for long-term contracts with foreign oil and gas companies to be renegotiated, suggesting 15 companies were between them exploiting international double taxation provisions to deny the government Rp 1.6 trillion (US$133 million) in tax payments to which it was entitled. The figures arose in testimony to a parliamentary hearing by Fuad Rachmany, a director of the tax office. Oil and gas production sharing contracts usually allocate 15 percent of profit for the contractor, with the balance going to the government, but according to Rachmany, oil and gas companies are using double taxation rules to boost their stake to up to 21.5 percent.

BP Migas's Raden Priyono pushed back, noting that "as soon as we do not honor contracts, we [Indonesia] will be disrespected by the world". Whether due to that argument or the short attention spans of some legislators, the proposal advanced no further.[237]

Four months later, the government flagged a plan to add a new clause to the Oil and Gas Law giving Indonesian companies priority access to take over the expired contracts of foreign companies.

Widjajono Partowidagdo, the Deputy Minister for Energy and Mineral Resources pushing the change, said explicitly that the new clause was intended to help Pertamina. Local private companies tipped to benefit from the new scheme were large energy firms MedcoEnergi, linked to businessman Arifin Panigoro, and Energi Mega Persada, affiliated with the Bakrie family. "It's most important to give national companies a chance to develop more oil and gas blocks in Indonesia," Partowidagdo said.[238]

Fueling resentment at the foreign energy companies was an inability to meet the oil output targets for the year set by government regulators and used in planning the national budget. In a June legislative hearing, representatives from three big players – Chevron Pacific Indonesia, ConocoPhillips and Total E&P – sought to explain why the targets were unrealistic given regulatory and operational challenges.

The government's target of 970,000 barrels per day, it emerged, was higher than the sum of the estimates lodged by each of the oil producers in their annual work plan and budget, which stood at 952,000 barrels per day. But even this target was proving difficult: as of April the output stood at 916,000 barrels per day. Clearly the government's wishful thinking was not enough to boost output. For its part, Total E&P was struggling to meet the target of 94,000 barrels per day set by the government, producing only 89,100 barrels per day as of May. Pertamina quietly admitted that it too would fall short of its target.[239]

The shortfall in gas output at Mahakam was also on the radar of the regulator, BP Migas. Production had fallen to 1,800 million standard cubic feet per day (mmscfd), 11 percent below the 2,020 mmscfd target for the year, and BP Migas had expressed fears that production could dip by as much as 35 percent from the goal. In May 2012, BP Migas established a special team to keep an eye on production activities at Mahakam to limit the drop to no more than 150 mmscfd. Total E&P's Elisabeth Proust appeared cognisant of the concerns. "We will need to mobilise all resources to boost production to the maximum level," she said.[240]

Keen to break through the stalemate that had emerged, Widjajono Partowidagdo, the deputy minister, acted as a go-between to bring Total E&P and Pertamina closer to a deal. In seeking to make progress on Mahakam, his message to Total E&P was that Pertamina ought to be the operator beyond 2017, with investment costs shared between the companies. "We have to make a decision as soon as possible," he said in November 2011.[241]

Sadly, the deputy minister would never get a chance to follow through. One Saturday in April 2012, Patrowidagdo was hiking up the famed Mount Tambora in the West Nusa Tenggara island of Sumbawa when he had a heart attack and died. The death of the adventure-loving official at age 60 was yet another blow to those craving certainty in Mahakam.

New approach

By 2012, Total E&P was becoming increasingly frustrated at the lack of progress. Many of its investment decisions involving Mahakam would only achieve a return beyond the 2017 contract expiration, and it wanted certainty. As an energy player with projects in dozens of countries around the world, Total E&P is frequently weighing those projects against each other in determining where it would be most sensible to invest. Investing more in Indonesia was already a tough case to make to head office – while the country was second in terms of production for Total E&P across all the countries in which it operates, it ranked seventh for revenue. The fog of uncertainty meant that it was increasingly difficult to make the case internally to invest in Mahakam.

The company tried a new approach to push the government towards a decision. It took a group of senior journalists from Jakarta to visit Mahakam, allowing them to appreciate the scale of the project first-hand and the consequences of a lack of certainty. Senior company executives were made available to put their case, including a barely concealed frustration at the government go-slow.

One executive used the event to point to one of the problems that may emerge if a state-controlled company, presumably Pertamina, was to take charge of a project requiring a large investment for uncertain returns. Will its executives face trial if they approve costly exploration but are unable to find commercially viable hydrocarbon resources, mused

Arividya Noviyanto, Total E&P vice president for human resources, explaining that state companies need to account for their use of state funds.[242]

The resultant coverage sent a signal to the government that it risked being embarrassed at home and abroad if it failed to get its act together.

At the same time, Pertamina was becoming increasingly bold in putting its case for taking a controlling stake in Mahakam, rather than just a minority interest. Senior executives talked openly about the plan, and some figures in the government appeared sympathetic.

Activists with an economic nationalist streak also found their voice, talking up the case for Pertamina to take charge. One activist, Marwan Batubara from think tank Indonesian Resources Studies (Iress), took an unconventional route. He organised a petition, signed by people including Reformasi-era government ministers Kwik Kian Gie and Rizal Ramli, as well as Muhammadiyah Islamic group chairman Din Syamsuddin, urging the government to gift Mahakam to Pertamina. "The block still has some 12.5 trillion cubic feet of natural gas left, potentially generating a gross revenue of around Rp 1,700 trillion [US$142 billion], under current natural gas prices," the group said in a statement.[243]

Later, Batubara, who has links to the Islam-based Prosperous Justice Party (PKS), reported senior energy regulators to the powerful Corruption Eradication Commission (KPK), accusing them of creating policies that may benefit foreign companies operating in Indonesia.[244]

Provincial officials in East Kalimantan also voiced their support for Pertamina, complaining that they were being neglected by Total E&P and wanted an Indonesian firm in charge.

East Kalimantan Governor Awang Faroek Ishak used the January 2013 opening of the new South Mahakam field to express his opposition to the renewal of Total E&P's contract. "I reject the company's contract extension and I urge the Mahakam block to be managed by the government," he told an audience that included Total E&P's Elisabeth

Proust. He added his frustration that the energy-rich province was still experiencing intermittent power failures, and called for Total E&P to allocate 50 percent of its income from operations in the block towards the development of the province.

In response, Proust talked up the company's contribution to the local economy. "There are 3,700 Indonesians working in the company, so it's crucial for the government to make a quick decision since this case involves the interests of those Indonesian workers," she said.[245]

The East Kalimantan government, along with the regency of Kutai Kartanegara, in which Mahakam sits, were also seeking a 10 percent stake between them in the project. With the discussion with government regulators and Pertamina already protracted, Total E&P had little desire to bring yet another party to the negotiating table. "We signed the Mahakam block contract with the central government and thus any request from the locals should be accommodated by the government," Total E&P spokesman Kristanto Hartadi told a media briefing in Balikpapan in March 2013.[246]

Split at the top

The discussions over Mahakam revealed a schism in the cabinet room. Two of President Susilo Bambang Yudhoyono's most senior ministers were at odds over just what role Pertamina should play in its future.

State Enterprises Minister Dahlan Iskan, a colourful former media executive whose ministry oversees Pertamina, argued for the company to take over the whole production operation at Mahakam. He sought to tap into national pride to bolster his case. "Assuming the Mahakam operations would be a quick way for Pertamina to become equal to or perhaps even larger than Petronas in terms of revenue," he said, referring to Pertamina's Malaysian counterpart. "Indonesia has already outperformed Malaysia in the palm oil sector and our flag carrier, Garuda Indonesia, has surpassed Malaysia Airlines. However, we have yet to find a way for Pertamina to do the same."

Jero Wacik, the veteran Democratic Party politician serving as Energy and Mineral Resources Minister, was of a very different view, doubting that Pertamina had the technical capabilities to take control on its own. "Imagine if Pertamina is granted operation of Mahakam. Will they be able to maintain the annual investment for the block? We have to consider so many things right now," he said.[247]

Shaping the thinking over what stake Pertamina would have in Mahakam were two recent experiences – its problematic attempt at a complete takeover of the Natuna oil and gas block in the Riau Islands province east of Sumatra, and its more successful taking of a minority share in the offshore North West Java block.

Pertamina was in 2008 given the right to operate Natuna, a block rich in natural gas reserves, after its previous holder, ExxonMobil, failed to reach an agreement with the government. Two years later, Pertamina found it had little choice but to partner with ExxonMobil, Total E&P and Petronas to bankroll the US$40 billion investment needed to develop Natuna.[248]

In the case of the offshore North West Java block, Pertamina in 2009 purchased a 46 percent stake from British energy giant BP, at a cost of US$280 million. It went on to operate it successfully, boosting production to 36,000 barrels per day by 2013, up from 20,000 barrels per day when BP ended it period as operator.[249]

The experiences created doubts that Pertamina had the capacity to go it alone at Mahakam.

Pertamina itself appeared to acknowledge the risk of it overreaching in its quest for Mahakam. In an interview with the *Jakarta Globe* in October 2012, Sugiharto, a former State Enterprises Minister now working for Pertamina, laid out some of the company's concerns.

"Pertamina, as a state-owned enterprise, must manage its assets prudently, meaning that we must distribute the risk into different productive assets with calculated risk," he said. "As we have issued global bonds, Pertamina must follow several covenants that compel us to carry out meticulous calculation before making any investment decision."

Sugiharto went on to note that the Mahakam block's rate of production decline was high. "We cannot be greedy," he said. "We must assess whether any investment plan will provide the ultimate return for Pertamina." It would be foolish for Pertamina to take on all of the substantial risk associated with the Mahakam block. Instead, he argued, the risk should be distributed among several parties. "There are no single oil and gas fields with high risks that require large amounts of investment being handled by a single operator," he said.[250]

The Ministry of Energy and Mineral Resources appeared to be on the same page. In November 2012, deputy minister Rudi Rubiandini said the government was considering making Pertamina and Total E&P the block's joint operators from 2017 to 2022, after which Pertamina would become the sole operator.[251] Earlier, the ministry's highly respected director general of oil and gas, Evita Legowo, urged Pertamina to learn from Total E&P. "Pertamina should seek experience in operating the Mahakam block," she said.[252]

Bolt from the blue

Just when the decision-making vehicle appeared to be spinning its wheels ineffectually in mud, the wheels themselves came off.

BP Migas, the oil and gas regulator, had for a decade brought a new level of professionalism to the administration of the nation's natural resources, making evidence-based policy decisions at arm's length from the government of the day.

But its approach had left a few noses out of joint, particularly among those observers who felt it was unsympathetic to the wishes of local companies. One frustrated organisation, Muhammadiyah, the nation's second-largest Muslim religious group, launched legal action to challenge the authority of BP Migas – and won.

In November 2012, the Constitutional Court ruled as unconstitutional key parts of the legislative act under which BP Migas operated, the 2001 Oil and Gas Law, because it delegated authority that under the founding law of the nation must reside with the government itself. The court affirmed that decisions BP Migas had previously made would stand, but that it had no right to make future decisions.[253]

Embarrassed by the ruling, the government disbanded BP Migas and hastily established a new regulator, SK Migas (and later SKK Migas), which would no longer be at arm's length from the government – instead, it would reside inside the Ministry of Energy and Mineral Resources and be headed up by the portfolio's minister, Jero Wacik.

Rudi Rubiandini, the deputy minister who was also previously a key figure at BP Migas, was appointed to lead the body, which would now notionally decide Mahakam's future.

The court ruling was seen by some observers as a boost for Pertamina. The ruling had hinted at a narrow reading of the national interest with regard to government decisions over natural resources, such that any foreign company would struggle to make its case against a local rival. And any progress Total E&P had made in discussions with BP Migas now counted for little, although many of the staff from the disbanded body were transferred to its replacement. Certainty over Mahakam would be some time away yet.

Diplomatic offensive

As 2013 rolled around, Total E&P sought fresh ways to nudge discussions along. In February, Energy and Mineral Resources Minister Jero Wacik, already thought to be sympathetic to its cause, met with Total E&P executives in Paris. "It turned out that they really want to continue the partnership with Indonesia," he said afterwards. "If the current 'husband' matches with the 'wife', why should the 'wife' find another?"

The minister sketched out the government's key considerations: revenue flow to the state, the allocation of output for domestic consumption and efforts to maintain, or even increase, production level. "In principle, the national interest remains our top priority," he said.[254]

A month later, Total E&P stepped up its efforts to persuade SKK Migas of the merits of its claim. It met with executives of the regulator in Balikpapan, East Kalimantan, telling them that a maturing block meant new extraction projects at Mahakam "have more and more marginal economics". The development of Mahakam's Tunu and Peciko fields was being held in a "standby" position amid the uncertainty of the concession, it added.[255]

Part way through the year the French ambassador to Indonesia headed to East Kalimantan to make the case for Total E&P, and then in August the visit to Jakarta of French Foreign Minister Laurent Fabius helped the company escalate the issue within the government. In discussions with his Indonesian counterpart, Marty Natalegawa, as well as Wacik, Fabius discussed the future of the Mahakam project, and amid the diplomatic niceties made clear that the issue was a concern.[256]

The next month, Inpex sought to push for an answer. Inpex chief executive Toshiaki Kitamura visited Jakarta from Tokyo and gained an audience with President Susilo Bambang Yudhoyono, with the issue on the agenda. (Also on Kitamura's agenda was a call for a production sharing contract extension on Inpex's project in the gas-rich Masela block in the Arafura Sea, south of Papua. The 30-year contract on the massive block, which has an estimated 18.5 trillion cubic feet of proved and probable gas reserves, does not expire until 2028. Inpex, it seems, has learned that plenty of time needs to be set aside for such discussions.)[257]

With the government leaning toward giving Pertamina a major role in Mahakam, discussions centred on competing ideas for how that role should be structured.

Pertamina proposed that it be given a 51 percent stake in the block and Total E&P pay the government US$500 million for a 49 percent interest if it wished to continue to develop it.[258]

The existing operators proposed another compromise: a transition period of five years to transfer skills and expertise to Pertamina, during which Total E&P and Inpex would reduce their stakes to 35 percent each. At the end of the five years, it would be up to the government to decide whether Total E&P and Inpex could remain part of the new consortium taking over the block.

Total E&P senior vice president Jean-Marie Guillermo put the proposal to Wacik, the Energy and Mineral Resources Minister, in a meeting in July 2013. "A decision has to be taken now. I am not sure people actually realise what is at stake," Guillermo said in a statement issued after the meeting.

To slow the decline of the block, Guillermo said, the company planned to invest about US$7.3 billion before 2017. "That is a lot of money and to justify such an investment, we need to have some visibility on what will happen to us after 2017 since a large part of the return on this investment will only be generated by the post-2017 production," he said.

Guillermo put a further sting in the tail, quantifying just how the uncertainty would hit output beyond that inevitable with the maturing of the field. He said current production stood at about 1.8 billion cubic feet per day (bcfpd), and that even if the necessary investments are made, production will still decline to between 1.1 and 1.2 bcfpd. "But if we cut from the investment the portion of it which cannot be justified due to lack of visibility, the production might fall to 0.8 bcfpd," he said.[259]

But as such arguments were being made, the regulator's attention was elsewhere. Rudi Rubiandini, the deputy minister heading up SKK Migas, was in mid-2013 arrested and accused of receiving more than US$1 million in kickbacks from a Singapore company seeking import contracts from the regulator. Again, the organisation was paralysed.

Stumbling through

Over four decades, Total E&P had invested more than US$25 billion in the Mahakam product sharing contract, drilling more than 1,655 wells and generating US$77 billion in net revenue for the state. But in line with the maturing of Mahakam, Total E&P's gas output for Indonesia fell 16 percent in 2012.

This maturing has prompted Total E&P to look further afield in Indonesia to maintain its pipeline of oil and gas from the country, including taking over exploration projects in the offshore Bengkulu basin, southwest of Sumatra, and in the Salawati basin in the province of West Papua.

Some development is proceeding closer to the main block. In October 2012, Total E&P and Inpex started operations in their condensate gas fields in South Mahakam, intended to offset the maturity of other parts of the Mahakam block. The South Mahakam project, at a cost of US$830 million, aims to increase gas production from the block by 100 million metric standard cubic feet per day.

But the future of Mahakam remained unresolved, with Energy and Mineral Resources Minister Jero Wacik saying only that the issue would be settled some time before the end of Susilo Bambang Yudhoyono's term in office in October 2014.[260]

Hoping to put relations with the government on a better track, Total E&P in early 2014 announced the appointment of Hardy Promono to succeed Elisabeth Proust as general manager, making him the first Indonesian to lead the unit. It also announced it had set aside US$2.5 billion for Mahakam for the year. "The main priority is to restrain declining production in the Mahakam block," the 30-year company veteran told the *Jakarta Post*.[261]

Tamba Hutapea, the deputy chairman of the Investment Coordinating Board (BKPM), said the woes afflicting the regulator – first the Constitutional Court ruling and then the arrest of Rudi Rubiandini – were responsible for the delays to the decision over Mahakam. "We

are not proud of that. The delay means a negative economic impact,"
he said in an interview, acknowledging concerns over drops in oil and
gas production. But he denied that Pertamina would get preferential
treatment, saying it operated like a private company and had lost out in
open bidding processes in the past.[262]

The implications over the decision in East Kalimantan will be
profound. Mahakam is one of 29 oil and gas concessions due to expire
between 2013 and 2021. Among them are the South Natuna Sea Block
B operated by ConocoPhillips Indonesia, the Southeast Sumatra block
operated by China National Offshore Oil Corporation and the East
Kalimantan block operated by Chevron Pacific Indonesia, all in 2018.

Keith Loveard, the Jakarta-based risk analyst, noted that the national
government was enthusiastic about foreign investment when it involved
technical capabilities beyond the reach of state companies, including
Pertamina. "[But] if an Indonesian company – and particularly Pertamina
– can do the job and has the capital to handle it, there will be very little
chance for a foreign investor to play a role," he said in an interview.[263]

The tightening of government regulation surrounding the oil and
gas industry, and the trend towards nationalisation of assets, can in part
be explained by the fact that production is struggling to keep up with
the surge in local demand. A decade ago Indonesia was a net exporter
of oil and a member of the Organisation of the Petroleum Exporting
Countries (OPEC), but since then it has shifted to being a net importer,
a trend likely to continue. In these circumstances, governments – in
Indonesia or abroad – are naturally keen to take a tighter grip on what
assets they do have available for exploration.

Indonesia still has huge oil and gas reserves, but they are located in
deepwater basins that will rely on expensive exploration activities to
quantify and access. If global energy prices stabilise, like they have in the
early part of the 2010s, or head downwards in the coming decades, the
economic case to access those reserves will be harder to make.[264]

In the slew of major contract decisions to come, investors will watch with keen interest to see whether Indonesia can institute robust processes to ensure a decision is made in a timely and transparent way. It will likely have a major influence on future investment decisions, and with that the ability for the country to gain the most value out of the abundance of natural resources with which it is blessed.

8

A Port in a Storm

Wander along the northern shoreline of Jakarta and you will see a container ship every hundred metres or so anchored in the still, grey waters of the Java Sea with little sign of movement. Those several dozen vessels – some laden with cargo to disgorge and others waiting to pick up their load – are the most obvious physical manifestation of the shortcomings of Tanjung Priok, the port that for more than a century has been the main shipping gateway to Jakarta.

Patience is a virtue, or perhaps just a necessity, in shipping in or out of the capital. Wait times there compare very unfavourably with other ports in Asia, and many large ships intending to make several stops in the region avoid Jakarta altogether, instead unloading their Jakarta-bound cargo in Singapore and sending it over on a separate vessel. And it's not just on the water that a queue forms. The port is served by just a single major road, along which a trail of smoke-belching trucks snake around the clock, their drivers idling away the hours with kretek cigarettes.

With about 60 percent of all international shipping to and from Indonesia passing through Tanjung Priok, its dysfunctionality is a major bottleneck. And despite universal agreement that the port is in need of a major expansion, in recent years government plans for a public-private partnership were abandoned and instead a contract was given to a state-owned company. For thousands of exporters and millions of consumers, the future of Tanjung Priok is vital.

The story of Tanjung Priok's origins give some clues as to the problems it would face more than a century later.

When the Dutch colonial administrators in the early 1600s established Batavia, the city that would become Jakarta, they used a stretch of the northern shore as the port that would connect the new city with global trade. In those early days ships would anchor at the head of the mighty Ciliwung River, which meanders through the city, while a slew of smaller vessels, called lighters, came to load and unload the ships.

But as silt accumulated at the river mouth over the decades, large ships had to anchor further out at sea. Cargo had to be transported longer distances between the ships and Batavia's warehouses by lighters. The process was slow and dangerous, particularly during the wet season, and the lighters' business was highly lucrative. Traders keen to move goods had little alternative.

The inadequacy of facilities at the old port prompted frequent calls for improvement. Two key developments in the 19th century turned the murmurs of frustration into a cacophony – the 1819 establishment of modern Singapore provided Batavia with a local shipping rival, and the opening of the Suez Canal in 1869 sharply increased traffic.

Finally the Dutch administration acquiesced and chose Tanjung Priok as the site of the new port, nine kilometres from the existing Batavia port. But the decision, which was ultimately made by an independent commission, came after much wrangling with the local chamber of commerce, which was keen to protect the lighters' business and the traders operating around the existing port.

Work on the new harbor commenced in 1877, concluding nine years later. It went on to become a modern bustling port equipped with the mod cons of the day, serving steam ships from the Netherlands and those with whom it was on friendly terms, including England, Japan, Germany, Italy, Sweden, Russia and the United States. Its growth over the decades matched that of the city it served, helping to transport agricultural and manufacturing products from Java to the world, and bringing the island the imported goods its increasingly wealthy citizens craved.[265]

The port's name came from Mbah (Grandfather) Priok, an Islamic figure revered in the area. According to folklore, Mbah Priok – born Al Imam Arif Billah Hasan bin Muhammad Al Haddad in Palembang, South Sumatra, in 1727 – was an Islamic scholar who came to Jakarta to spread the world of Islam, dying while under attack from the Dutch colonialists. A 20-square-metre tomb honouring Mbah Priok still stands on the site and is fiercely protected by his self-proclaimed heirs when it is put at risk in any port expansion efforts.[266]

Troubled giant

These days, Tanjung Priok is the jewel in the crown of Pelabuhan Indonesia II, a state-controlled port operator managing at a dozen sites across the country. The company has long been known to many Indonesians as Pelindo II, but in 2012 sought to rebrand itself as the Indonesian Port Corporation. Under an earlier legal structure, the company was established under President Sukarno in 1960 as one of eight companies charged with responsibility for operating the nation's ports.

Heading up IPC now is Richard Joost Lino, a live-wire executive who has become something of a poster boy for the next generation of commercially focused leaders of state-owned enterprises. Lino, who was 56 when he was appointed to lead the company in 2009, was born on the Maluku island of Ambon and like many from the region has sea water flowing through his veins. He went on to study civil engineering at the Bandung Institute of Technology and later received a master's qualification from the Institute of Hydraulic and Environmental Engineering in Delft in the Netherlands.

Much of his early professional career was spent at Tanjung Priok, where he worked in management from 1978 to 1990, suggesting the port is far more than just one of many commercial assets under his watch. Immediately before taking the lead role at IPC, Lino spent three years working in China as managing director of the Guigang port in Guangxi. Unusually for leaders of state-owned companies, Lino's experience goes well beyond the government sector, with stints in private consulting and logistics companies along the way.

Lino made quite an impact when he was headhunted to lead the organisation in 2009, seeking to shake up a lethargic culture among long-serving staff. "I challenged them to try and dig themselves out of their weakness and their low morale. Most importantly, I told them I wanted initiative and innovation," he later recalled in an interview with *Globe Asia* magazine. "I didn't care about the criticism this created. As a leader you have to be a little bit of a dictator. You have to have the guts to shake things up for the sake of the nation and the company."[267]

The Tanjung Priok that Lino managed early in his career was a quieter place than it is today. Tanjung Priok is the busiest port in Indonesia, handing about 60 percent of the flow of goods into and out of Indonesia. IPC declares the port a "barometer of the Indonesian economy" in its marketing material.

The site is vast, almost a city in itself, with the processing facilities stretching over about 630 hectares of land and containing a berthing area for ships of another 422 hectares. Container terminal facilities take up another few hundred hectares.

But in recent years, Tanjung Priok has become a byword for Indonesia's lagging infrastructure, too small in its capacity and plagued with inefficiencies in its administration. The dwell time, which measures the time from the moment a container is unloaded from a vessel until it leaves the gates of the container terminal, stood at 6.4 days in November 2012, up sharply on the 4.8 days recorded in October 2010. And the pressures are only going to intensify – total container traffic forecast is expected to grow by over 160 percent by 2015, according to IPC estimates. "As trade and the traffic of shipping containers continue to grow, Indonesia's main port of entry appears to be buckling under the pressure to keep up," a 2013 World Bank-backed study found.[268]

The port area itself has become filled with government and corporate offices that have nothing to do with the port's operations, crippling efficiency and falling foul of the International Ship and Port Facility Security (ISPS) Code.

A report a few years ago from the Japanese Development Institute was particularly damning, noting that Tanjung Priok "does not have efficient facilities to handle the volume of the trade Indonesia deals with now. Especially, the port is facing the problem of limited land unable to hold containers and shallow depth (currently 12 metres which needs to be dredged to [at] least 15 metres) for the berthing of larger size ships now commonly used. This situation piles up the transportation costs in terms of extra time and expenses which not only prevents new investments but also induces the withdrawal from existing business."[269]

Ports measure their capacity in twenty-foot equivalent units (TEUs), the size of most shipping containers. The port in Shanghai, for example, handled 29.1 million TEUs in 2011, nudging it ahead of Singapore, at 28.4 million TEUs, to make it the world's busiest. Tanjung Priok came in 25th on the list, compiled by the International Association of Ports and Harbors, handling 4.7 million TEUs that year.[270]

At that time the Jakarta port's capacity was estimated at between four and five million TEUs, the upper limit of which it was fast approaching. Sure enough, it soon exceeded that capacity, and by 2012 it squeezed through 6.2 million TEUs, according to company figures. So rapid was the growth that the 2012 figure was up more than 60 percent on that achieved just three years earlier.[271]

Hard facts and anecdotal evidence about the port's shortcomings were in abundance. In 2008, the access toll road only reached to Cakung, falling 15 kilometres short of the port itself, forcing an estimated 5,500 trucks a day to use Jalan Cilincing Raya, a dilapidated public road that was just two lanes wide, according to a Pelindo II official quoted in a *Jakarta Post* story at the time. "In good road conditions, a container truck can make up to three trips a day. But now it can only make a trip a day," the official, Hendra Budi, was quoted as saying. "It can take a truck 24 hours on busy days – Thursday, Friday and Saturday – just to get to the port from the industrial area in Cakung."[272]

Business groups seized on the port as one of the country's key trade bottlenecks, and campaigned relentlessly for its expansion and an overhaul of its administration. Leading the charge was the Indonesian Chamber of Commerce and Industry (Kadin) and the Indonesian Employers Association (Apindo).

"Jakarta needs one more port," Sofjan Wanandi, who as chairman of Apindo has long been Indonesia's strongest voice for the private sector, told the *Jakarta Globe* in 2010. "I think the effort to make Tanjung Priok more efficient will still not be enough to improve export activities because of how crowded it is."[273]

Change is coming

In 2010, the campaign yielded some success. In August that year, the government announced a plan for four new terminals at Tanjung Priok to improve handling capacity, booting out organisations such as oil and gas company Pertimina and water supplier PAM Jaya to make room. With IPC the operator of Tanjung Priok, the government opted to give it the green light to take charge of the expansion, the cost of which it put at Rp 22 trillion (US$1.8 billion).

But it was the second prong of the announcement that was perhaps more significant. Acknowledging the physical limitations of Tanjung Priok, the government gave new life to a previously mooted plan that a new port would be constructed at Kalibaru, a site about seven kilometres along the shore. A target date of 2025 was set. But the financing and ownership arrangements of the new port were yet to be decided.

On paper, these plans seemed to go a long way towards easing the congestion that was strangling the port. The Tanjung Priok expansion alone promised to more than double its capacity. Richard Lino, the affable head of IPC, released back-of-the-envelope calculations that the existing capacity of 4 million TEUs of the port would hit 10 million TEUs, assuming each of the four new terminals had a capacity of 1.5 million TEUs.[274] But the key to the success of the plans would be execution.

At the 2010 announcement, Finance Minister Agus Martowardojo declared his intention that the Tanjung Priok expansion would involve both domestic and overseas private companies under public-private partnership schemes. Under PPPs, the Indonesian government's preferred model for building infrastructure, the government maintains a stake in the project while tapping into the funding and expertise of private partners.

"This project will be led by port management company PT Pelindo [IPC] and involve many partners from the private sector," said Martowardojo, one of the leading voices for economic discipline in Susilo Bambang Yudhoyono's cabinet before he was appointed to lead Bank Indonesia, the central bank. Other senior government figures made clear they understood the urgency and the scale of the work that needed to be done. "Congestion is the main problem. If it's not solved, industrial development could be hampered. Businesses will think twice about growing their capacity," said Hatta Rajasa, Yudhoyono's Coordinating Minister for the Economy.[275]

IPC gleefully accepted its role in the Tanjung Priok expansion, and despite Martowardojo's declaration that private companies were to be major players, sought out a slew of partners among state-controlled companies. IPC formed a joint venture with Pembangunan Perumahan, a state-owned company whose primary role is housing construction. It also enlisted three state-controlled banks – Bank Mandiri, Bank Negara Indonesia and Bank Rakyat Indonesia – to help finance the Rp 6.5 trillion (US$542 million) it said it needed for the first phase of the project.[276]

In early 2011 the government released its Master Plan for the Acceleration and Expansion of Indonesia's Economic Development (MP3EI), a watershed 207-page document that sought to spell out the government's development plans for the decade and a half to 2025. Unsurprisingly, infrastructure was identified as key to the country moving towards prosperity.

The document divided the country into six geographic corridors, and identified key industries that each should focus its energies on. Java was identified as a driver for national industries and service provision. For Tanjung Priok, MP3EI backed the development of new terminals, noting that a new car terminal was critical to the development of the nation's automotive industry and also calling for improved connectivity around the port.

On financing new projects, the MP3EI document had this to say:

> The government has very limited funds to finance development through its state budget. Thus, to foster the economic growth in Indonesia, it will depend on the private sector participation which includes state-owned enterprises, and private domestic and foreign investors.
>
> Government policy must be streamlined to allow a bigger participation from private sector. Regulations must be clear, and without possibilities for misinterpretation, in order to encourage trust and maximum participation from investors to build much needed industries and infrastructure. In order to achieve the above objectives, all existing regulatory frameworks must be evaluated, and strategic steps must be taken to revise and change regulations.
>
> The spirit of Not Business As Usual should also reflect in the implementation of important development elements, such as the infrastructure development. The old thinking suggests that infrastructure must be built using government funding. However, due to the limitation of government funding, the old line of thinking resulted in the slow fulfillment of adequate infrastructure

to support rapid development. Under the new way of thinking and working, cooperations between the government and the private sector under the public-private partnership (PPP) scheme is expected to bring in much needed investments.[277]

Such a statement – in a document endorsed by the president, no less – was music to the ears of the economists, development experts and businesspeople who had urged the government to steer, not row, in the pursuit of economic growth.

With infrastructure back on the agenda, the government shifted its transportation focus to the new project at Kalibaru, since rebranded New Priok Port, up the coast from Tanjung Priok. The project would consist of two phases. The first phase would be the construction of three container terminals with a combined capacity of 4.5 million TEUs and two fuel oil terminals and a gas terminal with a combined capacity of nine million tons per year.

The second phase would involve the addition of four more terminals, bringing the total container handling capacity of New Priok to 13 million TEUs. All up, the total capacity of Tanjung Priok would more than triple, from about five million TEUs to 18 million TEUs.[278]

Through deepening the port, the project aimed to allow so-called Triple-E class vessels, those container ships carrying up to 18,000 TEUs, the largest category in shipping, to dock at Jakarta. The existing capacity was just 5,000 TEUs. Finally, the need to stop in Singapore to move cargo to a smaller ship would be eliminated.

Reaching out

The government announced in June 2011 that a swift tender process would be used to determine who would get the contract to build and operate the new port. Ideally, the tender would attract world-class port developers, both to ensure that a quality facility was built and that the process had the necessary competitive tension.

The government pledged that the outcome of the tender would be announced in October the same year, and in August released a short-list of five consortiums still in the running, including several from outside Indonesia. The value of the tender was put at about US$1.3 billion.

Then the government fell silent. The October deadline came and went with the bidders none the wiser on the outcome. Then the new year arrived, with still no word on the outcome. Finally, in late January, came a bombshell.

The Transportation Ministry called representatives from each of the bidders to a meeting – and told them the tender had been scrapped. Under the original plan, the government was to stump up Rp 3.5 trillion (US$292 million) for roads and bridges to improve land access to the port. But an inability to find the funds to meet this obligation had forced it to abort the prequalification tender, the government said.

Instead, a state-owned enterprise would be given the go-ahead to build the new port, using its own finances rather than relying on the government. (IPC was not explicitly identified as the state-owned enterprise in question, but it was pretty clear who the government had in mind.) In a face-saving maneuver, an official said the shortlisted candidates would be given priority in another tender to build a port in West Java, at Cilamaya, Karawang.[279]

Participants in the aborted tender vented their frustration to the *Jakarta Globe*.

Bernardus Djonoputro, the president director of Nusantara Infrastructure, which bid for the project through an international consortium that included Taiwan's Evergreen Group, Japan's Mitsui & Co. and local company 4848 Global System, said the cancellation was "not good for the government's image ... and investment climate". Djonoputro said the government's lack of preparation made investing in Indonesia's infrastructure through public-private partnerships "risky". "Companies could lose US$1 million to US$2 million spent on a feasibility study to participate in a tender if the tender is cancelled," he said.

Also irritated at the process was Garibaldi Thohir, the Indonesian tycoon who serves as president director of Brilliant Permata Negara, a company that bid for the project through Jakarta New Port Consortium. He said the cancellation "will definitely diminish investors' trust in participating in government-backed projects, despite Indonesia receiving investment grade [ratings] from various rating agencies".

Jakarta New Port Consortium included Salam Pacific Indonesia Lines, Cosco Shipping and Hutchison Ports Indonesia. Thohir said his consortium had reached the point of arranging finance: "We had prepared enough funds to finance this Kalibaru project. Four overseas lenders and Bank Mandiri had given commitments to us."[280]

Observers were damning, and some doubted the government's explanation for the scrapped tender.

"This is one reason foreign investors steer clear of infrastructure projects. There are too many vested interests who frankly do not want foreign investment in infrastructure," an unnamed veteran consultant on foreign investment in Indonesia told *Asia Sentinel*. "The problem is that the Tanjung Priok port is OK now and maybe for two to three years but this kind of thing slows down getting new facilities built and in three years it will be inadequate at current rates of growth. For investors, the best sectors are those that are the farthest away from government."[281]

Progress amid uncertainty

Despite the dysfunction of the tender process, two years later there are signs that IPC is making progress in its execution of the Kalibaru/New Priok project.

A presidential decree in April 2012 affirmed that IPC was the sole developer of the project, and by late that year, the company had estimated that the total investment needed for the two-part project was US$4 billion. The first phase, the construction of three container terminals set for completion in 2014, was set to cost US$2.5 billion; the second phase, the development of two fuel oil terminals and a gas terminal from 2018 to 2022, would cost US$1.5 billion.

IPC said the New Priok facilities would reduce reliance on feeder ships via Singapore by doubling channel access to 300 metres and offering draft alongside berths of up to 20 metres, 6 metres deeper than current depths and adequate for almost all container vessels. Dani Rusli, the man appointed chief executive of Pengembang Pelabuhan Indonesia, the company IPC established to develop the new port, pledged that it would cut port costs to users by between 20 and 30 percent compared to the existing Tanjung Priok site.[282]

The awarding by the government of a 70-year permit to operate the NewPriok port at Kalibaru means IPC's position there is entrenched.

"This is a historical moment for Indonesia because we have not expanded [the existing] Tanjung Priok Port for 130 years despite container traffic increasing at around 24 percent annually," Richard Lino said at the start of work for the New Priok port in March 2013.[283]

Despite the gifting of the contract to IPC, foreign operators were not shut out from the process entirely. "How can you finance an expansion plan when the government budget will not stretch that far?" Lino asked rhetorically in a *Globe Asia* interview. "The only way was to open up the plan to a join venture with a foreign investor." Japan's Mitsui & Co, one of the participants in the original aborted tender, beat Maersk Line and MEC to become the building partner, taking a 49 percent share in construction and operation at New Priok.[284]

Acknowledging the potential for the project to become mired in corruption, Vice President Boediono, an economist by training, lent on IPC to establish a supervisory committee. Leading the committee is a former deputy chairman of the graft-busting Corruption Eradication Commission (KPK), Erry Riyana Hardjapamekas, while its members include a representative from Transparency International Indonesia and respected independent economist Faisal Basri.

"We need independent and credible people to monitor Kalibaru and ensure every process of the port development is in accordance with good corporate governance," Lino said at the launch of the committee in early 2013, seeming to gloss over the questionable practices that had already taken place.[285]

The committee, whose initial tenure runs for two years with a prospect of extension, has the right to access any information about the port and can attend directors meetings. It is empowered to report any irregularities in the process to the Transportation and State Enterprises Ministries, and even to the KPK if corruption is suspected. Whether it is a watchdog or a lapdog remains to be seen.

In a far less encouraging sign, the clutter afflicting the original Tanjung Priok port remained in 2013, despite acknowledgement of the problem and a pledge to act four years earlier. "What needs to be redesigned is the layout of the port," Finance Minister Agus Martowardojo said in January 2013. "From our point of view, there are too many entities doing business in the port." His colleague, Coordinating Minister for the Economy Hatta Rajasa, added: "In the Priok port, you can find anything from photocopy service providers to welders."[286]

In an effort to improve efficiency, or at least create the impression of improving efficiency, the Transportation Ministry in mid-2013 established a committee charged with boosting performance. The team, including representatives from the Customs and Excise Office, the harbour master and quarantine office as well as IPC, was given the task of cutting dwell time to three days and the yard occupancy ratio to 65 percent. At the end of June 2013, when the body was established, the dwell time had blown out to 8.7 days, and YOR, a measure that reflects spare capacity, stood at 106 percent.

Problems in administering the port extend into the surrounding infrastructure. Hutchison Ports Indonesia, a Hong Kong-based member of the Jakarta New Port Consortium in the abandoned tender, has had a partnership with IPC stretching back to 1999 to operate the nearby

Jakarta International Container Terminal. But chief executive Stephen Ashworth has noted that improvements in performance were constrained by the provision of utilities. "If you can't run enough electricity to the terminals, or face problems with traffic congestion, you can't run the business," he said in April 2012.[287]

The shortage of port capacity extends well beyond Jakarta. Industry giant APM Terminals estimated in 2011 that, with five of Indonesia's six leading container ports currently operating above capacity levels and suffering from congestion, at least six million TEUs of new capacity would be required by 2015, and a further 15 million TEUs by 2020.[288]

One solution may lie 65 kilometres inland at Cikarang, where a privately owned dry port has been established with a capacity of 400,000 TEUs. Accessible by road, the West Java port can process goods 50 percent faster than Tanjung Priok can, and a World Bank study found the costs for users were 50 percent lower at Cikarang than at its coastal rival. The 200-hectare Cikarang dry port, which has customs and quarantine services in place, is near the industrial areas of Bekasi and Karawang. But uptake at the port has been sluggish, with only 9,869 TEUs of volume realisation in the first half of 2013, just a small fraction of its capacity.[289]

Any longer-term solution needs to involve channelling a smaller proportion of Indonesia's foreign goods trade through Tanjung Priok. Even when it is fully functional, New Priok is unlikely to go too far in relieving the burden. "If we look at the forecasting, New Priok isn't enough in relation to the capacity of this country," Tamba Hutapea of the Investment Coordinating Board (BKPM) lamented in an interview. Instead, he argued, ports in East Java, Sumatra and North Sulwawesi needed to be developed to shoulder a greater share of the burden.[290]

In the wake of the tender cancellation announcement, Nusantara Infrastructure's Bernardus Djonoputro proposed one way to ensure that public-private partnerships that make it to tender do actually materialise. He suggested that the government establish a clearing house directly under the president to manage PPP projects, including marketing, business development, tendering, negotiations and financial completion.[291]

The volume of major projects in the pipeline suggests that Djonoputro's suggestion is worthy of urgent consideration.

9

Facing Jail for Doing Business

Eight years is a long time to be sentenced to prison, all the more so when you're a well-respected corporate executive, the crime for which you've been convicted is standard practice in your industry and your actions were explicitly endorsed by a government minister in evidence tendered to the court.

But living that nightmare is Indar Atmanto, the former president director of telecommunications company Indosat Mega Media, who in July 2013 was convicted by the Jakarta Anti-Corruption Court and given a four-year jail sentence – later doubled to eight years – and a Rp 200 million (US$16,700) fine. While the case was still winding its way through the appeals process six months later, even if Atmanto is ultimately exonerated the case has proved scarring.

Atmanto's conviction for corruptly misappropriating 3G telecommunications spectrum put on display the unpredictability of the Indonesian court system, especially when cases involve regulatory or technical issues. The verdict prompted outrage in the telecommunications industry, including fears that commercial arrangements that are common in the sector could grind to a halt and many other executives could face prosecution for actions that were thought to be innocuous.

Talent groomed within

Jakarta-born Indar Atmanto is a softly spoken businessman who rose through the ranks of Indosat, one of three companies that dominate

Indonesia's telecommunications sector, to join its team of senior executives. Like so many Indonesians who achieve success in technical fields, he was a graduate of the Bandung Institute of Technology, completing his bachelor degree in industrial engineering in 1986. He later went on to receive a master's degree in business administration from the University of Miami.

The father of two was seemingly one of Indosat's great success stories, starting in the lowest ranks of the company in 1990 with limited connections and using a mix of hard work and good networking abilities to advance his career. His mix of technical, commercial and communications skills led him to a slew of interesting roles – he served as the company's general marketing manager, product development manager and corporate secretary.

The fact that his success did not come easy made him particularly cognisant of the importance of showing respect to more junior employees, and listening to their ideas. "At the beginning of my career I was simply an ordinary employee, so I know very well the demands and needs of employees on every rung of the ladder," he told the *Jakarta Post* in a profile interview in 2008. "My principle is that work is a responsibility that is entrusted to me and has to be carried out seriously. That way, if someone works well, they will automatically be rewarded by management."

The influence of management gurus Robert Kiyosaki and Jack Welch, whose works Atmanto told his interviewer he read keenly, is evident in his approach to getting the most out of his staff. "I always emphasise to the employees and my colleagues that we are one team. A company can only succeed if the teamwork is good. That way the company does not depend on me alone," he said.

Atmanto was in his mid-40s when he was appointed president director of Indosat Mega Media in June 2006, a role he explained he hoped to use for national development as well as company profit. "I want everyone here [in Indonesia] to be connected to the internet so that they can access knowledge easily for the sake of the nation's progress," he told his profiler.[292]

Indosat seems like a wise place for a budding telecommunications enthusiast to build a career. The company is a major player in the Indonesian industry, offering the typical suite of services ranging from mobile phones to internet, and has used its "challenger" status to spur innovation. Across the industry, Indosat sits second, behind the government-controlled Telekomunikasi Indonesia (Telkom), but ahead of Malaysia-backed XL Axiata. As Alexander Rusli put it in a *Globe Asia* interview to mark his November 2012 ascension to the head of Indosat, the company wants to be known as "the operator of choice for smart devices".[293]

Indosat has an unusual mix of owners. Holding the biggest stake is Ooredoo ("I want" in Arabic), the company formerly known as Qatar Telecom and owned by the Qatar government, with 65 percent. The Indonesian government holds a 14 percent share. Norway-based mutual fund manager Skagen, with six percent, leads the private investors holding the rest of the company. Indosat's board has since 2008 been led by president commissioner Sheikh Abdullah Al Thani, a senior Qatari who has long been chairman of Ooredoo.

Plans for the future

At the dawn of the new century, Indosat established Indosat Mega Media, branded as IM2, as a wholly owned subsidiary to develop its internet and subscription television businesses, particularly to customers seeking to be at the cutting edge of technology. With the national economy making rapid progress in recovering from the Asian Financial Crisis that crippled it just two years earlier, in 2000 Indosat committed to a capital spending program of up to Rp 15 trillion (US$1.3 billion) over the following five years.

But progress was on the internet front was sluggish, and IM2 struggled to gain significant market share. Keen to support the growth of its offshoot, Indosat in 2006 made available to IM2 a stretch of telecommunications spectrum it had paid to access through a tender process administered by the Indonesian Telecommunication Regulatory Body. The spectrum – in the 2.1 gigahertz (GHz) band – was best suited to providing mobile phone services, but was also capable of supporting 3G data services, just the sort of thing IM2 desperately needed to attract customers. Mobile broadband was in its infancy, and IM2 had a chance to stake its claim. It would be one of several internet service providers to cooperate with Indosat to access spectrum in a similar way.

For Indar Atmanto, who had been appointed the president director of IM2 not long before the deal was struck, the spectrum would give the company a fighting chance in the growing Indonesian ISP industry. IM2's cooperation deal with Indosat was formalised in a letter, dated November 24, 2006.[294]

Within months, IM2 launched new products to capitalise on the wireless network it had accessed. As part of its Broadband Anywhere suite, the company unveiled a range of packages – ECO!, YOU!, PRO! and MAX! – that offered users high-speed wireless broadband access in about 10 cities, with different data limits and price points. "ECO!, in this respect, could be seen as a solution, particularly for students who need to regularly access the internet on a budget," Atmanto said at the product launch. The digital pioneer who saw access to knowledge as key to the nation's development was in his element. From a low base of 14,000 wireless broadband customers, the company reported scorching monthly growth of 20 percent in the early days, with most customers coming from the big Java cities of Jakarta, Bandung and Surabaya.

The use of a wireless network was a creative solution to Indonesia's lack of fixed-line internet support infrastructure, such as a decent national cable grid. Using technology known as High-Speed Downlink Packet Access (HSDPA), IM2 allowed users to go online either through their mobile handset, or by plugging their phone card into a so-called dongle, a device connected to a computer.[295] Many rivals were doing the same, using the networks of Indosat, Telkom and XL Axiata.

For the next four years IM2 posted sustained growth. A surge in customers – a seven-fold increase to 350,000 in 2008 – even took its toll on the operator's technical performance for a while, with data-hungry users claiming service standards on its mobile wireless network were becoming patchy.[296] Licks of capital investment to bolster the number and capacity of base transceiver stations eased the bottlenecks over time and made future growth sustainable. In 2009, IM2 was given international kudos, when industry group the World Broadband Alliance recognised it as the world's most innovative wireless broadband company.

Trouble strikes

As IM2 soon learned, no good deed goes unpunished. In October 2011, a man by the name of Denny AK, an activist with a group called the Indonesian Telecommunication Consumer (KTI), reported Indosat and IM2 to authorities in West Java.[297] The crime, according to Denny, was the transfer to IM2 of spectrum that had been granted by the government to Indosat. The fact that IM2 was a wholly owned subsidiary of Indosat appeared to count for little.

Law enforcement authorities took the complaint seriously: the initial investigation by the West Java prosecutor's office was within three months passed to the national Attorney General's Office for further consideration. (As AGO prosecutor Andhi Nirwanto put it, "The scene of the crime is not limited to West Java."[298]) Five days after the AGO took on the case in January 2012, Indar Atmanto was officially declared a suspect and charged with two counts of corruption.[299]

In essence, the accusation was this. In winning a government tender to use the 2.1 GHz spectrum, Indosat was required to pay a series of fees (an "upfront fee" and a "frequency fee"). By allowing another party, in this case IM2, to use the frequency, Indosat was in effect "sharing" it, an action that should trigger a fresh set of fees for the additional party. By constructing the deal so that IM2 cooperated with Indosat to access its frequency, the two companies had allegedly engaged in corruption that deprived the state of Rp 1.36 trillion (US$113 million) – the funds it would have gained had the second set of fees been paid.

The AGO cited a 2000 Communications Ministry regulation limiting the ability of firms to pass on allocated frequency. The AGO also claimed the 1999 Telecommunications Law and a 2006 Communications and Information Technology Ministerial Regulation on the 2.1 GHz frequency had been breached.[300]

But Indosat and its supporters argued that the 2000 regulation permitted cooperation between a network operator, like Indosat, and a service provider, like IM2. Indosat denied any wrongdoing, arguing that a cooperation agreement between the company and IM2 allowed for the cooperative use of the 3G licence. It also denied there had been any losses to the state through the spectrum transfer, arguing it had paid all fees, charges and obligations mandated by the government.[301]

Central to the dispute is the difference of opinion on exactly what the cooperation agreement entailed. The AGO's position was that it involved IM2 using the frequency held by Indosat, an action that would trigger a new set of fees. The defendants countered that IM2 was instead just using Indosat's 3G network, not directly accessing the frequency itself. Conceptually the distinction was a fine one, but legally it was very significant.

The repurposing of the telecommunications spectrum is commonplace in Indonesia and elsewhere, as telcos seek to generate the best return on their investment. Often a company that acquires spectrum has no immediate need for it, but other parties without their own spectrum do have such a need. Such trading leads to the efficient use of a scarce resource – spectrum – and fosters competition and innovation among companies motivated to make the most of the assets they have available to them. Were every service provider required to construct its own network, prices would be prohibitively expensive for consumers and competition would dwindle. In the case of IM2 and Indosat, the fact that the former was owned entirely by the latter ought theoretically to quell any lingering concerns.

As Gatot S. Dewa Broto, a spokesman for the Ministry of Communications and Information Technology, said in January 2012: "Cooperation or agreements between operators to rent networks are perfectly legitimate." He added that up to 90 percent of Indonesia's estimated 180 service providers, including IM2, rent their networks from the 20 cellular operators registered with the government, of which Indosat is one.[302]

The IM2 case came amid a wider debate within the Indonesian telecommunications industry about repurposing for internet access spectrum initially intended for mobile phone use. Differences in spectrum prices meant canny ISPs could gain cheaper access than if they were to access spectrum earmarked for internet access. Semuel Pangerapan, chairman of the Indonesian Internet Service Provider Association, explained the reason behind the trend. "The internet is a combination of networks," he told the *Jakarta Globe*. "Not all ISPs have fixed networks to cover their market area. The 3G network helps connect the area."[303]

The trend also created openings for opportunists keen to exploit the inability of the law to keep up with developments. In February 2013, a hitherto unknown group calling itself Actual Implementation of Eradicating Collusion, Corruption and Nepotism (KKN RIP) filed a report to the Attorney General's Office accusing 16 ISPs, including IM2, of illegally using cellular frequencies on their internet networks, costing the state licensing revenue.

High stakes

As jitters about Indar Atmanto's legal troubles grew, in May 2012 he left his position as president director of IM2 after six years in the role. He would continue to serve as the company's president commissioner, effectively the chairman of the board, and also continue in the lower-profile role of Indosat's chief corporate services officer. The stakes for Atmanto, personally and professionally, were high: prosecutors were seeking a 10-year jail term for him, along with Rp 500 million (US$42,000) in fines.

Despite the backlash from the industry and parts of the government, the Attorney General's Office continued its investigation into IM2 and Indosat. Determined to cast the net wider than just Atmanto, the AGO named former Indosat president director Johnny Swandi Sjam as a suspect in November 2012 following a meeting between prosecutors and auditors from the Finance and Development Supervisory Agency (BPKP). Sjam, who served as president commissioner of IM2 from 2006 to 2007 before going on to be Indosat president director in 2007 and ultimately defecting to rival Telkom in 2009, was immediately hit with a six-month international travel ban.[304]

During its investigation into IM2 and Indosat, the AGO interviewed more than 30 witnesses, including Basuki Yusuf Iskandar, who chaired the Indonesian Telecommunication Regulatory Body in 2006 when the tender for the spectrum in question took place.[305]

The size of the supposed loss to the state from the actions of Indosat and IM2 was murky. In the early stages of its investigation, the AGO put the figure at Rp 3.8 trillion (US$317 million), perhaps in search of an easy headline. The body later revised down its figure to Rp 1.3 trillion, relying on a report from BPKP, the government oversight body. But even that figure was disputed in court by lawyers for Indosat: the BPKP report had also previously been undermined by a Jakarta State Administrative Court ruling, which found it was legally flawed, and the report itself did not take into account a submission by Indosat, relying only on government data. Given it disputed the essential nature of the charge, Indosat did not offer its own alternative figure.[306]

As the AGO investigation rolled on, Denny AK, the man who had first blown the whistle on Indosat, was having legal troubles of his own. In February 2012, he wrote to Indosat claiming he had identified several legal irregularities in the company's operations separate from the accusation he had already made and threatened to publish the details unless a company director would meet with him within 72 hours. The company ignored his approach, and Denny decided not to follow through on his threat. Instead, he bombarded Indosat staff with text messages and phone calls, seeking to extort funds from the company in exchange for going quiet on his allegations.

Initially the company ignored his overtures, but later opted to report him to authorities. Police decided the best way to prosecute Denny was to catch him in a sting operation. On a Friday afternoon in April 2012 they arranged for Indosat representatives to deliver an envelope with US$20,000 to him at the plush Plaza Indonesia mall in Central Jakarta. Police swooped. Denny was convicted in October that year and sentenced to one year and four months in jail. But the investigation into the initial claim he had made against Indosat and IM2 had taken on a life of its own, so his downfall did little to stop the case's progress.[307]

Court hearing

In January 2013, prosecutors at the South Jakarta District Court formally indicted Indar Atmanto, accusing him of fraud and tax evasion. Outside the hearing, hundreds of IM2 staff mobilised by their union gathered to express their anger, claiming the charges were bogus. Rent-a-crowd demonstrations are common in Indonesia, but in the case of this gathering those in attendance had a genuine interest in the outcome – an unfavourable ruling could put jobs at risk.

Among the key witnesses was Sofyan Djalil, the Communications and Information Technology Minister at the time of the spectrum auction, who told the court that IM2, as a service provider, had no obligation to pay an upfront fee and frequency fee to the government. Indonesian internet pioneer Onno Purbo endorsed the position in his evidence.

The case attracted the interest of the Qatar government, which held a 65 percent stake in Indosat through Ooredoo. During the investigation process, the Qatar government wrote to its Indonesian counterpart about the case, although diplomacy dictated that both parties keep the contents of the correspondence confidential.

The progress of the case, and the implications should the verdict be a conviction, was causing concerns in Indonesian government ranks. In April, the Coordinating Ministry for Political, Legal and Security Affairs convened a meeting of bureaucrats and academics to discuss the case. Eddy Satriya, a deputy at the Coordinating Ministry for Economic Affairs, told the meeting that a guilty verdict would endanger the government's goal of achieving a 30 percent broadband internet penetration rate for 2014. Asep Warlan Yusuf, a legal academic from Universitas Katolik Parahyangan, said the case was evidence of a lack of coordination between government agencies. "When there is no coordination, then it means there is no legal certainty," he said. (Minutes of the meeting were obtained by the *Jakarta Globe*, with detail published after the verdict was delivered.)[308]

Concern extended to the Ministry of Communications and Information Technology, which launched a campaign to reassure investors in the sector that the passing on of spectrum could continue.

Tifatul Sembiring, the Communications and Information Technology Minister, wrote a letter to the Attorney General's Office on November 13 explaining that Indosat and IM2's actions were completely legal and backed by his ministry. IM2 was not obliged to pay an additional fee for the spectrum nor did it need to secure additional permits because Indosat had already acquired the necessary permits, his letter said. In essence he reaffirmed that Indosat was entitled to farm out its 3G frequency to IM2.[309]

The spokesman for the ministry, Gatot S. Dewa Broto, publicly reinforced the minister's message, seeking to assuage the concerns of companies increasingly fearful that they might be next to be prosecuted.

"As regulators [the ministry] must be able to provide peace of mind. We are asking the telecommunications industry not to panic and continue their service to consumers in line with the Telecommunications Law," he said. The spokesman also called on the Attorney General's Office to be more proactive in explaining its actions. "We don't want to intervene between the AGO and the investigation process against IM2. A dialogue [between AGO and industry players] is out of the ordinary but dialogue is needed to provide clarity."[310]

The willingness of prosecutors to continue the case despite the letter was a damning indictment of the minister's authority, and the respect that government agencies had for one another. "If there is no trust among government institutions toward some other government agencies, then this is a bad precedent for the country," noted Setyanto Santosa, chairman of the Indonesian Telecommunications Society (Mastel).[311]

Swift backlash

Ultimately, the Indosat defence case fell on deaf ears. In July 2013, a panel of five judges at the Jakarta Anti-Corruption Court unanimously found Indar Atmanto guilty and sentenced him to four years in prison, with a further fine of Rp 200 million (US$16,700) or an additional three months in jail. The judges said the sentence for Atmanto was lighter than that sought by prosecutors – 10 years in jail and a Rp 500 million fine – because he was not found to have enriched himself through his actions. IM2 was ordered to pay Rp 1.36 trillion – the amount the state was found to have been deprived through the transaction – in compensation within one year.[312]

The verdict sparked howls of outrage among the telecommunications industry. "If IM2 was declared to be guilty, then there are more than 200 internet service providers that also apply the same business model that have to be declared guilty," thundered Semuel Pangerapan, chairman of the Indonesian Internet Service Providers Association.[313] "The verdict also threatens to thwart efforts by the industry to pump up internet usage in Indonesia. It's a very bleak day for the industry."[314]

Turina Farouk, a spokeswoman for XL Axiata, Indonesia's third-ranked telco, said the court's verdict was regrettable. "We are all in grief. Why did things get so complicated?" she wondered aloud to the *Jakarta Globe*, adding that the verdict was a sign of the industry's inability to properly explain its business practices.[315]

The AGO, and the judges who sided with it, had seemingly failed to understand the distinction between a network operator, which typically participates in spectrum auctions effectively as a wholesaler, and a service provider, which cooperates to use that spectrum to meet the needs of customers. It has also taken what was essentially an administrative matter and elevated it to a criminal one amid the euphoria of the battle against corruption.

Mastel's Setyanto Santoso said the verdict "could trigger loss in confidence from the public as well as investors in the sector". The organisation was so outraged by the disregarding of the Communications Minister's letter that it reported the panel of judges to the Judicial Commission, the government body responsible for ensuring legal rulings are honest, transparent and professional.[316]

Adding to the perception of misconduct by the judges was the fact they allowed state prosecutors to revise the indictment during the trial – from an allegation of frequency sharing to one of illegal use of the frequency – even through the law says that any change must be made at least seven days prior to the start of a hearing.[317] Observers at the trial noted that the judges often appeared bored or distracted: talking among themselves, using a laptop computer and closing their eyes.

Luhut Pangaribuan, a lawyer for Atmanto backed by Indosat, expressed disbelief that his client had been targeted personally in the lawsuit. "The defendant Indar Atmanto does not have any capacity nor intention to use the frequency; the agreement that he signed on behalf of IM2 with Indosat is for the use of the cellular network, not the frequency," the lawyer said in a statement. "Therefore, the action that he did was simply to carry out his fiduciary duty as a member of the board of director[s] of IM2. If there is any wrongdoing the sanction should be imposed on the corporation and not on the defendant personally."[318]

For its part, Indosat in the wake of the verdict revealed that it had delayed contracts worth at least US$300 million due to the case.[319]

Enraged that his letter had apparently been disregarded, Communications Minister Tifatul Sembiring spoke up to express his bewilderment at the court ruling. "This will definitely affect the investment climate in a very negative way, and many foreign investors will question the legal certainty of doing business here," he said.[320] "We need to prevent the telecommunications industry from being killed, especially since we issued the licence the company obtained that was then considered false by the court."[321]

His words sparked a rebuke from the Attorney General, Basrief Arief, who said the minister could be accused of interfering in the judicial system by violating the separation of powers between the executive and judicial wings of the government.[322]

Amid the cloud of uncertainty created by the verdict, the Indonesian Telecommunication Regulatory Body halted the licensing processes.[323]

Emboldened by their court victory, prosecutors soon announced that the net had again widened, and former Indosat president director Hari Sasongko was now a suspect in the case. He joined on the list of suspects Johnny Swandi Sjam, whose case had not yet proceeded, as well as companies IM2 and Indosat.

Not long after the verdict was delivered, Indosat and Atmanto said they would appeal. Alexander Rusli, the president director of Indosat, said that if necessary the company would consider global options to achieve justice. "We will keep on fighting the ruling both through local and international courts," he said in a statement.[324]

The first round of appeals did not go well. In December 2013, the Jakarta High Court decided to double Indar Atmanto's sentence to eight years, while keeping the fine at Rp 200 million. Indosat, however, was exempted from its Rp 1.36 trillion fine because the appeal court found it could not be punished for a case in which it was not the defendant. The appeal verdict appeared to catch Indosat by surprise. "We only heard about [the latest verdict] on the news," Indosat spokesman Adrian Prasanto told the *Jakarta Post*. He said the company was likely to appeal the case to the Supreme Court, although he added that it was open to arbitration.[325] In the meantime, Atmanto remains outside of prison and is serving as Indosat's head of strategy.

Regardless of the final outcome of the appeals process, the case serves as an illustration of the unpredictable nature of the Indonesian legal system, and of the way that seemingly strong assurances of the legality of an activity can be undermined. The decision by prosecutors to pursue individual executives personally appears capricious given the number of instances of commercial malfeasance in which the courts opt not to pierce the corporate veil. For executives and companies keen to stay free of prison and fines, independent advice beyond that offered by government ministries and industry bodies is necessary for extra reassurance, and even then there are no guarantees.

10

Hunger Pangs

Travel around the kampungs of Indonesia for a little while and you'll soon spot poor and downtrodden people nursing empty bellies. Often it's skinny men, all bone and muscle, gathered on the side of the road, hang-dog eyes giving a distant stare as they rest their chin on a sinewy knee. Then there are the children, gaunt and tired as they cling to the emaciated frame of their mother, the age of the youngster often much greater than a bystander might guess by observation alone.

About one in 10 Indonesian people face malnutrition, and about half the population lives on less than US$2 a day, leaving many poor people spending up to a third of their incomes on food.[326] These are the people who would stand to benefit from policies that seek to make food cheap and plentiful, but instead are the victims of a policy that deliberately limits its availability. On the flip side are farmers in Australia, Asia and North America who have the capacity to produce the food stocks Indonesia needs, but are prevented from doing so by policies of dubious benefit but obvious cost.

Tapping into deep wells of popular nationalism, the government of Susilo Bambang Yudhoyono has sought to make the country self-sufficient in major food commodities by 2014. While part of the strategy to get there involves supporting the development of local farms, the major tool is a pernicious quota system that tightly controls the volume of imports. Such quotas have had the effect of driving up prices for consumers and creating an allocation system that is rife with corruption and political favouritism. Nowhere is this more evident than in the public policy saga surrounding the nation's beef industry.

While there were small signs of hope in 2014 that rules surrounding beef imports might be relaxed, policy-makers remained willing to sacrifice the interests of consumers in order to keep a small number of well-connected producers happy. But even then, self-sufficiency remained elusive.

Constitutional grounding

Indonesia has viewed reliance on its own resources as a core part of its national identity since it threw off the shackles of colonialism in the 1940s. Article 33 of the Constitution decrees that: "The land and the waters as well as the natural riches therein are to be controlled by the state to be exploited to the greatest benefit of the people." Later in the same article, "self-sufficiency" is identified as one of a half-dozen principles that should guide the organisation of the national economy.[327]

For Indonesia, with a history of being exploited by outsiders and anxious about its standing in the world, being able to feed itself is not just perceived as a means of improving security, but is also a source of national pride. Throughout its independence era, Indonesia has revered its farmers, whose commitment to hard work was seen variously as a beacon of socialist selflessness by President Sukarno, or a symbol of patriotism by President Suharto.

The New Order leader also embraced the self-sufficiency ethos, launching a successful rice self-sufficiency program in the 1970s. Able to impose his will on those who served him, the president achieved the objective through establishing a floor price for the grain, allocating more irrigated land, setting prices for fertiliser and pesticides, and providing credit schemes.[328]

But campaigns that champion self-sufficiency, rather than a comparative advance and prosperity through trade, have a history of failure in Southeast Asia. Over the decades efforts have been launched by countries in the region to achieve self-sufficiency in a range of heavy industries and agriculture, but only in energy have some countries in the region been successful. The problem often lies in the need for foreign capital and technology inputs such as fertiliser, as well as an inability to achieve the output needed to achieve economies of scale. As historian Norman G. Owen notes of 20th century trends: "The urge for autarky remained strong, yet almost every effort to achieve it resulted in retarding economic growth."[329]

In Indonesia, agriculture has long been an integral part of the economy, with a substantial proportion of the population, particularly in densely packed Java, being employed in the industry. Farmers have come to recognise the power of their place in the national psyche, forming an influential lobby group that since 2004 has been led by former military general and presidential aspirant Prabowo Subianto. What's good for the nation's farmers is good for the nation, goes the message.

By 2010, agriculture represented about 15 percent of Indonesia's gross domestic product. Indonesia stood as the world's 10th largest agricultural producer despite being the world's fourth most populous country, a reflection of the fact that it has just one-third of the world average of agricultural land per person. The country was home to about 42 million farmers, representing 40 percent of the workforce, although their dependants swelled the number of people dependant on the sector. About two-thirds of farmers work on Java, with Sumatra home to most of the remainder.[330]

The forces of urbanisation mean that since the 1990s many farmers have left the land and headed to factory jobs in the new industrial estates popping up across Java. Even through this trend came at the same time as output from the nation's farms increased, the rise in productivity still left Indonesia well short of its Southeast Asian neighbours in the yield it achieved from its agricultural industry. In releasing a 2013 study on farm productivity, Bambang Kristianto, an analyst at the Central Statistics

Agency, lamented that "when we talk about technology, Indonesia is up to 10 years behind Malaysia, because Malaysia is much better in terms of their development of agricultural technologies".[331]

Fresh energy

The desire for food self-sufficiency was pursued with renewed vigour by Susilo Bambang Yudhoyono when was reelected for his second term as president in 2009. For Yudhoyono, the issue made sense politically and economically. The Indonesia that Yudhoyono had inherited was one that was down on its confidence, no longer sure of its place in the world and feeling a lingering humiliation after it was brought to its knees by the Asian Financial Crisis. Self-sufficiency would signal to the world that Indonesia could feed its own and need bow to no master.

The nation's economic advancement also relied on it improving its balance of trade position, particularly with the country's shift from being a net exporter of oil to being a net importer. While stimulating exports was the ideal method of achieving an improved trade position, curbing imports was a blunter tool that could achieve similar objectives. More pragmatically, the farmers lobby was one that the president would rather have on his side than opposed to him.

The terms of Yudhoyono's commitment to self-sufficiency were stark: by 2014, the president pledged, Indonesia's farming sector would be able to meet at least 90 percent of demand for five key foodstuffs: beef, corn, rice, soybean and sugar. Getting there would involve a mix of encouraging local farming production (he pledged 45,000 hectares of land to be set aside to support food security, reversing a trend in which about 100,000 hectares had been converted from agricultural to industrial use) and incrementally reducing quotas for imports.[332]

Quotas are Indonesia's preferred tool for keeping watch on imports. Many products, including some far removed from agriculture, can only be brought into the country if an export quota is obtained; the packages of goods slowly rotting at Tanjung Priok and other ports across the country are a testament to the seriousness with which the quota requirement is enforced. To the government, curbing quotas was an effective method of ensuring the movement away from food imports and towards home-grown produce.

But the use of quotas has brought on a series of headaches so significant that they have seriously undermined the policy's credibility, even among those who support it in principle.

The problems were most evident in the beef industry. Indonesians are not heavy consumers of beef but tend to eat small amounts regularly. The meatballs in bakso, the ubiquitous hearty broth sold by the sides of roads across the country, are made using cheap cuts of beef. More expensive cuts tend to be in the diets only of the middle class and wealthy, although for festive occasions such as Idul Fitri at the end of Ramadan, premium beef products are often on the menu. All up, annual consumption stood at 2.2 kilograms per person in 2013, up from 1.9 kilograms a year earlier, both among the lowest in Asia. Across Indonesia's 240 million people, that left demand for 2013 at 549,000 tons.[333] When the price and availability of beef changes, it doesn't take long for most Indonesians to feel the impact.

The beef import trade comes in two forms: as live cattle, with animals fattened in Indonesia before slaughter; and as boxed beef, with the animal already slaughtered and cut into portions. The biggest source of imports are Australia and New Zealand, from which cattle, boxed beef and offal sales to Indonesia reached a record US$700 million in 2009.[334] Canada and the United States are also big players.

The drive towards beef self-sufficiency kicked off in earnest in 2011, a time when beef on average sold for somewhere south of Rp 50,000 (US$4) a kilogram. The scale of the transformation to the nation's beef industry that the government was trying to achieve through its quota system is breathtaking in its audacity. For live cattle, the government slashed import quotas by 20 percent in 2011, 32 percent in 2012 and a further 30 percent in 2013. The boxed-beef import quota was cut by nearly two-thirds in 2012 and by six percent for 2013. That left the life cattle import quota at 267,000 head of cattle in 2013, and the total beef import quota at 32,000 tons. The local industry, the government reckoned, would rush in to fill the gap.[335]

Quota quandary

Ideally under the policy, the volume of import quotas for a given year should be the gap between anticipated demand for the product and the anticipated domestic supply, assuming a price that rises at, say, the rate of inflation. But discovering the likely domestic demand and supply has proven a tricky business, in part due to the lack of sophistication in data collection methods, which often involve little more than aggregating the guesses of industry participants. Through 2011, for example, official estimates of the size of the national herd varied widely: part way through the year the number was put at 12 million, but in December Agriculture Minister Suswono put the number at 14.5 million. Independent estimates put it at closer to 10 million.[336]

While cattle numbers should be reasonably predictable from year to year, erratic movements in numbers (in 2008 in East Java, for example, the head count increased inexplicably from 2.7 million to 3.4 million[337]) suggest some political interference is at play. Some industry observers believe agriculture officials are keen to maintain the perception that the move towards self-sufficiency is progressing, and so inflate local cattle numbers.

There's also evidence that the figures have frequently underestimated the growing demand for beef: while Indonesians consume modest amounts at present, demand is steadily growing as more consumers reach the middle class, and increasing numbers of foreign visitors bring with them a desire for the product. Problems with estimates are evident in the fact that actual beef demand for 2010 stood at 493,000 tons, but the Ministry of Agriculture's projected demand for 2011 was only 456,000 tons, indicating a highly unlikely fall in consumption, according to a report at the time.[338]

The price rises brought about by a shortage have created a vicious cycle. Early in the self-sufficiency drive, some cattle farmers slaughtered their female breeding cows to meet demand and make some quick cash, crippling efforts to increase head counts in future years. Even though the Ministry of Agriculture sought to halt the practice, the impact lingered. One meat importer quoted in a 2011 *Globe Asia* report estimated that "80 percent to 90 percent of what's been killed at the moment in Indonesia is productive breeding females".[339]

Experience on the ground put paid to the government's figures, with ranch operators complaining of the difficulty of finding stock. Pudjantoro, a commissioner at Tanjung Unggul Mandiri, a company that fattens cattle before slaughter, told Trade Minister Gita Wirjawan directly that his company needed to import up to 24,000 cows, but was only allowed to import 13,000. "It is very hard to find local cows," he said.[340]

Regardless of the noble intentions of the policy, its consequences were proving painful. Consumers were finding beef was in short supply.

H.S. Dillon, an agricultural economist serving as President Yudhoyono's expert on poverty alleviation, was incredulous at the chaos brought about by the policy. "It's pure politics," he told the *Straits Times* in an interview in late 2012. "Self-sufficiency is nonsensical. They wave figures around and set objectives, but they don't provide the means to achieve them."[341] Thomas Sembiring, chairman of the Indonesian Meat Importers Association (Aspidi), agreed: "The government is being stubborn. Politically, they are afraid that its self-sufficiency efforts have not been achieved and the public will question the government's work."[342]

The next problem brought about by quotas was the abundant risk of corruption in their allocation. With the process for granting quotas largely opaque, bureaucrats and government ministers were left with sweeping authority to make decisions that had a major impact on the profitability of importers. Even in countries with a good track record on questions of integrity, placing such authority in the hands of a small number of people was bound to test their skills of self-control. In Indonesia, the process was a green light for kickbacks and payoffs. As Khudori, an agriculture analyst from the Indonesian Economy and Politics Association, told *Tempo* in early 2013: "Quota setting for importers has not been transparent. It's unknown why certain importers receive a bigger quota than others. The public is never informed. Such a closed mechanism is prone to manipulations."[343]

It was unsurprising, therefore, when the case of Ahmad Fathanah emerged. Fathanah was an aide to Luthfi Hasan Ishaaq, the chairman of the Islam-inspired Prosperous Justice Party (PKS) that has Agriculture Minister Suswono as one of its most senior members. In a case that transfixed the country for much of 2013, Jakarta's Anti-Corruption Court heard claims that Fathanah received, on behalf of his boss, Rp 1.3 billion (US$108,000) in kickbacks from beef importer Indoguna Utama in exchange for the PKS chairman using his influence in the party to try to increase the company's beef import quota by 8,000 tons. Were the scam to have continued unabated, the company pledged to pay Rp 40 billion for its quota increase, amounting to Rp 5,000 per kilogram. Fathanah was convicted of the corruption charges and in November 2013 sentenced to 14 years in prison, while Luthfi and Indoguna Utama president director Maria Elizabeth Liman were still awaiting their trials the next year.[344]

Politicians from rival parties sought to exploit the allegations of wrongdoing against PKS officials, but they missed the essential point: the corruption was a product of a deeply flawed system, not a deeply flawed individual. The scramble for quotas privileges a handful of politically well-connected Indonesian companies, who can use the artificial scarcity to improve their negotiating position with foreign beef producers on one hand, and wholesaler buyers on the other.

The quota system also created the prospect of a black market in beef, as importers unable to obtain a quota sought to circumvent the system. A January 2013 report in *Tempo* found that one importer had brought in 2,000 tons of beef from Australia in the first half of 2012, well in excess of the 300-ton quota it had been allocated for the period. After the excess meat sat on the docks at Tanjung Priok port for six months, it somehow found its way onto the market.[345]

Paying the price

So with the import quota inadequate to fill the gap between domestic supply and demand and some importers paying kickbacks for their quotas, it was inevitable that beef prices would rise. In 2013, as consumers grappled with a 33 percent hike in the price for the fuel they put in their cars and motorcycles, they found the price of what they put on their plates was rising too. Beef prices approached Rp 100,000 (US$8.35) per kilogram, about double the price two years earlier. And it wasn't just beef prices that were heading northward. The price of onions, garlic and chillis, all key ingredients in Indonesian cuisine, were also rising sharply. It is perhaps unsurprising that imports of those products were also subject to a quota system. (Using the system for garlic was particularly absurd, given 90 percent of Indonesia's supply is imported. In the first three months of 2013, the price tripled to Rp 60,000 per kilogram.[346])

Also causing concern among ordinary Indonesians was volatility in supply and pricing of soybeans, the main ingredient in the staple foods of tofu and tempeh. It is a quirk of history that the Indonesian diet is so rich in soybeans, given that it is not a tropical crop and so is ill-suited to being grown in Indonesia. These circumstances have left the country as Southeast Asia's biggest soybean importer, bringing in about 75 percent of its soybean needs, amounting to 2.1 million tons in 2013/14, most coming from the United States. Through 2013, a weak rupiah and high global prices pushed up domestic prices of soybeans.[347]

Feeling the heat on the food-price issue was Gita Wirjawan, Indonesia's urbane Trade Minister. The Harvard-educated minister has proven difficult for many political and business figures to read: while grounded in the economics of free trade, the former Goldman Sachs and J.P. Morgan investment banker has shown a tendency to make the case for protectionism of local industries. Appointed to Yudhoyono's cabinet at age 46 in 2011, Wirjawan had previously served the government as chairman of the Investment Coordinating Board (BKPM). While talking up the benefits of trade when fronting international audiences and speaking in English, he has an unashamed populist streak in communicating with Indonesian audiences. A brief tilt at the presidency in 2014 may go some way towards explaining why.

Keen to quell growing public anger on beef prices, Wirjawan in May 2013 introduced a policy that in effect acknowledged that the quota system was buckling under the strain. He took part of the live cattle import quota that had been set aside for the third quarter of the year and allowed it to be used to import cattle in the second quarter. And he also exempted premium-quality Australian beef imports from the quota.

The policy was welcomed by major trading partners, but some of them likely sensed that it was merely a tactic to delay confronting the substance of the quota problem. A month later, Wirjawan announced that registered importers would be allowed to bring in up to 45,000 head of cattle over the following two months, in addition to the allocated quota. Bulog, the state logistics agency, was told to do what it could to stabilise beef prices at Rp 75,000 a kilogram.[348]

The policy changes had little short-term impact. Across the country, inflation was starting to bite: it ended 2012 at a rather benign 4.3 percent, but by July it stood at 8.6 percent, its highest in nearly five years and well beyond the government's target range of 3.5 percent to 5.5 percent. The problem was more acute for individual commodities: the price of shallots climbed from US$1.20 to US$7 in March alone.[349]

Consumers were growing irate, with tempers rising at fresh-food markets, shoppers taking to Facebook and Twitter to vent their frustration and traditional media outlets documenting the outrage. Writing in the

Jakarta Globe, Farid Harianto, an economist, captured the mood. "The higher food prices indeed are the product of failed policies," he wrote. "And as long as the government continues to rely on ad hoc policies of import measures to curb food prices, the country will remain vulnerable to seasonal stints of wild food price volatility."[350]

Some vendors, keen to avoid passing on price increases to their customers, cut back the proportion of their meat that was beef and quietly substituted other products, including pork, much to the indignation of consumers whose religion forbade the consumption of such a product. The arrival of Ramadan in early July intensified the strain on food supplies.

Later, Concord Consulting analyst Keith Loveard argued that the shortages of garlic, shallots and beef were blatant attempts to invoke nationalist sentiment to legitimise attempts by a small group of importers to maximise profits. "Indonesia must at some stage abandon its entire system of import licensing, since it is nothing more than an invitation to corruption at the expense of the Indonesian people," he said in an interview.[351]

With food prices rises being just the sort of catalyst to bring people to the streets in protest, the government knew it had to act, and act fast. (In May 1998, government action to raise the price of oil products triggered a big riot in Medan and fed the momentum that ultimately ousted Suharto from the presidency within weeks.[352])

President Susilo Bambang Yudhoyono called together senior government officials and made clear his displeasure at the continued price rises. The targets of his anger were Agriculture Minister Suswono, Trade Minister Gita Wirjawan and State Logistics Agency (Bulog) chief Sutarto Alimoeso. "Have you people seen the situation in the markets?" Yudhoyono asked the three officials, according to an official account. "Mr. Agriculture Minister, Mr. Bulog chief, Mr. Trade Minister, you must have a sense of crisis, a sense of urgency and a sense of responsibility."

Yudhoyono was incredulous that a previous instruction to Bulog ordering it to intervene in the beef market in an effort to stabilise prices had not yet been acted upon. Bulog explained that it had been stymied in its efforts to import beef to stabilise prices by the Trade Ministry, which had been slow to issue permits. It should be little surprise that Bulog was struggling to move fast. This beef shipment was to be its first ever, and marked a major expansion of its traditional role as a stockpiler of rice. Nonetheless, like a father disciplining errant children, Yudhoyono warned the three senior officials not to blame each other for the soaring prices and to focus on tackling the issue as a team.[353]

Out of favour

The weight of evidence against the quota system was considerable. A panel of economic advisors hand-picked by the president produced a report in February 2013 that found that food import quotas encouraged bribes and price spikes, and argued for them to be replaced with import tariffs. "Instead of giving imports through quotas, just open these markets," said Hermanto Siregar, an economist and a commissioner at Bank Rakyat Indonesia serving on the panel. "Excess demand drives prices very high, and importers see a good prospect for profits and are willing to bribe to get licences or quotas. If you still want some control, put in place tariffs, which is more market friendly." He added in an interview with *Reuters*: "When the number of players are very few, it is easy for them to do price setting or fixing."[354]

A year earlier the Organization for Economic Co-operation and Development (OECD), a grouping of developed nations, was damning towards the quota policy, saying in a report that it hurt impoverished consumers. It called on Indonesia to open its domestic food market to international trade and move away from its self-sufficiency objectives, which it blamed for a rise in food prices. "Such measures undermine rather than improve access to food for poor consumers, a group which includes a majority of farmers who are net buyers of food staples," the report said. While many Indonesian policy makers equate food security — where each person has access to adequate nutrition, regardless of its source — and food self-sufficiency, the OECD report indicated how the two can be in conflict. In striving for self-sufficiency, the country was unwittingly putting its food security at risk.[355]

The policies were even causing a diplomatic stir. The United States decided that the red tape imposed by Indonesia was an unreasonable restriction of trade, and in January 2013 challenged the Southeast Asian country's policies on the import of horticultural and animal products at a World Trade Organization tribunal. "Indonesia has created a complex web of import licensing requirements that, along with quotas, have the effect of unfairly restricting US exports," the US Trade Representative's Office said in a statement.[356] Within four months Indonesia waved the white flag on the issue of horticultural products, agreeing not to impose quantity restrictions on imports. But, for the time being at least, it held the line on animal products. (Freeing up the import of fruit had a swift impact. In the month after the quantity limit on imported apples was scrapped, allowing produce to move from Surabaya port to wholesale markets, the price of an 18-kilogram box of US apples fell 68 percent to Rp 320,000 (US$27). "It's great because now everyone can buy imported fruits," East Jakarta fruit vendor Sri Asih told *Tempo* at the time.[357])

It is not clear just how seriously the Indonesians were taking the case. One observer noted that Indonesia would engage in stalling tactics like regularly making small iterative changes to regulations in the hope of resetting the clock on any tribunal hearing, or sending along inadequately briefed junior staff who could do little but report back to Jakarta on any developments.

As beef prices surged after the mid-July start to Ramadan to a national average of Rp 93,000, up 20 percent on recent prices, Trade Minister Gita Wirjawan was forced into making fundamental changes to the policy. Importers of beef, he announced, would no longer need to access quotas to bring their product into the country. The restrictions they had previously faced would be suspended, with the aim of achieving domestic beef prices of about Rp 75,000 a kilogram. Other foods that had also been facing price pressures, like shallots, chilli and soybean, also had their quota requirements suspended. In seeking to sell the policy, Wirjawan said: "It's noble to consider the interests of live cattle breeders and local beef sellers but it's more noble to reduce the price of beef back to its normal level for the sake of the people."[358] It was not clear how long the new policy would be in place, given it was described by Agriculture Minister Suswono as a response to an "emergency situation".[359]

The same day, it was announced that Indonesia would import 25,000 ready-to-slaughter cattle from Australia, with that number set to rise to 75,000 by the end of the year. (But the process wasn't all smooth. Desperate to get the Australian cattle moving quickly, Indonesia sought an urgent visa to send a quarantine officer to Darwin to begin the inspection program before the cattle boarded ships. Once he arrived in the rowdy northern capital, however, the inspector went missing for several days, according to one source.)

The decision was clearly a win for consumers keen to avoid straining the household budget to put food on the table, and also for importers keen to complement the output of local producers.

The beef industry was not the only one to grapple with a rapidly shifting set of import rules. The phalanx of policy changes for the import of soybeans amid sharp price rises and mass protests reveals the sorts of levers the government is willing to reach for in order to boost supply. After a bout of pressure the government scrapped the quota system for the import of soybeans, but kept in place a requirement for importers to hold a permit. Then it turned to forcing traders to buy domestic supplies and imposing a floor and ceiling price for buyers and sellers. When traders found that the issuing of permits was too slow to react to spikes in demand and was prone to corruption, that too was scrapped.

Coordinating Minister for the Economy Hatta Rajasa then went one step further, ditching the five percent soybean import tariff, a move backed by the Ministry of Trade. But the move was too much for President Yudhoyono, who within days reinstated the tariff, perhaps with a view to his government's deficit budget. Also in play was an investigation by Indonesia's antitrust authority, the Business Competition Supervisory Commission (KPPU), into cartel behaviour in the soybean industry. Likely the watchdog had in its sights FKS Multi Agro, the agribusiness giant with a 60 percent stranglehold of the soybean import market.[360]

The instinct among Indonesian political leaders to take a command-and-control approach to the economy is strong. Just a few months after the beef quota requirements were suspended, President Yudhoyono was again playing his role as the nation's farmer-in-chief, bumping up targets for domestic production of corn, sugar, rice, soy and beef in the wake of extreme weather hurting harvests overseas. While some increases involved modest and likely achievable targets, others seemed absurdly ambitious: Yudhoyono set a 2014 target for sugar of 3.1 million tons, a whopping 35 percent increase over the amount expected to be produced in 2013. In selling the case for boosting local production, Yudhoyono drew on his credentials as an environmentalist. "In facing climate change and global food market volatility, the solution is to improve our supply, not import," he said.[361]

New approaches

Alongside the stuttering efforts to achieve self-sufficiency, other projects have sought to develop the Indonesian agricultural sector. Programs to improve the efficiency of Indonesian farms, many of which are still very traditional and labour-intensive in their operations, have been implemented widely. Among them is the private-public scheme Partnership for Indonesia Sustainable Agriculture (PISAgro), which aims to implement best practice in the farming of rice, corn, soybeans, dairy cattle, potatoes, coffee, cocoa and palm oil. Its goal is to achieve a 20 percent higher crop yield, eliminate poverty among farmers and reduce carbon emissions by 20 percent by 2020.

Indonesia has also sought to buy land in northern Australia for the breeding of cattle. Under the plan, which depends on the approval of the Australian government, Indonesia would cut back on its reliance on Australian-owned farms for its cattle, instead taking control of supply much like Chinese companies have taken control of Australian mines in a bid to achieve better security of supply of key minerals. A consortium of state-owned Indonesian firms spent part of 2013 exploring investment prospects in Australia, the acquisition of which is not only intended to boost supply but also help Indonesian companies learn how to develop ranches. "We really need to have cattle farms in Australia so that we can supply the beef demand in Indonesia as our demand is expected to rise significantly over the next few years, while our ability to provide it domestically is insufficient," Bulog chief executive Sutarto Alimoeso told *Reuters* in a moment of candour.[362]

In part the impetus for Indonesia buying Australian cattle stations came from the events of 2011, when an investigative report on Australian television broadcast alarming footage documenting the distressing conditions inside Indonesian abattoirs that had received Australian cattle. The public outcry was such that the Australian government quickly suspended the live cattle trade, which at that stage amounted to 750,000 head of cattle a year.[363] While Indonesia had intended to scale down live cattle imports over time as part of its quota system, the suspension brought on the fall at breakneck speed. The Australian suspension reminded Indonesia of its food supply vulnerabilities, and in part prompted it to take a more active involvement further up the supply chain.

Despite the policy changes of 2013, food self-sufficiency remains the government's stated objective. But the odds of the goal ever being achieved, let alone by the 2014 target date, are increasingly unfavourable. In 2012 the government conceded it would not meet the target date for sugar, and early the next year conceded it would fall considerably short

on soybean. The reason given for both by Agriculture Minister Suswono
was a shortage of available agricultural land. For soybean plantations,
1.1 million hectares would be needed compared to an existing 600,000
hectares, while for sugarcane farmland 800,000 hectares would be needed
compared to the current 450,000 hectares, the minister told *Reuters* in
a March 2013 interview. (He was, however, confident that domestic
rice output would meet 90 percent of the country's needs by 2014, the
government's benchmark for self-sufficiency.)[364]

Australian farmer Michael Sheehy has been working in Indonesia for
more than a decade seeking to improve agricultural trade links between
the two countries. In his mind, the quota system is deeply flawed, with a
trader playing by the rules having little chance of getting a decent import
quota. As well as hurting consumers, he pointed out, quotas actually hurt
farmers in the long run because it shields them from competition and
gives them no incentive to improve productivity, such as by pooling their
assets to achieve economies of scale.

Instead, he advocates scrapping the quota system and replacing it
with technical expertise such as consultant agronomists to help farmers
boost the yield from their land, as well as improved infrastructure to
help get perishable products to consumers quickly. "You need to have
leaders who have the courage to roll it out, because it's what needs to be
done," he said in an interview at the Jakarta office of Natural Resources
Indonesia, the company where he serves as the chief operating officer.[365]

While some members of the political elite realise how the quotas
and import restrictions are hurting consumers and farmers, they remain
on the margins of the policy debate. Among them is Farid Harianto, an
economist advising Vice President Boediono, who wrote a column in
the *Jakarta Globe* offering a searing analysis of the absurdity at the heart
of the government's long-running policy. It is worth quoting at length:

> The heart of policy discourse in this country rests on the
> presumption of what national social welfare is and how to measure

it. The political rhetoric being advanced in this case is a populist one, namely to provide protection for domestic producers, farmers or SMEs [small and medium enterprises].

Yet students of Economics 101 are acutely aware that social welfare is measured as consumer surplus, and the biggest surpluses arise from open, competitive markets. Any deviation from competitive equilibrium, be it in the form of inadequate supply or from government intervention such as administered quotas, will only result in greater benefit to producers — to the detriment of consumers, in the form of higher prices and lower consumption.

Our current problems can be traced back the famous article 33 of our original constitution of 1945, which emphasises the importance of production in our economic system, and puts the control of key natural resources in the hands of state to achieve 'maximum social welfare'. It has never been made explicit what this social welfare is, and it has since become a contested terrain politically. The standard bearing of populist argument has always been that social welfare is equivalent to protecting the weak and underprivileged, in this case farmers, SMEs and informal sectors, but not the poor as consumers.

In the name of protecting local farmers, the ministries of trade and of agriculture have imposed an ad hoc quota regime, in which import licences are arbitrarily allocated with administered prices. It doesn't take a genius to figure out that such arbitrary policies have created opportunity for cronyism and rent-seeking. That is what's been happening with the beef scandal, and trade in other commodities, such as soybeans.[366]

For voices like that of Harianto to prevail require decision-makers to be willing to stare down the powerful business figures who dominate agriculture as well as those who have a stranglehold on import quotas. The millions of Indonesians who go hungry at night depend on it.

11

Bankers' Bluff

Perhaps the most popular destination in many of Jakarta's glitzy malls is a space labelled "gallery". But it's not art that fills the valuable stretch of commercial real estate; instead automatic teller machines from a dozen or more banks line the walls. It's the most tangible example of just how fragmented Indonesia's banking system is, with more than 120 banks servicing retail and business customers. The high number of banks has long been a concern for the Indonesian central bank, which worries that too many small banks lack significant reserves and so are vulnerable in a downturn, and too few large banks compete to offer services to customers.

So when Singapore's DBS bank hatched a plan in early 2012 to take over mid-sized player Bank Danamon in order to expand its existing Indonesian operations, it would appear to be a step towards the consolidation that regulators craved. Bank Danamon was already in the hands of Singaporean owners (sovereign wealth fund Temasek Holdings, which had majority control of the Indonesian bank, was also a big shareholder in DBS), so it would not involve a local asset being newly sold off to foreign owners.

But instead the deal became ensnared in the broader Indonesian debate about boosting local control of the major players in the nation's banking sector. For more than a year the central bank, Bank Indonesia, mulled over the transaction, during which time new rules were introduced that shifted Indonesia from being one of the most open banking environments in Asia towards the middle of the pack. Along the way an assessment process that is normally an administrative one became mired in politics, as regulators sensed an opportunity to use the case as leverage to increase the access Indonesian state-owned banks could have in the Singaporean market.

Ultimately Bank Indonesia refused to let DBS Group Holdings take control of Bank Danamon unless Singaporean regulators eased restrictions. The ruling has left deals involving other foreign banks on ice, and with matters of ego and capital constraining local banks from merging with one another, there has been little progress on consolidation in the sector.

Forged in adversity

When the winds of the Asian Financial Crisis blew through Indonesia in the late 1990s, everybody hurt. The rapid depreciation in the rupiah meant the value of many people's savings collapsed, the price of imported goods skyrocketed and the ability of companies to finance loans disappeared. As newly impoverished people took to the streets to vent their anger, and ultimately bring down the president, the nation's bankers looked on in horror at their own circumstances. The banking system was manifestly incapable of handling the stress of a plummeting rupiah and a steep economic contraction, and individual banks were at the point of insolvency.

Desperate to stave off the collapse of the banks as the economy shrunk 13 percent in 1998, the Indonesian government and its phalanx of international advisers did all they could to keep the banks afloat. Restrictions on ownership of local banks were lifted so that any single entity, foreign or local, could hold up to 99 percent of an Indonesian lender, allowing some foreign buyers to pick up assets on the cheap. The Indonesian Bank Restructuring Agency was established to take some of the troubled banks under state control, with the aim of merging unviable lenders and reviving survivors with great licks of capital, and then selling them off. In total, more than 80 banks failed or were nationalised or recapitalised.

One of those banks bought up by IBRA was Bank Danamon, an Indonesian lender established in 1956 as Bank Kopra and in the hands of tycoon Usman Admadjaja when the crisis struck. The bailout amounted to Rp 47 trillion (US$3.9 billion). Determined to keep Bank Danamon alive, the government owner in 1999 decided to combine it with eight smaller lenders to give it adequate scale. Come 2003, things were looking more promising. The rupiah had stabilised and economic growth was nearing its pre-crisis level. More pragmatically, the government was facing a ballooning budget deficit. IBRA decided to put a 51 percent stake in Bank Danamon up for sale, and received plenty of interest. Ultimately it was Singapore's Temasek Holdings that prevailed, with Germany's Deutsche Bank taking a smaller stake.

Established by the Singaporean government as a repository for its stored wealth, Temasek has become a giant in the city-state's economy, with its US$170 billion in assets sprawling across financial services, telecommunications, consumer goods and energy. Keen to reduce the risk of a downturn in the economy of its home country, the sovereign wealth fund has looked abroad with increasing ambition in recent decades, snapping up assets around the world that offer a steady return, and in some instances allow it to make use of its considerable depths of corporate expertise.

The Singapore company has a complex relationship with Indonesia that reflects the tensions between the two countries. Many Indonesians respect the advanced state of development of their northern neighbour, but their admiration is tainted by frustration at the way the country has provided safe harbour for fugitive Indonesians, particularly corruption suspects. Under a long-standing deadlock, Singapore is seeking access to Indonesian land for military training exercises in exchange for increased cooperation on law enforcement. No deal has been reached.

In the seven years after its Bank Danamon acquisition, Deutsche Bank sold out and Temasek gradually increased its holding to 67 percent. The balance was held in small chunks, the largest of which was 6.4 percent in the hands of US-based Franklin Templeton Investment Funds. By this point the Indonesian bank had established itself as a major player in consumer lending and microfinancing, which accounted for two-thirds of its loan book. But come 2010, Temasek decided the current arrangement with Bank Danamon was not meeting its needs, standing as an asset on its own and carrying significant risks rather than being part of a broader strategic plan. The company quietly took soundings among big local companies to see if there was much interest in buying out its holding in Bank Danamon, but came back empty handed.[367]

So it considered another plan. Temasek already held a 30 percent stake in DBS Group Holdings, a bank with a big footprint in Singapore but only a niche player in 14 other Asian nations, including Indonesia, where it set up shop in 1989. Were DBS to take control of the holding in Bank Danamon, Temasek would retain its exposure but in a way that fitted in with its broader strategic plans. DBS, which had set itself a long-term target of generating half of its revenue from outside Singapore compared to 38 percent in 2011, was keen on the idea.[368]

Leading DBS through the takeover attempt was Piyush Gupta, a graduate of the Indian Institute of Management who had been with DBS for little more than two years since moving across from Citigroup. His background in consumer and corporate banking gave him a good grasp of detail, skills that would come in handy in executing the takeover, but his standing as a visionary leader had yet to be thoroughly tested.[369]

A bold plan

In early April 2012, DBS Group Holdings revealed its takeover plan. Its proposal was for DBS to take Temasek's 67 percent stake in Bank Danamon Indonesia in exchange for giving Temasek new shares issued in DBS valued at US$4.9 billion. (Temasek's stake in DBS would increase from 29 percent to 40 percent.) DBS would then seek to buy almost all the remaining Bank Danamon shares for Rp 7,000 each, a hefty 52 percent premium on their trading price before the deal was announced, for a total of US$2.3 billion. Under the plan, DBS would come to hold 99 percent of Bank Danamon, the most allowed under the law.[370] The total value of the deal was put at US$7.2 billion, making it the largest banking takeover in Southeast Asia in more than a decade, according to *Bloomberg* records.[371]

"Indonesia is an exciting Asian market and we believe that we will be able to contribute towards the growth of the Indonesian banking sector, especially in areas such as infrastructure financing, project financing, trade finance and shariah banking," DBS chief Piyush Gupta said in a statement.[372] "The 52 percent premium is not cheap. On the other hand, Indonesia is a high-growth country. We expect to pay a full price to be able to expand our franchise here," he added at a media briefing in Jakarta.[373] In the deal, DBS was paying 2.6 times the book value of Bank Danamon, compared with a median of 2.2 for deals worth more than US$1 billion in the global banking industry over the previous five years, *Bloomberg* data showed.[374]

To DBS, taking over Bank Danamon was a neat fit. DBS's existing presence in Indonesia consisted of fewer than 40 branches, and building the network of clients and branches necessary to reach the upper echelons of the banking sector would be a slow process. But Bank Danamon was already the sixth biggest bank in Indonesia by assets, with a network of 3,000 branches servicing six million customers, more than the entire population of Singapore. As a merged entity operating under a single brand, a likely outcome under the plan, it would become the fifth biggest Indonesian bank by assets.[375]

By using Bank Danamon's existing network and DBS's deep pockets and international expertise, the Singapore lender figured it could make major inroads in Indonesia, challenging the big established players. The lenders' existing operations complemented each other well. While Bank Danamon held a significant market share in lending to consumers and small and medium enterprises, DBS had the skills to expand its corporate lending. And as DBS said in outlining the "strategic rationale" for the deal, it could help Danamon "increase its resilience to withstand credit cycles".[376]

The company also spelled out how it believed the deal would benefit Indonesia: providing access to capital from abroad to support infrastructure and development, thereby developing financial markets; enabling Indonesia to capture a greater share of the value of its trade flows; and helping customers and businesses in Indonesia to grow regionally.

The management of Bank Danamon appeared receptive to the takeover proposal. Henry Ho, the Indonesian bank's president director, noted in a statement that "in the event the transaction proceeds, Danamon and DBS should be complementary in many ways", and that "Danamon will work closely with DBS to become a dynamic Asian banking franchise".[377]

Knowing how long approval might take was fraught with difficulty. DBS said it "expected" it would receive regulatory approval by the end of the year,[378] but analysts were doubtful it would be that swift. Another would-be acquirer of an Indonesian bank, Malaysia's RHB Capital, had been awaiting Bank Indonesia's approval on its Rp 3.1 trillion (US$258 million) takeover of Bank Mestika Dharma since October 2009.[379]

What was it that made the Indonesian market so attractive? The high growth that Gupta mentioned is a big part of the story, underpinned by favourable demographics and rapidly rising domestic consumption. Annual loan growth across the industry was rising at beyond 20 percent a year as the economy itself grew at six percent a year, both of which were impossible to achieve in developed nations.

But there was more to the country's appeal than just a high rate of growth. The presence of 120 commercial banks in operation might lead to the conclusion that the market is overserviced. The reality, however, is that most hold only a small market share, and lack the capital to expand geographically or by market segment. Some 140 million people (about four in five adults) are categorised as "unbanked" by the World Bank in that they do not have a bank account and the financial security it brings.[380]

Among the major players, meanwhile, the top 10 banks control 80 percent of total bank assets.[381] Three of the five biggest lenders are owned by the national government and so are reluctant to compete too aggressively against each other. Adding to the problem is the fact that Indonesian banks rely heavily on deposits to fund their lending.

The effective oligopoly among major players has left the Indonesian banking system with the highest margins of any banking system in the world's 20 largest economies, meaning the interest paid by borrowers is much greater than the interest paid to savers, or the central bank's official cash rate.[382] In October 2011, for example, when Bank Indonesia's policy interest rate stood at six percent, loans for working capital and investment stood at 12 percent. The difference, six percentage points, compares rather unfavourably with the two-percentage-point gap in Malaysia and one percentage point in the Philippines.[383]

Darmin Nasution, the governor of Bank Indonesia, used his 2011 speech at the annual Banker's Dinner to explain how he feared that a paucity of banking services was hurting the economy. "The scarcity of financing is among the most binding constraints of investment activity," he told the gathering. "Surveys pointed to financing constraint suffered by business players, particularly difficulties in accessing bank loan, resulting from too high lending rate, too demanding collateral obligation, and too complicated administrative requirement." He went on to note that the difficulty of accessing credit meant that bank loans accounted for only 21 percent of funding for Indonesian companies' investment, while 61 percent came from internal financing.

When expanded across the whole of the economy, the result was growth that fell short of potential. Nasution noted that as of September 2011 credit as a ratio of gross domestic product stood at 29 percent in Indonesia, compared to Malaysia's 114 percent, Thailand's 117 percent and China's 131 percent. While a lack of access to credit might have reduced the prospects of Indonesia experiencing an asset price bubble, it was also constraining the ability of firms to grow.[384]

University of Indonesia economist Lana Soelistianingsih explained how large banks, many of which are owned by the state, are the big winners. "Many of Indonesia's big banks are enjoying 'abnormal profits' because of the oligopoly that governs them," she told the *Jakarta Post*. "If there is a strong new player in the market, then more competition will be injected and these existing big banks will no longer be able to apply such high lending rates as they do at present."[385]

The DBS-Bank Danamon deal had the potential to significantly shake up the market for lending to the nation's 55 million small and medium enterprises, 70 percent of which lack access to finance and some of which face an exorbitant 30 percent interest rate on microcredit.[386] Bank Danamon was struggling to take on the market leader, the state-owned Bank Rakyat Indonesia, but a takeover would likely change the landscape. "In the short-run, Danamon might not be able to topple the dominance of BRI, which still has an unrivaled network of SMEs, but the acquisition would still promote healthier competition in the industry," Creco Consulting banking expert Raden Pardede told the *Jakarta Post*. "Danamon, with stronger capital provided by the DBS Group, would be able to boost its credit penetration in the SMEs segment."[387]

DBS was adamant that it wanted a controlling stake in its target. The company took ownership in banks so that it could run them, rather than just so it could pocket dividends. And global banking rules known as the Third Basel Accord preference controlling stakes over majority interests when calculating the capital used in capital adequacy ratios, a key measure of a bank's financial health. Basel III requires that banks deduct minority investments of 10 percent of more from their capital, but majority acquisitions do not trigger capital deductions. For DBS, getting stuck part way was not an appealing option.

The reaction among investors to the proposal was mixed. Most acknowledged the potential for great profits in the Indonesian banking sector, but questioned whether DBS was paying too much to tap into them. To critics, the premium of 52 percent on the value of Bank Danamon shares was a hefty one.[388]

Some Indonesian commentators recognised the opportunity that the takeover provided to Bank Danamon to become more competitive. "Strategic investors and owners such as DBS, with good reputations and huge capital resources, will accelerate the operational restructuring of Bank Danamon to provide comprehensive financial services, notably credit – the lifeblood of the economy," columnist Vincent Lingga wrote in the *Jakarta Post*.[389]

As for the ratings agencies, they were positive. Fitch Ratings put Bank Danamon under watch with a view to a ratings upgrade, arguing that the backing of a substantial new shareholder made the company a safer bet.[390]

But persuading investors of the merits of the deal was not DBS's major challenge: instead, winning over regulators and politicians was. It was no small task given the rising sentiment of economic nationalism and the suspicion with which Singapore, and in particular Temasek, was viewed in Indonesia.

Regulatory battle

Tasked with deciding on the fate of the takeover bid was Bank Indonesia. Like most central banks, it operates at arm's length from the government of the day, but that does not mean it avoids the skirmishes of political debate given its officials are held to account by the House of Representatives.

Since the Asian Financial Crisis the objective of Indonesian banking regulators was to avoid such disasters in future through bolstering lenders' prudential status and only conducting bailouts as a last resort. The central bank recognised that the best way to achieve stability was to encourage larger banks to take over smaller ones, and minnow rivals to merge among themselves, so that they had deeper wells of capital to draw upon and were less sensitive to downturns in particular parts of the economy. The central bank was seeking to reduce the number of commercial banks from 120, where it stood in 2011, to about 70. But progress in consolidation was slow, with the leaders of many banks reluctant to integrate because they feared it would put their job status and security at risk. Also, the many provincial governments that owned banks feared they would lose the ability to encourage finance of local development projects were their control over the bank to be diluted.

Alongside the objective of consolidation, Bank Indonesia had two other significant goals in its approach to regulating banking: it wanted to strengthen local ownership of banks operating in Indonesia, and also extend banking services to the tens of millions of people who lack access to them. Sometimes these objectives would work in tandem with each other, and sometimes in competition, but all entered into the calculations surrounding the central bank's regulatory decisions.

In wooing Bank Indonesia, DBS appeared to get off on the wrong foot. The takeover plan caught the central bank by surprise given DBS had opted to not forewarn the regulator that the proposal was in the pipeline, perhaps worried that details might leak.[391]

Under the law as it stood, DBS was able to take over Bank Danamon so long as Bank Indonesia approved its capital structure and corporate governance. But Bank Indonesia sensed an opportunity in the takeover proposal.

One recurring irritation among Indonesian banks is the difficulty they have in achieving access in Singapore's US$33 billion financial services market, one of the least open banking systems in Asia. Singapore law limits the number of branches and automatic teller machines that foreign banks are able to operate there, and also imposes extremely high capital requirements – S$1.5 billion (US$1.2 billion) in paid-up capital as a minimum, equivalent to the cost of opening up hundreds of branch offices in Indonesia. (In contrast, the minimum capital requirement for banks operating in Indonesia stands at only Rp 100 billion – about US$8.3 million.)

While one Indonesian bank, Bank Negara Indonesia, is among the 26 foreign banks that have managed to leap over the hurdles to gain a full banking licence in Singapore, three others operate under restrictions that cap their number of branches and ATMs. Bank Mandiri operates as an offshore bank in Singapore, while Bank Central Asia and Panin Bank have just a single representative office each. Bank Rakyat Indonesia was also reportedly keen to do business in Singapore but thwarted by the restrictions. The circumstances were particularly galling for Indonesian banks given that their own government imposed few restrictions on the operations of foreign banks.

This issue was central to the response of politicians and local banks to the DBS takeover proposal. "At the moment, nothing is legally standing in their way to acquire Danamon," Golkar Party legislator Harry Azhar Azis told the *Jakarta Globe*. "However, our bank, Bank Mandiri, when they want to expand to Singapore, they [the Singapore government] make it difficult. That's not fair."[392] Bank Mandiri chief financial officer Pahala Mansury voiced the frustrations of some Indonesian banks. "We need to see equal treatment in other countries and in Indonesia. Frankly, we are still facing obstacles to develop in Singapore now," he said.[393] The proposal also exposed broader fears about Indonesian banks being marginalised in their home market, where six of the top 15 banks were already in foreign hands.[394] "We are concerned that Indonesian institutions only become the branches of foreign banks," Deputy Finance Minister Mahendra Siregar said.[395]

The central bank decided to make reciprocal access to the Singapore banking market a condition of approval of the DBS application. Soon after the takeover proposal was announced Bank Indonesia wrote to its counterpart, the Monetary Authority of Singapore, to advance the issue, and followed up a few weeks later with a meeting in Washington.[396] The plan to push for reciprocity won approval from some analysts. "Singapore is probably the most protectionist banking sector in Asia," Jim Antos, a Hong Kong-based analyst at Mizuho Securities Asia, told *Bloomberg*. "The Indonesian government is right in making their little pitch and I would do the same if I were them."[397]

This would not be the first time a foreign regulator had sought to use this kind of leverage with the Monetary Authority of Singapore. When banks from Singapore sought to open their doors in India, regulators there denied them the right to because Indian banks faced tight restrictions in Singapore. Ultimately, Singapore regulators eased the way for the entry of Indian banks, and now State Bank of India and the ICICI Bank are among those allowed to operate in the city state.[398]

Were Bank Indonesia to consider the DBS proposal under the existing law, where its review was limited to largely cursory matters, it would have little opportunity to use the case for leverage in discussions with the Singapore central bank. But Bank Indonesia had been working on a plan of its own, this one to tighten the laws surrounding the ownership structures of banks.

The changes sought to address two issues that were causing angst among regulators. The first was that the rule allowing foreign investors to hold up to 99 percent of local banks, a legacy of the Asian Financial Crisis, was considered detrimental to the local banking sector. Neighbours Malaysia and Vietnam had set a limit of 30 percent, while China, India and Thailand had also limited foreigners to minority stakes in local banks. A 2011 Indonesian proposal to cap foreign control at 50 percent was shelved after the government feared it would scare off investors for the sale of Bank Mutiara, formerly Bank Century, which the state had acquired as part of a controversial rescue a few years earlier.

The second concern was that banks were financially vulnerable if they relied on too small a pool of owners. By forcing banks to have greater diversity in their ownership, the institutions would be more robust and not reliant on the financial fortunes of a small number of investors. While in most parts of the world major banks are publicly listed companies with a diverse ownership base, that is not the case in Indonesia. Eight of Indonesia's top 11 banks by market value are either controlled by foreign banks, business families, private equity firms or wealth funds, according to *Reuters*.[399]

New rules on these issues were still several months from being released, but the central bank decided to defer consideration of the Bank Danamon takeover until then. If Bank Indonesia had greater power to approve or decline the DBS application, its bargaining power with its Singapore counterpart would surely increase. In case DBS was in any doubt, it now knew that the path to regulatory approval would not be an easy one.

A few weeks after the bid was unveiled, DBS executives fronted the company's annual general meeting in Singapore. Doubts were growing among investors on the ability of the company to navigate the deal through the regulatory process. Looming large over the thinking of investors was a failed attempt the previous year by bourse operator Singapore Exchange to take over the Australian Securities Exchange. The foreign takeover was rejected by the Australian government, a decision some analysts attributed to the company's failure to communicate early and openly with government decision-makers. Was DBS making the same mistake, investors wondered. DBS chief executive Piyush Gupta sought to dispel the fear, saying that DBS has "talked to a lot of people in Indonesia at all levels" and was working with the country's regulators to get approval. "There are clearly concerns around the whole nationalism situation … It's something we're going to have to work [on] with the regulators and the leaders to make sure people understand this transaction is actually very good for Indonesia," he said.[400]

New rules

In July 2012, the central bank released the terms of its new bank ownership rules. Under the rules, a single financial institution could own up to 40 percent of a bank; a single non-financial institution could hold up to 30 percent; and an individual investor could hold up to 20 percent. But exemptions to the cap were allowed, at the discretion of Bank Indonesia, for those owners deemed to be sound, have strong capital, be publicly listed and hold recommendations from their supervisory authorities. "There needs to be a policy that organizes bank-ownership structures to increase banks' strength – this is achieved by increasing the financial soundness and quality of corporate governance – and to consolidate the banking industry," the central bank said in a statement announcing the new rules.[401]

The later release of further detail spelled out how the policy would work in practice. Acquirers of banks could go through a reasonably straightforward assessment process to take a stake up to the threshold limits. If the acquirer could demonstrate its financial soundness emphatically, it could then be approved to gain a greater stake straight away. In less definitive cases, however, the acquirer would face three tests of financial soundness spread over 18 months. Only if these tests were passed could the acquirer take the greater stake.

The new rules did not overtly alter the current 99 percent foreign ownership caps on local banks. While the central bank had the power to introduce new regulations on this front, it calculated that the matter was best left to the legislature. Officially, at least, the new bank control rules were blind to the nationality of the owner, applying equally to foreign and local investors. But as the chief executive of an Indonesian bank later revealed, the rule would still be used as a tool of economic nationalism. "This ruling on ownership cap is basically directed at foreign banks. I've been told by the central bankers but they can't say that publicly in order to avoid problems with other countries," the chief executive told *Reuters*, speaking on condition of anonymity. "Local banks, especially the major banks, will be the ones who benefit from this regulation as they can buy the smaller banks easily and cheaply."[402]

The new ownership limits would also apply not just to new acquisitions but also to current arrangements, meaning that some existing owners could be forced to sell down their stakes by a 2019 deadline. Sigit Pramono, chairman of Indonesia's National Banks Association (Perbanas), expressed his approval, saying: "The rules give incentives for healthy banks, while unhealthy banks are given disincentives by being forced to divest their stake holdings."[403]

The rules moved Indonesia from being one of the most liberal banking regimes in Asia towards the midpoint of its counterparts. "Indonesia is returning to normal by shutting the door, whereas other Asian countries are returning to normal by opening up more, so Indonesia just looks worse," Edward Teather, the senior Southeast Asian economist at UBS, told *Reuters*.[404]

In terms of DBS's application to take over Bank Danamon, the new rules meant that approval for acquiring 40 percent looked likely but getting the nod for anything higher would be at the discretion of the central bank. Even though the Singapore bank looked well-placed to meet the exemption criteria, it appeared that other factors would enter into consideration. Still, analysts remained upbeat about the prospects of the deal advancing. "We believe the new regulation will pave the way for DBS to conclude its proposed acquisition of Bank Danamon and other planned acquisitions by foreign banks," Tjandra Lienandjaja, an analyst at BNP Paribas Securities Indonesia, wrote in a report.[405]

The new rules now on the table, the central bank quietly went about assessing the DBS application. For months it said little in public, and DBS, keen to not antagonise the organisation deciding the fate of its proposal, stayed quiet.

The push for easier access into Singapore was being spearheaded by three large state-owned Indonesian banks: Bank Mandiri, Bank Negara

Indonesia and Bank Rakyat Indonesia. The trio were keen to establish or expand their operations in Singapore and saw this case as the opportunity to remove the regulatory hurdles. Bank Mandiri president director Zulkifli Zaini spoke for the three when he enthused about the opportunities for growth in Singapore. "We are not worried about competition with big, foreign banks in Singapore, as we have proven that we can grow rapidly here in Indonesia," he told the *Jakarta Post*. "Just give us access there and let's do banking in an open system."

But analysts were more sanguine about the Indonesian banks' prospects, noting that their Singapore operations were unlikely to go beyond managing the assets of wealthy Indonesians living in Singapore, and others who have cross-border business interests. Gadjah Mada University economist A. Tony Prasetiantono noted that capital is the biggest barrier to expansion in Singapore. "Foreign banks [in Singapore] are huge in terms of capital, hence they are more efficient and can afford to have modern banking technology," he said. Bank Mandiri, Indonesia's largest bank, sat only seventh on the list of Southeast Asian lenders by capital size.[406]

There was a whiff of hypocrisy to the outrage of Indonesian state-owned banks at the takeover proposal. They had been given a chance to make an offer for Bank Danamon when Temasek indicated it was keen to sell down its direct stake, but had baulked at the considerable control premium that would need to be paid, according to a later account in the *Jakarta Globe* citing an unnamed banker. Perbanas chairman Sigit Pramono acknowledged that it was tough for state-controlled lenders to make big acquisitions. "As you know, you have to go through the government's approval, securing lawmakers' permission. It has never been easy," he told the *Globe*.[407]

Unstated in the public discussion over DBS's takeover application was that it would likely serve as a test case for other foreign banks keen to increase their presence in Indonesia. For the big local banks, fostering hostility to foreign banks had several benefits. By keeping smaller competitors weak, the big players would continue to face a lack of competitive pressure and would likely be able to keep Indonesia as the banking market with the biggest margins of any among the world's 20 largest economies. And by making acquisitions by foreign companies more difficult, the big banks would be able to keep down the premium they needed to pay to buy up the minnows. The interests of consumers, particularly the significant proportion of the population that is unbanked, and smaller banks were at risk of being sacrificed.

Months ticked past with little sign of progress. Early in the process DBS had expressed confidence that it would know the fate of its application by the end of 2012, but that deadline loomed without any hints on the outcome. Asked why no regulatory decision had been made eight months after the deal was announced, Lin Che Wei, an analyst from the Independent Research Advisory Indonesia, noted: "The fact that the deal was announced by the DBS Group without prior consultation with BI may have offended the central bank."[408]

In early December, Bank Indonesia governor Darmin Nasution provided an update of sorts, saying that discussions with the Monetary Authority of Singapore were ongoing. "This is a process of persuasion [between Singaporean and Indonesian central banks]. It's a political process. We will just see how it develops," he told reporters.[409]

While Bank Indonesia's handling of the case won it support from politicians and state-owned banks, it also drew its share of criticism from people who feared that the interests of consumers were being ignored. Among them was Vincent Lingga, the columnist with the *Jakarta Post*, who launched a swingeing attack:

> It is regrettable that BI has not been sufficiently transparent about the benefits of the DBS-Danamon merger for improving competition in the banking market, which seems to have been gripped by an oligopoly of the nation's five largest banks, three of which are state banks. The central bank should have made clear the economic logic of the deal to politicians and the general public,

and educated people as to how the merger would contribute to strengthening the banking sector and invigorating Indonesia's economy, which is still largely under-banked.

Such transparency and public education would have helped improve public opinion and protected the central bank from political meddling. Indonesia, especially its banking industry, will benefit greatly from the transfer of skills from the merger, not to mention from the external expertise in risk management and other best practices of good governance and access to a new big source of international financing.[410]

The first anniversary of the announcement of the takeover came and went with little fanfare. Governor Nasution provided a brief update that indicated that little progress was being made in discussions with the Monetary Authority of Singapore. "Some of our national lenders want to establish a presence over there. That's what we are discussing," he said. "If it is clear and there is a commitment [from the MAS], then that's when we will decide."[411]

Decision time

By late May 2013, Darmin Nasution was entering his final days as Bank Indonesia governor. While his successor, Finance Minister Agus Martowardojo, had indicated that he shared the incumbent's view on the need for reciprocity from Singapore in assessing the DBS application, Nasution decided a definitive announcement was needed under his watch. With the MAS showing little sign of budging, the governor announced the outcome: DBS could for now only acquire 40 percent of Bank Danamon. "If they want more … we want to see a realisation from MAS regarding our need for reciprocity," the outgoing governor told reporters.[412]

Though the central bank had failed to get the shift in policy it sought from MAS, Nasution said the greater ability to vet applications given by the new bank ownership cap worked favourably. "There's an extremely valuable lesson to be learned in this case: Don't talk about reciprocity when we have nothing to support it," he said. "There must be a clear reason for why we can say 'no' – if there isn't then the [other party in the negotiation process] can just laugh at our demands."[413] For its part, MAS gave Bank Indonesia some hope that change may come in the future. "In the case of Indonesian banks in Singapore, this will be by way of a broader provision of financial services, both in wholesale banking and to, for example, Indonesian students and work permit holders in Singapore," the regulator said in a statement.[414]

Holding out hope that it might still be able to guide the deal through, DBS twice extended the deadline it set itself to complete the transaction. The latter of these deferrals set a final date of August 1. A deal insider gave some insight into the debate going on inside the bank. "Increasingly, this is becoming an inefficient deal for DBS from an operational and capital perspective. And at some stage, it also becomes a question of credibility for DBS," a person familiar with the process told *Reuters*. "It's a messy situation and the debate within DBS is whether to live with the short-term pain or walk away."[415]

As the latest deadline approached it became clear there was little change on the horizon. Rather than prolong its struggle, and tie up the capital involved in financing the deal, on the final day of July the company announced it was letting the plans for the transaction lapse. In line with its control-or-nothing approach to the deal, DBS opted to not take any stake in Bank Danamon.

Keen to stay on good terms with Indonesian regulators, the company offered a face-saving statement to the market. "We would like to express our deepest appreciation to the regulators in Indonesia and Singapore for giving the transaction due consideration," DBS chief executive Piyush Gupta said. "We are positive about Indonesia's long term potential and will continue to grow our DBS Indonesia franchise, while remaining open to opportunities as they arise."[416] He acknowledged in a news conference the next day that it would take DBS about five years to expand its own operations in Indonesia to match Danamon's US$400 million in profit.[417]

Balancing act

On one level, the actions of Bank Indonesia in seeking to gain leverage in discussions with a fellow regulator are understandable, and reflect an organisation mindful of its role in pursuing the national interest. But on another it shows how notionally administrative decisions can become politicised and be used by powerful interests – such as nationalist politicians and growth-hungry state-owned banks – to further their own causes.

The policy decision to restrict takeovers will inhibit the consolidation that the banking sector needs, and also limit the competition among major players that will likely drive down margins and give consumers better value. As Fitch Ratings noted in the wake of the collapse of the deal: "This could limit potential buyers of Indonesian banks to investors with less commitment to the country and who may be looking essentially for capital gains … We believe the collapse of the deal is likely to discourage some long-term foreign buyers looking to establish and build a local franchise."[418]

While state-owned banks can be confident that Bank Indonesia was taking their needs into account in handling the DBS application, can Indonesia's banking consumers – and potential consumers – share the same confidence? The consolidation needed to ensure the prudential stability of participants in the fragmented banking sector seems as elusive as ever. And in lending to small and medium enterprises, Bank Rakyat Indonesia's dominant position, and hefty margins, remain unchallenged. The collapse of the DBS deal denied access to a major source of reserves for Bank Danamon to tap into in expanding its lending to SMEs. A few months after the deal was called off, the World Bank's International Finance Corporation offered up a US$75 million loan to Bank Danamon to allow it to expand its lending to small businesses. To some extent, it was filling the breach left by DBS's absence.

The tensions inherent in Bank Indonesia's approach to regulation were evident when new governor Agus Martowardojo stepped up in

November 2013 to deliver his inaugural address at the Bankers' Dinner. Continuing his predecessor's push for consolidation, he noted that: "Banks must escalate their business scale in order to achieve a higher level of economic of scale and concurrently an improved governance." But lest foreign banks prepare themselves to help Indonesia achieve that aim too quickly, he went on to warn: "In principle, these [foreign] investors can play a role in the national banking industry. However, it must be carried out in a proportional and reciprocal manner and delivering benefits to the economy."[419]

The case also jolted members of parliament into action. After howling at Bank Indonesia to do something to curb foreign takeovers, nationalist legislators decided to propose a new law on the matter. Under the draft of the law set to come into force in 2014, foreign ownership of local banks would be capped at 51 percent and the branches of foreign banks operating in Indonesia would be compelled to become locally incorporated subsidiaries.[420] The unintended consequences could be jarring. As economist Fauzi Ichsan argued, compelling banks to divest stakes in a market with little appetite to buy could trigger a collapse in the value of banks, while forcing local incorporation could lower banks' credit ratings to the level of Indonesia's sovereign rating, driving up the banks' cost of funding from the global money market and ultimately raising Indonesian companies' cost of funding.[421] Politicians pursuing tighter regulation should be careful what they wish for.

The combination of the 2012 ownership caps, the way they were applied in the case of DBS's application and the proposed new law has had something of a chilling effect on merger and acquisition activity in the Indonesian banking sector. In May 2013 *Bloomberg* put at US$10 billion the value of looming banking deals targeting Indonesia, with Japan's Mitsubishi UFJ Financial Group and the China Construction Bank among those studying acquisitions.[422] But as the year came to an end, none of those transactions had materialised.

12

Not Ready for the World

"Indonesia is probably the least well recognised of the major Asian economies. Today it's remarkable to me that there is no Indonesian company listed on the main market in London."

They were the words of Nathaniel Rothschild in late 2010 upon partnering up with the Bakrie family to list a US$3 billion coal company on the London Stock Exchange.[423] Within two years, he had a pretty solid explanation for his observation.

The short-lived corporate marriage and subsequent messy divorce between the scion of one of Britain's wealthiest families and an Indonesian family steeped in the country's business traditions is on one level a swashbuckling corporate tale of alpha-male egos butting heads over 10-figure sums of money. But on another it reflects the chasmic gulf between the way business is often done in Indonesia and the standards expected by the developed world's stock exchanges.

The deal heralded the first time major Indonesian assets had been listed on the London Stock Exchange, and so acted as a test case to see whether the country's companies were able to achieve the probity and transparency necessary for foreigners to be confident their investment is being used diligently. But soon after the deal was consummated evidence emerged of soft loans being given to related parties, hundreds of millions of dollars in assets being unaccounted for, directors reluctant to challenge powerful wealthy owners and the interests of minority shareholders being trampled upon. The deal's ultimate failure was a sign that the corporate habits of patronage, loose financial controls and opacity were no mere relics of the past but instead animated current business practices, and made the next effort to list a company with Indonesian assets abroad all the more difficult.

Perfect match?

The partnership between Rothschild and the Bakries dates back to 2010. Nathaniel Rothschild was just 39 at the time but schooled in generations of business experience in his family stretching back to an ancestor who funded Britain's battle against Napoleonic France. After spending his formative business years in hedge funds and serving as the co-president of New York-based Atticus Capital, the London-based Rothschild was keen for something fresh, and started Vallar Plc, an investment vehicle listed on Britain's bourse. Rothschild's bold plans for acquiring resources companies struck a chord with investors and he was able to tap the market for £707 million (US$1.13 billion at the time), funds raised on the understanding he would consider acquisitions of up to £5 billion.[424]

With Rothschild known to be on the lookout for investments, he was approached by Ian Hannam, an investment banker at J.P. Morgan Cazenove, who had a tip. Hannam pointed Rothschild towards Bumi Resources, a company controlled by the Bakrie family that was rich in Indonesian coal but facing serious debt troubles.[425]

In the seven decades since it was founded as a trading company in Sumatra, the Bakrie Group had become a vast Indonesian corporate empire spanning steel, plantations, real estate and telecommunications. For the company, started by Achmad Bakrie and now in the hands of the next generation, the coal in its Bumi Resources subsidiary was a prized asset given rapid energy-hungry growth at home and in nearby

Asian markets. The coal, much of it extracted in East Kalimantan by subsidiary Kaltim Prima Coal, had helped Bumi Resources reach a market capitalisation of Rp 54 trillion (US$4.5 billion) in Jakarta.[426] Playing senior roles in the Bakrie Group were Achmad's sons Indra and Nirwan Bakrie, while their brother Aburizal, Indonesia's fourth richest man, kept one eye on business affairs while also pursuing the Golkar Party presidential nomination for the 2014 election.

On the surface, the logic of the deal was compelling. Vallar Plc was cashed-up and had already passed through the fraught regulatory process to gain a listing on the London Stock Exchange. Bumi Resources was flush with coal assets but struggled, particularly outside Indonesia, to access the cash it needed to properly develop them (Bumi Resources had to pay an eye-watering 19 percent interest rate to access a US$1.9 billion loan from China Investment Corporation in 2009). Into the mix was thrown Berau Coal Energy, a notional Bumi Resources rival but one with links to the company. Also keen for better access to funds, it sought to hitch a ride on the deal.

Bumi Resources was the largest coal producer and Berau Coal Energy the fifth largest in Indonesia, a country that since 2005 had been the world's leading exporter of power-station coal. Between them, the companies had control of 12 billion tons of coal.[427] International coal prices were trending upwards, bouts of melancholy amid the Global Financial Crisis notwithstanding, and the more they rose the more compelling the deal would be.

Within weeks of Ian Hannam pitching the idea to Nathaniel Rothschild, the young entrepreneur met with Nirwan Bakrie in Los Angeles. So amicable was the meeting that a handshake agreement was reached, and three weeks later a subsequent meeting in Singapore committed the US$3 billion deal to paper.[428]

The terms of the pact were that Rothschild's Vallar Plc would use cash and shares to eventually buy a 29 percent stake in Bumi Resources and 85 percent in Berau Coal Energy. The transaction, a reverse takeover, left the

Bakrie Group as the biggest shareholder in Vallar Plc, with 55 percent, while Rothschild's stake had shrunk to about 15 percent. Reflecting the extent to which this was a company-defining deal for Vallar Plc, the company would be renamed Bumi Plc. (To avoid confusion, this text will refer to Bumi Plc and Bumi Resources by those fuller names.)

And just who was behind Berau Coal Energy? The company, with a market capitalisation of Rp 18.2 trillion (US$1.5 billion) at the time of the deal, was under the control of Indonesian entrepreneur Rosan Roeslani, who also served as president director. Started in 1983, by the time it listed in 2010 the company had three mining sites in coal-rich East Kalimantan that it predicted would reach 30 million tons of extraction a year by 2015, and its location positioned it well for exports to elsewhere in Asia. Bumi Plc insiders ran the ruler over the company and figured it could clamp down on some inefficiencies within Berau Coal Energy to help boost margins. Roeslani's holding was via another company, Bukit Mutiara, which was itself a unit of Recapital Advisors. The US- and Belgian-educated Roeslani would hold 13 percent of Bumi Plc under the terms of the transaction.[429]

The extent of Rothschild's due diligence on his partners before the deal was done was later the subject of some scrutiny. Rothschild engaged another part of his business empire, Vallar Advisers, to conduct a due diligence on the Indonesian assets and report back to the board of Vallar Plc. Rothschild later told *Bloomberg* that Vallar Advisors' assessment involved it seeking the wisdom of 50 experts and consultants who scoured thousands of documents, including prospectuses from Berau's August 2010 Indonesian initial public offering and a September 2010 US bond issue for Bumi Resources, both of which were marketed by J.P. Morgan and Credit Suisse Group. J.P. Morgan, whose Ian Hannam had first pointed Rothschild towards Bumi Resources, was engaged by Vallar Plc to advise it on the transaction, meaning the US investment bank had links to both sides of the deal. Later, when trouble struck, Rothschild would say that one of his blunders was "relying far too much on the supposed relationship that Hannam and J.P. Morgan had with the Bakries".[430]

Many remained doubtful at Rothschild's wisdom. "I was shocked that Rothschild would get into such a venture," Mark Mobius, who oversees US$50 billion at Templeton Emerging Markets Group, later told *Bloomberg*. "I am not saying the Bakries have done anything wrong, but given their history of corporate governance, I was surprised."[431] The structure of the deal struck some observers as risky. Majority control of London's Bumi Plc would rest with the Bakries, and the Indonesian family would directly hold a majority stake in Jakarta's Bumi Resources. The Bakries would have the whip hand, and the ability of Rothschild and other Bumi Plc investors to influence the Indonesian operations would be limited.

Corporate governance would be the topic on the lips of many commentators watching the pairing. Corporate governance is defined as the rules and mechanisms that guide the relationship among interested parties within a corporation, especially owners, boards and senior executives. In practice, it involves the way the company approaches thorny issues like accountability of staff, fulfillment of fiduciary duties, protection of minority shareholders and management of the firm's reputation. While many issues of corporate governance are determined by the law of the land, or the requirements of lenders and stock exchanges, other parts are at the discretion of the board of the company involved. As academics Peter Verhezen and Natalia Soebagjo wrote in a paper on corporate governance in Indonesia: "The board should make sure all shareholders are fairly treated and that shareholder rights are protected, including minority shareholders. The legitimate concerns of relevant stakeholders and social obligations should also be taken into account in making strategic decisions."[432]

In November 2010, the deal was announced to the stock market. Like a newlywed bride and groom, the two sides were effusive in their enthusiasm for the union. "We are listing it on the London Stock

Exchange and we're giving UK investors the opportunity to participate in this extraordinary growth story," Nathaniel Rothschild crowed. "[The listing] will enhance our international profile, provide a currency and platform for development in the region and put us in a much stronger position to build on the organic growth that our combined assets already provide," Indra Bakrie gushed.[433]

Market analysts seemed to recognise the merits of the arrangement. "A London-listed, large scale, pure play Indonesian coal play should offer a unique commodity exposure and have strong investment appeal," Liberum Capital analysts wrote in a report soon after the deal was announced.[434] Others noted that the Indonesian companies' alliance with Rothschild gave them access to European financiers, bankers, investors and markets. "They just can't rely on Indonesian banks for borrowing. They must, must seek funding from outside Indonesia," said Adrian Rusmana, a broker at Sucorinvest Central Gani in Jakarta.[435]

With the Bakries the biggest shareholders in Bumi Plc, they took the lead in appointing board members and senior executives. Indra Bakrie took on the position of chairman, while loyal lieutenant Ari Hudaya became chief executive. Rothschild took a position on the board.

Chummy lending

It wasn't long before problems started to emerge. Bumi Resources was heavily indebted at the time of the transaction – US$3.8 billion in June 2010, up six-fold on three years earlier[436] – but not all its borrowings were going towards developing the business. Bumi Resources had extended loans to companies linked to Rosan Roeslani, the president director of Berau Coal Energy who also served as a non-executive director of Bumi Plc. It emerged in November 2011 that Roeslani's Recapital Asset Management had received a US$231 million loan from Bumi Resources, while affiliated company Bukit Mutiara had a US$251 million loan.[437] As debt collectors go, Bumi Resources was hardly a strict one, allowing delays to repayments.

The practice of offering loans to related parties is still a common one among Indonesian conglomerates. While allowing a lender to offer a rate of interest below what the borrower would otherwise be able to achieve, it also serves a deeper purpose. Extending loans serves as a way to build trust, return favours and develop the goodwill essential in markets where personal connections are paramount and the enforcement of contracts is weak. For a private company, or one listed on a bourse where the practice is commonplace, related-party loans might be tolerable, but for one listed on a developed world market, it serves as a corporate governance red flag.

Not content to settle the matter internally, Rothschild wrote a letter to Ari Hudaya, Bumi Plc's chief executive, excoriating him for his apparent negligence in the matter. In the November 8, 2011 letter, which was made public by Rothschild, he demanded a "radical cleaning up" of the finances of Bumi Resources. He sought a timetable for the "repatriation of funds deposited with connected parties". He argued that the related-party loans had left Bumi Resources over-leveraged and led to a "corporate governance discount" in the value of Bumi Plc shares, which had fallen 15 percent since their July 2010 debut compared to a 10 percent rise in the benchmark FTSE 100. With Bumi Resources declining to accept Bumi Plc representatives on its board despite the London-listed company's 29 percent stake, Rothschild argued, Hudaya was the company's main hope of improving the corporate culture of the Indonesian miner.[438]

The publication of the letter was humiliating for the Bakries on several fronts. Not only had its debt troubles once again entered the public spotlight, but so had its cosy relationship with some borrowers. And for such issues to be championed by a foreigner was particularly painful.

Within weeks Rothschild met with Indra Bakrie in Singapore to press his concerns. The outcome of the meeting was that Bumi Resources agreed to a time frame in which loans extended by the company to related parties would be repaid, and those repayments would then go towards reducing the company's debt burden. The timetable involved Recapital Asset Management repaying its loan by the middle of 2012, and Bukit Mutiara settling its debt by the end of 2013.[439] (Sticking to the repayment schedule proved tricky, with Recapital Asset Management failing to meet the deadline.[440])

After the meeting both parties made comments that seemed to suggest the relationship was all smiles, although in retrospect it is apparent that teeth were gritted. "Indra and I had a very constructive meeting," Rothschild told *Bloomberg News*. "I am delighted that our partnership is back on track. We clarified a number of issues and we are completely aligned going forward." He added: "The Bakries are fully committed to an early repayment of shareholder loans, and the improvement in governance that was always promised as part of this transaction." For his part, Indra Bakrie said: "Our views are completely aligned on the importance of strong corporate governance and we agreed to work closely together to take the steps that will create value for all our shareholders."[441]

Bumi Resources arranged for US$600 million of its US$1.9 billion loan from China Investment Corporation to be refinanced elsewhere at a vastly more favourable rate.[442] But even that, combined with repayment of the related-party loans, was not going to be enough to ease the financial pressure on the Bakrie Group. A falling global coal price was weighing down on the Bumi Plc share price, which was down to £8.50 in October 2011 after listing a little over a year earlier at £10. The fall prompted a margin call on US$1.35 billion in loans from Credit Suisse Group, leaving the Bakries in need of some quick cash. The solution it found was to sell half of its stake in Bumi Plc, amounting to 23.8 percent of the company, to another Indonesian miner, Borneo Lumbung Energi & Metal, for $1 billion in cash.[443]

The deal represented a rescue of the debt-laden Bakries by Samin Tan, Borneo Lumbung's savvy president director. Tan represented a

classic rags-to-riches story, starting as an entrepreneur in his home village
before becoming a tax advisor of some renown and then making a fortune
on Borneo Lumbung's 2010 stock listing. Within months Tan, whose
connection with the Bakries goes back to his days as a tax consultant,
was appointed as Bumi Plc's chairman. Though he borrowed heavily to
fund the transaction, Tan insisted it was a commercial transaction rather
than a helping hand.[444]

Balance sheet blues

Not long after the loans issue became public another problem emerged.
Bumi Plc's financial report for the year to December 2011, released
the following April, included US$637 million in write-downs in the
Indonesian operation after auditor PricewaterhouseCoopers said it was
unable to verify the value of the assets. The write-downs (a reduction in
the estimated value of a company's assets on its balance sheet) involved
US$390 million in exploration and evaluation assets and US$247 million
in business development funds.[445] Some of the spending was supposedly
taking place at Bumi Resources' iron ore mine in Mauritania in West
Africa and its oil field in Yemen in the Middle East, but neither were
yet producing. Rothschild had flagged problems with the development
funds in his November 2011 letter, based on the most recent half-year
financial results, and the latest numbers appeared to back his suspicions.
Not long before the financial report came out, Ari Hudaya stood down
as Bumi Plc chief executive, but he remained on the company's board.

The revelations put the Bumi Plc board in a tricky position given
the boardroom dominance of appointees by the Bakrie family and their
ally, Samin Tan. In such circumstances it is usually incumbent upon
independent directors to assert themselves and seek answers from
executives at troubled parts of the business.

But Rothschild believed the Bumi Plc board was complacent in getting
to the bottom of the matter and ensuring such loose financial controls
are not able to continue, so he stayed on the case. Into his possession

came a slew of documents allegedly detailing financial irregularities not just at Bumi Resources and its subsidiary Bumi Resources Minerals, but also at Berau Coal Energy. In September 2012 he presented the dossier to the board of Bumi Plc, which had little choice but to act.

The company engaged London-based law firm Macfarlanes to undertake an independent probe into "potential financial and other irregularities" at the companies in the group. It also took the information to financial regulators in Britain and Indonesia.[446] Bumi Resources said it was not given any advance notice of the probe. The investigation prompted Ari Hudaya to go a step further than he had earlier in the year, quitting the Bumi Plc board altogether.[447]

Just where did the documents that Rothschild presented come from? The Briton explained that they had been offered to him on an unsolicited basis, but declined to publicly reveal how that came about.[448] The accessing of the documents would go on to be a source of great consternation.

For its part, Bumi Resources sought to portray the airing of possible impropriety as part of the cut and thrust of an increasingly rancorous dispute between shareholders with widely divergent visions for the company. "The present situation is unfortunate and is an internal issue between a few shareholders who have chosen to go external, managing media through innuendo," Bumi Resources director Dileep Srivastava said in a statement, suggesting it was part of a campaign by Rothschild to buy out his partners on the cheap. "This appears to be an attempt to damage the inherent value of our business by orchestrating internal issues and leaking them publicly, for motives which appear dubious."[449]

Nonetheless, the corporate governance allegations renewed fears among investors that Bumi Resources had overextended itself on credit. Its shares were down 69 percent for the first 10 months of 2012, compared to an 11 percent rise for the benchmark Jakarta Composite Index. The slew of allegations and debt concerns also prompted the ratings agencies to downgrade Bumi Resources: from a stable outlook to a negative one for Moody's Investors Service, and a one-step demotion to BB- by Standard & Poor's.[450]

A missing billion?

By January 2013, the Macfarlanes investigation had reported back to the Bumi Plc board. The company revealed that the report had found circumstantial evidence backing up the claims in the leaked documents of impropriety at both Bumi Resources and Berau Coal Energy. While the company did not put a figure on the amount possibly misappropriated, Rothschild said the report put it as high as US$1 billion, which he urged Bumi Plc to seek to recover. Bumi Plc said it would pursue potential claims where there was a prospect of recovery.[451]

The decision by Bumi Plc to not release the report, citing "exposure of unacceptable legal risks", reignited curiosity over the origins of the documents. Bumi Plc commissioned an investigation into where they had come from, and found evidence of e-mail hacking. Rothschild explained that the documents were obtained by an internal whistle-blower, though how this person got his or her hands on them was unclear.[452]

Rothschild's anger was not just directed at those involved in Bumi Resources and Berau Coal Energy, but also at Bumi Plc figures who had failed to take action. "Samin Tan knew about financial irregularities involving the Bumi Plc group before he joined the board, yet in his role as chairman did nothing about it," Rothschild's NR Investments said in a statement following the release of the report. "This calls into question compliance with his legal and fiduciary duties as a UK Plc director."[453] By this point, Rothschild was an outsider at the company he had founded, and had little faith in a Bumi Plc board dominated by people in the Bakrie camp.

It had become apparent that the Bakrie-Rothschild partnership was doomed to failure. The gulf in business cultures was so great that no financial imperative would be adequate to breach it. The only question was just how the company should be divided up. Mining industry veteran Nick von Schirnding was appointed as chief executive of Bumi Plc at the end of 2012 to oversee a split, and several new faces joined him on the board.

'No clear business purpose'

The explosive Macfarlanes report prompted Berau Coal Energy to launch an audit into past spending and to verify that the company's payments to contractors were legitimate. Fears of loose financial controls had led to worries that poorly documented spending at the company may have spiralled out of control. The audit, which involved consultancy heavyweights Ernst & Young and PricewaterhouseCoopers and included about 60 participants, was damning. It found US$201 million in spending at Berau Coal Energy with "no clear business purpose". The funds included US$79 million attributed to roads and construction, US$42 million in land-related payments and US$5 million of goodwill, while an additional US$24 million of consulting costs were reclassified to other exceptional costs.[454]

"This happened at various levels in the organisation, it happened around procurement, around certain contracts, and so we are investigating those parties," new Bumi Plc chief executive Nick von Schirnding told *Bloomberg*. "We are doing quite a significant amount of work in terms of getting restitution. I'm not here to be popular, I'm here to sort out this mess." Rothschild leapt upon the audit's findings as a sign of "clear fraud" at Berau Coal Energy and accused the Bumi Plc board of being "astonishingly slow" to act.[455]

The scrutiny of Berau Coal Energy also flushed out the fact that its former president director Rosan Roeslani, who also served on the Bumi Plc board, had received a substantially larger salary than the company had stated in its annual report. In 2011, Roeslani's salary, bonuses and other benefits amounted to US$3.8 million, rather than the US$700,638 initially stated. Furthermore, Roeslani, who left Berau Coal Energy when allegations of wrongdoing first emerged, received a termination payment of US$322,971 from the Berau Coal Energy board without the knowledge of the Bumi Plc board.[456]

Bumi Plc committed to try to reclaim the US$201 million that had been misspent by Berau Coal Energy, and so their attention turned to Roeslani. While Bumi Plc might have had a legal case against the former president director, it decided that discretion was the better part of valour. The two parties struck a deal in June 2013 under which Roeslani agreed to transfer to Berau assets and cash valued at US$173 million while Bumi Plc agreed to waive potential claims against him over the missing funds. The suite of assets Roeslani said he would relinquish included a shareholding in a company that transports all coal produced by Berau and another that owns the land it uses for its operations.[457]

Under the deal Roeslani made no admission of wrongdoing or liability. Rothschild was again infuriated at Bumi Plc's actions. "It is not up to the company to decide whether or not he can be exonerated," he told *Bloomberg News*. "The London regulators need to take action to send a message to foreigners who believe listing in London is a pushover."[458] But as one defender of the deal with Roeslani explained, the money was gone, legal action was unlikely to recoup it, and the company had to make the best of the circumstances.

Within months Roeslani appeared to be backsliding on the deal. After missing a September payment deadline for US$30 million, he claimed he had no obligation to meet the terms of the agreement. "Roeslani has now raised a number of issues as to the nature of his obligations, as a result of which he denies that he is in breach of those obligations and asserts that any outstanding liability to transfer any cash or assets under the Roeslani Agreement has been extinguished," Bumi Plc told shareholders, pledging to pursue arbitration to get their hands on the money.[459] (Roeslani did not appear to have any cash flow problems when, in October, he joined with two other Indonesians to buy a 70 percent stake in Italian soccer club Inter Milan.)

Messy split

If the marriage between the corporate interests of Rothschild and Bakrie had been an unhappy one, then the divorce was nightmarish. Once the split had become irreconcilable by late 2011, the two sides developed alternative visions for the future of the assets in the company. The Bakries were keen to essentially return things to how they had been prior to the deal, with their company taking back control of the Bumi Resources assets. Rothschild, however, was keen for Bumi Plc to buy out the Bakries so that it could retain the full extent of Indonesian exposure but run them in the way he wanted it to. Much of the battle played out in the form of efforts by both parties to stack the board with candidates amenable to its proposed resolution.

(In an intriguing twist, one of the people Rothschild proposed be appointed as a director of Bumi Plc was Indonesian businessman Hashim Djojohadikusumo, the brother of former military leader Prabowo Subianto, a rival to Aburizal Bakrie early in the 2014 presidential election campaign. Djojohadikusumo was unsuccessful in his tilt at the board.[460])

Ultimately the Bakries prevailed in that dispute. But the process of realising their vision, which involved the debt-laden Bumi Resources finding the cash to buy back its assets, was long and tortuous. More than a year after the Bakries got the nod from a majority of shareholders, they were still seeking to engineer a complex series of deals that would give them control of the mines and give Bumi Plc the funds to which it was entitled. Repeated calls by the Bakries to delay payment dates indicate that the company was struggling to find the money.[461] The delays made it all the more difficult for Bumi Plc, now reduced to a majority stake in Berau Coal Energy and a pile of cash, to move on.

Frederick Daniel Tanggela, an analyst at Bahana Securities in Jakarta, captured the mood of many market-watchers. "We had expected Rothschild's presence would help improve corporate governance at the Bakrie Group, Bumi Plc and its subsidiaries including Bumi Resources," he told *Bloomberg*. "But with the effort to oust Rothschild that hope has vanished."[462]

As the partnership unravelled and some investors faced losses as high as 75 percent, recriminations began in the Bumi Plc camp. The process by which the company had conducted a due diligence on the Indonesian assets it was acquiring, looking out for the very problems that later emerged, came under scrutiny. In January 2013 Bumi Plc announced it was undertaking an investigation into the role of advisers in giving the transaction the all-clear.[463]

Nathaniel Rothschild was rare among foreign investors in Indonesia in taking such a public approach to airing his grievances towards his local partners. From his leaked letter in 2011 to frequent comments to journalists, particularly at *Bloomberg* and the *Financial Times*, Rothschild came to offer a running commentary on the affairs of the company. But in a country where Javanese deference is still highly regarded and the maintenance of dignity a fundamental driver of action, an approach that sought to shame an adversary into action always ran the risk of backfiring.

In the wash-up, many observers in Jakarta have been critical of the approach taken by Rothschild throughout the transaction. "To my mind it shows extraordinary naivety on the part of Rothschild. I just don't know what he thought he was doing, getting into bed with someone like Aburizal Bakrie," one veteran business figure in Jakarta said in an interview.[464]

Perhaps the more significant issue to ponder is why it is that Indonesian corporate governance standards are so low that many foreign observers instinctively shudder at the prospect of an intimate business dealing with one of the great standard-bearers of the Indonesian economy. Some clues come from an observation from academics Peter Verhezen and Natalia Soebagjo. "We should not forget that Indonesia's corporate structure is dominated by insiders who control the board and major decisions within the firm," they noted grimly in their paper.[465]

Part of the weakness of Rothschild's position in the saga came from the fact that Bumi Plc was only a minority shareholder in Bumi Resources, with 29 percent of the company, leaving it unable to assert its values and expectations. Instead, the Bakrie Group was able to bend the board to its will and continue with questionable practices. Corporate governance expert Chris Leahy noted that generally speaking, tightly held Indonesian companies treat the presence of outside shareholders on their register as a source of kudos, but are reluctant to make substantive changes. "The idea that it's no longer just our business doesn't really take hold with these families," Leahy, who has done business in Indonesia for more than a decade, said in an interview.[466]

As for independent directors, the pool of people in Indonesia with the relevant expertise as well as a willingness to stand up to large shareholders is quite small. Adding to the difficulty is the reality that many listed companies in Indonesia, and indeed across Southeast Asia, are still dominated by single families and have a reflexive suspicion of outsiders in senior positions. Corporate rules require publicly traded companies in Indonesia to have just a single independent director (of boards that typically have up to a dozen members), compared to a requirement of 20 percent independent directors in the Philippines and 33 percent in Singapore.[467]

In the battle for improved corporate governance in Indonesia, there are some signs of hope. The Financial Services Authority (OJK) has launched a project to rate the corporate governance performance at the country's 50 largest companies, with criteria including the way companies treat minority shareholders and the roles played by board directors. "We'd like to see how companies implement sound corporate governance so investors are confident that these companies are in good hands," OJK chairman Muliaman Hadad told *Bloomberg* in a January 2013 interview. "The top 50 at least should reflect excellent qualities." The Harvard-educated official added: "Enforcement is key. Violations need to be followed up on, sanctions have to be clear and exercised."[468]

But a tick-the-box approach will not be enough to achieve a meaningful improvement. "Complying with procedural rules may improve board governance, but as long as the attitude of integrity and openness that creates trustworthiness in the capital market remains only lip service and compliance-oriented, processes and procedures may continue to be perceived as weak and superficial," wrote Verhezen and Soebagjo.[469]

The failure of the Bumi transaction serves as a salutary tale for others keen to bring Indonesian natural resources assets to developed markets. Certain ways of doing business are entrenched in Indonesia, and while some prove advantageous others are an anathema to global standards of corporate governance. At the heart of Bumi Resources' inability to ready itself for a listing abroad is not a failure of intellect or imagination – certainly the people making the decisions at Bumi Resources are shrewd, internationally experienced businesspeople – but instead one of culture.

For many of the elite families who control Indonesia's great conglomerates, their businesses are perceived as tools of achieving political influence, social acceptance and friendship. In deciding where to invest and who to lend to, commercial factors are only one of several considerations. The approach runs the risk wastefully deploying capital and propping up poorly run businesses, ultimately stifling innovation and hurting productivity across the whole economy. For conglomerates that remain in the family, the price might be one worth paying. But as these companies grow to the point where they need outside investors, the calculus becomes far more complex.

On one hand, local companies will often benefit from stock exchange listings, particularly abroad, because of the ability it gives them to access a new source of funds. But on the other hand a listing forces them to curb vanity projects and wasteful spending and sacrifice some of the control over their company that they have come to expect. Just which path Indonesian companies choose to go down will give great insight into how they perceive themselves, and the extent to which companies make the most of the resources available to them.

By early 2014, the separation between the Bakries and Rothschild was nearly complete. The Bakries looked set to end up with Bumi Resources, while Rothschild and the company he founded would keep control of Berau Coal Energy. Both parties appeared happy to be rid of the other. And Asia Resource Minerals Plc, the new name assumed by the company that started life as Vallar Plc and morphed into Bumi Plc, was on the hunt for new assets. But probably not in Indonesia.

13

Caging the Golden Goose

With an abundance of tin, copper, gold, nickel and coal all resting in its soil, Indonesia has long been a major international supplier of natural resources. Stretching back to the colonial period, various competing interests have sought to gain access to the rich bounty, using fair means or foul, with the country's location within easy reach of heavily populated Asian neighbours adding to the appeal. Used wisely, the country's natural resources can be a catalyst for economic advancement and improved living standards for all people, but if squandered they assist an elite few while pock-marking the environment and fuelling resentment.

Control of energy and mineral resources almost inevitable depends on control of political institutions, and this has proven to be the case in Indonesia. So when foreign miners fell out of favour with the national government, and local mining interests gained influence, it was unsurprising that a major policy shift was enacted. The consequences of that shift would be far reaching and in many cases unexpected. They put at risk a significant share of Indonesia's mineral exports while also sending the country to the top of the list when it came to foreign miners' assessment of risk. A suite of changes intended to help the country as a whole prosper seemed to instead help just a handful of local interests, and left workers and taxpayers little better off.

So how did Indonesia come to this point?

For much of his three-decade presidency, Suharto was a great friend of foreign miners. While in the early years he inherited the resource nationalist instincts of the socialist president he succeeded, over time he become increasingly acquiescent to the wishes of foreign mining companies, sometimes with little regard to the welfare of his own people.

The fundamental piece of law governing the operations of mining companies was the 1967 Mining Principles Law, rubber-stamped by the legislature. From then on, mining rules would be determined by successive waves of formal regulations issued from the presidential palace. So it came to be that in regulations introduced in 1994, Suharto relaxed the rules to the point that foreign miners could own up to 95 percent of a resources project.[470]

And that's how the mining rules operated in Indonesia until Suharto was removed from office. During the first decade of the Reformasi period there were few changes to the regulations, but many Indonesians were concerned about the extent to which the natural resources of their country were being exploited by foreign companies, and the terms on which it was taking place.

So with an election looming, President Susilo Bambang Yudhoyono decided to sweep a broom through the resources sector, modernising the system under which miners operated in order to increase the benefits that flowed to the state and the people. The outcome was the 2009 Law on Mineral and Coal Mining, legislation that sought to fundamentally rebalance the relationship between the state and the mining companies with which it did business. Gone were the chummy deals of the Suharto era, and in their place were tough rules that sought to increase local control of mines, ensure a steady flow of royalties revenue to the state and develop downstream processing operations. The law was scheduled to come into effect from 2014, meaning the country was in for a five-year countdown to what would either be a development masterstroke or a massive act of self-sabotage.

(Not all in the 2009 Mining Law was unfavourable to foreign

investors. The law did remove one long-standing frustration: it allowed foreigners to hold mining licences directly, where previously they had to strike deals with local companies who had little intention of using the licences themselves.)

Until this point mining companies in Indonesia had operated under Contracts of Work, long-term contracts that spelled out a company's rights and obligations with respect to all phases of mining operation, including exploration, pre-production development, production and mine closure. The legislation established a new legal instrument – Mining Business Licences (IUP) – and introduced a new geography-based licensing system involving a supposedly transparent tendering procedures across all levels of government. But the government was determined that holders of Contracts of Work should not get off easily even though the new law did not strictly speaking apply to them.

While officially the legislation sought to develop the resources industry, in practice it unleashed five years of uncertainty and a stuttering in investment. Mining amounted to about six percent of gross domestic product, but far from securing a future of sustained economic growth on the back of the industry, the legislation prompted a paralysis in mining company decision-making.[471]

Resources are a rapidly growing part of Indonesia's export base. In 2011, bauxite exports stood at 40 million tons, up from 16 million tons two years earlier, while exports of nickel rose to 33 million tons from 11 million tons two years earlier, and iron ore rose to 13 million tons from seven million tons.[472] (Indeed, it was the rapid pace of that growth, and the risk of over-exploitation of Indonesia's resources, that in part motivated ministers and lawmakers to reach for the brakes.) The country is a major player in global resources markets, being the world's top exporter of nickel ore, thermal coal and refined tin, fifth-largest copper producer and a significant player in gold. Mine exports in 2012 exceeded US$10 billion, accounting for five percent of the country's total export revenue.

If the mining industry had taken the legislation at its word, perhaps the introduction of the policy might not have proven so rocky. But Indonesia has a long history of mining industry rules coming and going, often before they've even arrived, so there was a high degree of uncertainty that the new legislation would ever materialise. Often rules are watered down, manipulated and thoroughly bent out of shape through later clarifications, such that the final outcome often bears little resemblance to the initial intention.

In the case of the 2009 Mining Law, by mid-2013 there had been five sets of government regulations and six other sets of regulations from the Minister of Energy and Mineral Resources.[473]

As each new regulation emerged, the industry became increasingly concerned at the beast that had been unleashed. The government sought to impose increasingly onerous restrictions on miners both foreign and local. The poor shape of the government's finances and the emergence of a trade deficit provided a more pragmatic incentive for squeezing miners.

The 2009 law and subsequent regulations had myriad impacts on the mining industry in Indonesia, but there were three aspects in particular that sharply elevated sovereign risk: the requirement for foreign mining companies to divest a majority stake to local interests; the forced renegotiation of existing contracts in line with the new law; and the ban on the export of raw minerals.

DIVESTMENT

Mining is an inherently risky enterprise. There's always the prospect that the lands on which you stake your fortune are barren rather than brimming, then there's the effort involved in shoring up a mineral reserve and the cost involved in establishing a mine, after which a slump in commodity prices may make the whole thing too costly to operate. Miners therefore need to know that they will be able to keep control of their mine in the long term, at least until they earn enough to cover the costs incurred in developing it in the first place, and hopefully enough to achieve a tidy profit in order to seed the next venture.

But this long-term certainty was put at risk with the 2009 Mining Law. Once the detail on the law became clear, it was evident that foreign miners could be forced to sell off more than half their holding in Indonesian mine projects to local parties within a decade of starting production, and they would receive few assurances on the price they would receive for the share they were forced to sell off. The change set the stage for a series of negotiations tilted towards opportunistic local miners keen to snap up a bargain from a distressed seller.

In February 2010, a little over a year after the law was passed, a set of regulations spelled out the terms of the new divestment rules. It said that at least 20 percent of a foreign-controlled mining company operating in Indonesia needed to be owned locally at the end of an incremental divestment scheme that had to begin by the fifth year of production and conclude within a further five years.

The regulation was a significant shift from the status quo, in which 95 percent of a miner could be foreign owned, but still compared favourably to other markets in Asia, where resource nationalism was a common refrain among lawmakers.

Two years after the initial regulations were released, the government had another go. It issued a further set of regulations on the 2009 Mining Law, and this February 2012 set had a much sharper edge than did its predecessor. Under these regulations, foreign mining companies would need to sell off 51 percent, not just 20 percent, starting no more than five years after production commenced and concluding within a decade.

The new rules shocked foreign mining companies, who viewed the 10-year time-span of the divestment as not nearly long enough to recoup their expenses, let alone achieve a decent return on investment. They argued that the divestment rules would hurt miners who had already spent large amounts, sometimes hundreds of millions of dollars, on exploration.

The chaotic approach to changing the rules on divestment incurred the wrath of the *Jakarta Post*, which published an editorial on the "arrogance" of the government's actions. "The government may think that foreign investors would stay put despite the harsher terms, given the profit windfalls they have been enjoying amid the commodity boom," the paper said. "True, Indonesia is rich in reserves of gold, copper, tin, coal, and several other minerals. But our country is not the only one with such natural resource endowments. Big risks are already inherent within the mining sector without legal uncertainty and policy inconsistency."[474]

Devil in the detail

It was not until mid-2013 that a new regulation on the Mining Law put flesh on the bones of the divestment price rules. Many of the industry's fears were confirmed. According to an analysis by Bill Sullivan, a Australian lawyer with Jakarta-based Christian Teo Purwono & Partners, the regulation gave little guarantee of a minimum price for the stake being sold. The fact that sellers had little choice but to offload their assets to a local party created every incentive for buyers to wait until they got a bargain-basement asset.

According to Sullivan, in cases where the government is the purchaser of an asset as part of a Mining Business Licence-holder's forced divestment, the purchase price under the regulations is no higher than replacement cost (less aggregate depreciation, amortisation and outstanding financial obligations). Such a crude calculation of the value of the asset denies compensation for the risk incurred, the goodwill that has been generated and the myriad other factors that ordinarily determine the value of an asset. By imposing this as a ceiling price, the regulation dramatically strengthens the hand of the government in price negotiations with forced sellers. In the absence of a private-sector buyer, companies are unlikely to make back the money they have invested.

"Denial of 'fair market value' compensation represents potentially huge loss to foreign investors," Sullivan said in a public presentation of his finding.

Furthermore, Sullivan found the regulation said that Indonesia Stock Exchange listings were not adequate to satisfy divestiture requirements. This limited the range of buyers to which a foreign miner could sell its assets to deep-pocketed individuals, companies and government investors, undermining efforts to develop the stock exchange as a source of capital and also to allow smaller investors to get easy exposure to mining companies.[475]

Given the legislation meant that many prime mining assets would soon be coming on the market, some observers wondered whether local buyers had the capital to fund purchases. Rather than a broad spread of buyers emerging to claim the assets, more likely was that a few wealthy local players would snaffle them. And with government entities able to use the regulations to push down the price paid for divested assets, privately funded government purchases, in which private investors bankroll an acquisition and effectively act as partners, became a particularly attractive proposition.

The mining divestment requirements, and the process by which they were developed, inspired little confidence among foreign miners. The commercial logic of investing in speculative projects in Indonesia was weak if a company was forced to sell off a majority stake before it had achieved a decent return. The campaign to persuade the government of this fact had fallen on deaf ears, and time will tell whether the investment slowdown materialises.

CONTRACTS OF WORK

With Contracts of Work making way for Mining Business Licences (IUP), the government was keen to find a way to ensure the tighter terms of the new law applied to those legacy contracts. If any benefits were to be achieved from the new policies in the short term, the government would need to ensure that the 42 Contracts of Work and 76 Coal Contracts of Work came under their scope. Otherwise, it would be a decade or more until higher royalty payments started to flow and divestitures started to kick in.

Seven generations of pro forma Contracts of Work have been in place since they were introduced in 1967, so each miner is on roughly similar terms. While contracts are held by many smaller miners, both foreign and local, two mining giants are the contracts' biggest signatories: Freeport Indonesia, which operates the Grasberg copper and gold mine in Papua, and Newmont Nusa Tenggara, which operates the Batu Hijau copper and gold mine in West Nusa Tenggara.

Even though these Contracts of Work still had years to run in some instances, the government declared it would bring the mining companies to the negotiating table to reset the terms of the contracts in line with the new legislation. The government's agenda in contract renegotiations featured six items: share divestment, the size of mining areas, contract extensions, the amount of royalties to be paid, obligations to process raw materials in Indonesia and the utilisation of local goods and services.[476]

In most instances, efforts by governments to forcefully reopen discussions on established contracts would lead to shrieks of sovereign risk. But given many of these contracts were settled in the opaqueness of Suharto's rule, there was some sympathy for the government's push even among advocates for the mining industry. And the contracts, the government was at pains to emphasise, did include a clause allowing for renegotiation under exceptional circumstances.

In February 2012, the government established a team dedicated to renegotiating contracts with the miners. Leading the team would be Hatta Rajasa, the charismatic Coordinating Minister for the Economy who during Susilo Bambang Yudhoyono's second term crafted a serious of protectionist development policies that collectively became known as Hattanomics.

'Moral obligation'

For President Yudhoyono, the contract renegotiations were an opportunity to right historical wrongs. "These contracts were signed 20 to 30 years ago and nowadays are found to be unfair. I have a moral obligation to make a change," the president told reporters in June 2012.[477] To the president and others angry at the extent to which the nation's resources were being plundered by outsiders, renegotiating contracts amounted to catharsis.

But it wouldn't be easy. The Contracts of Work holders were doubtful of the government's claim that the contracts could be reopened, and even when they did formally consent to renegotiations they were keen to stand their ground. While the government figured that it would have most sway over smaller miners, with whom the power imbalance was greatest, it knew the success or failure of the renegotiation strategy would hang on whether it could strike deals with the big players.

They don't come any bigger than Freeport Indonesia, the local arm of US mining giant Freeport McMoRan Copper & Gold, which has been operating in the restive Papua province for nearly half a century. Its 170,000-hectare Grasberg operation in Timika is the world's biggest gold mine and second biggest copper mine and employs about 24,000 people. The company has sought to steer clear of the complex politics of Papua, but it has inevitably become ensnared. Resentment towards Jakarta runs deep in Papua, and the presence of a mine backed by the national government, using police and military for security and relying significantly on workers from Java, stirs anxiety.

Despite its abundance of natural riches, Papua remains one of the poorest provinces in Indonesia, and anger over this reality is often directed towards the company. For its part, the company pays substantial royalties, taxes and dividends to the national government (US$7 billion over five years), has instituted a corporate social responsibility program in the province and hires local talent where available. Relations with its employees have also been tense – a three-month strike over wages and work conditions at the Grasberg mine in late 2011 turned violent, with at least eight people killed in ambush attacks and clashes with police.

The company signed its first Contract of Work in 1967, and this was renewed for 30 years in 1991 under a contract that was not revealed to the public until the fall of the Suharto regime seven years later. Today, Freeport McMoRan Copper & Gold owns more than 90 percent of Freeport Indonesia, with a 9.36 percent stake in the hands of the national government.

The uncertainty over its future contract was an unwelcome distraction for Freeport Indonesia as it mulled a major investment in underground mining facilities at Grasberg. The current operation is an open-pit mine to extract copper ore, but surface reserves are expected to be depleted by 2016, just five years before the company's current Contract of Work expires. A new investment, valued by the company at about US$15 billion, sought to allow underground mining to commence in 2017. A lack of certainty over its arrangements beyond 2021 made the investment a risky proposition.[478]

Joining Freeport as a major Contract of Work holder was Newmont Nusa Tenggara, the local unit of US miner Newmont Mining Corporation. Since 2000, it had operated the Batu Hijau copper and gold mine on Sumbawa Island in West Nusa Tenggara province. The company, which employs about 9,000 people either directly or on contract, has generally maintained good relations with the government and people despite the occasional worry over labour relations.

The uncertainty over Contracts of Work was taking its toll on Vale Indonesia, the country's largest nickel producer, which was 59 percent owned by the Brazil-based mining giant. The company said it needed to settle contract renegotiations before going ahead with a US$2 billion investment to expand its smelter in Sorowako, South Sulawesi, and to build a refinery in Bahodopi, Central Sulawesi. The proposal would double the company's production capacity in Sorowako to 120,000 tons of nickel matte and the refinery would process 18,000 tons. But if divestment was forced upon it and nickel royalty rates hiked from the current one percent to as high as the government's proposal of four percent, the investment may no longer be economical. "We have to have some security if we are going to fulfil our plan," Ricardo de Carvalho, president commissioner of Vale Indonesia, told the *Jakarta Globe*.[479]

Not bluffing

The push for contract renegotiations slowly gained traction as it became clear the government was not bluffing. In September 2011 the Energy and Mineral Resources Ministry's tireless director for minerals and coal, Thamrin Sihite, said that around 65 percent of mining companies operating in Indonesia had agreed to the government's request to renegotiate their contracts. "The renegotiation is the mandate of the law. The law is made by the people and the voice of the people is God's voice. We are proceeding with the renegotiation plan," he told the *Jakarta Post* during a flight of metaphysical fancy.[480]

The government said it was aiming to complete contract renegotiations by the end of 2013, but given more than 100 contracts were up for discussions, it would need to move fast. The government hoped that signing some renegotiated contracts early would create momentum and encourage some of the more recalcitrant miners to acquiesce.

But early victories were few, so the government resorted to talking up incremental advancements as evidence of progress. One such case was in July 2012, when renegotiation committee leader Hatta Rajasa announced that Freeport Indonesia had agreed to some concessions on matters of divestment, royalties and local content.

The company had agreed to prepare an initial public offering on the Indonesia Stock Exchange in order to boost its local shareholder base, although the size of the offering had yet to be determined. The company also agreed to increase its royalty payments, but again the extent remained undecided.[481]

Come October 2012, the government again sought to talk up its achievements. Some 14 small-scale coal miners (out of 76 holding Coal Contracts of Work) had settled on new deals, and Jero Wacik, the Minister for Energy and Mineral Resources who served on the government's renegotiation committee, said generally Contract of Work holders had "shown a willingness to renegotiate". But the process would go on for a while longer, he admitted.[482] Wacik's bureaucratic counterpart Thamrin Sihite gave some insight into the tone of the discussions. "The law stipulates that the old contracts are no longer allowed, but those miners were arguing for contract sanctity and delaying the ongoing talks," he said.[483]

Running on a treadmill

Negotiations with Freeport Indonesia and Newmont Nusa Tenggara ground on. It emerged that in both cases a major sticking point was the government's desire for the companies to process their ores locally before export. "Based on our studies, constructing a smelter is not feasible for the company," Newmont Nusa Tenggara spokesman Rubi Purnomo told reporters.[484]

Both companies already processed some of their ore at Indonesia's only copper smelter, a facility in Gresik, East Java, operated by a company called Smelting, a joint venture of Freeport Indonesia and Mitsubishi. Newmont Nusa Tenggara sent about half of the copper concentrate from Batu Hijau there, and Freeport Indonesia sent about 40 percent of Grasberg's copper concentrate. But Smelting was reluctant to expand its facilities after falling copper prices put a squeeze on margins, meaning the companies would need to look elsewhere.[485]

Gradually the terms on which Freeport Indonesia was willing to honour the partial agreement it had struck with the government the previous year emerged. The company said it had agreed to set the size of its initial public offering at 5 percent, which even when coupled with the 9.36 percent already in Indonesian government hands would leave the local stake well short of the government's desired level. On royalty rates, the company said it was willing to increase its copper royalty, which currently varied from 1.5 percent to 3.5 percent, to four percent, while it would increase its gold royalty from one percent to 3.5 percent, and silver royalty from one percent to 3.25 percent.[486]

As the second half of the year came and discussions with the major Contracts of Work holders remained deadlocked, a few more innovative approaches were tried.

Keen to mollify the government on raw exports, Freeport Indonesia and Newmont Nusa Tenggara in August each signed a Memorandum of Understanding with a pair of local smelters indicating they would supply them with concentrate. The two companies – Indosmelt and Indovasi Mineral Indonesia – said they intended to pour billions of dollars into the development of the smelters, but the plans had not yet left the drawing board. Given the preliminary nature of the plans, chief economics minister Hatta Rajasa was reluctant to give the miners a leave pass on the looming raw export ban just yet.[487]

Then in October, the House of Representatives commission that oversees mineral resources decided to try its hand as a deal broker. It summoned senior executives from the major Contracts of Work holders to learn of their latest position on the government's six contract renegotiation agenda items in a closed-door meeting, and then held a similar discussion with the government to learn of its position. The attempt to break the impasse was a creative one on the part of the lawmakers, who through their committee work have strong expertise in the policy area, and took advantage of the autonomy of Indonesia's legislature from its executive.

But the effort failed to yield a result. By the end of November, no resolution had been reached and the year-end deadline set by the government loomed. While some of the smaller Contract of Work holders had reached deals with the government, none of the major players had done so.

By this point it had become clear that most of the provisions of the Mining Law would in reality apply to the Contract of Work holders even if strictly speaking they were exempt. This was in part because the successful implementation of the ban on the export of raw materials, and hence the development of smelters, relied on the economies of scale achieved by having the big players on board. Given this, the interests of the contract-holders aligned very closely with the rest of the mining industry, and so they shifted their focus away from their own discussions. Freeport Indonesia and Newmont Nusa Tenggara joined the front lines of the industry's battle against the ban on raw mineral exports. While still vital to their future operations, the contract renegotiations would have to wait.

RAW EXPORTS

Miners in Indonesia are adept at extracting mineral resources and shipping them to countries in Asia hungry for materials to feed their growth. But much of the bounty is exported as ore, still largely as it was extracted from the earth, before the complex processes that convert it into the forms sought by end users. It is in these latter stages that much of the value is added to the material, and the price paid by buyers increases.

By selling the material in its unimproved form Indonesia is missing out on the chance to add value, and therefore selling price, to its exports. If Indonesia could be more involved in the downstream processes, it would boost the value of its exports, improve the sophistication of its industry and boost government revenues. No longer would Indonesia just be Asia's quarry – it could be its mineral processing hub as well.

It was this thinking that motivated perhaps the boldest change in President Susilo Bambang Yudhoyono's pack of 2009 mining industry reforms: a ban on the export of raw materials from 2014, requiring mining companies to instead work with smelters in Indonesia to develop the product before selling it abroad.

The government's justifications for the law widened over time. While
the need to develop downstream industries was the foremost explanation,
it was later joined by other apparent benefits. Bayu Krisnamurthi, the
Deputy Trade Minister, explained it like this a few years later: "When
the Indonesian government wanted to make this law, there were good
reasons. First, sustainability issues. Without different arrangements, we
just exploit the face of the earth and see the damage of that exploitation.
The second, of course, is value-added activity. For local people in the
regions where mining is located there must be positive economic impact.
We have seen stories where decades after mining there is no [positive]
impact on the local communities. Third, because this is a nonrenewable
resource we have to be careful because it will be lost forever once it is
taken out of the ground."[488]

Despite the apparent concern with the environmental impact
of mining operations, a legitimate fear given the mines that pock the
landscape, the law did little to directly regulate the volume of mining
activity nor introduce measures to ensure that sites were chosen carefully
and that operations met high environmental standards.

Instead, the regulations, which applied to raw commodities ranging
from precious metals like gold to base metals like tin and the energy
mainstay of coal, would involve a massive scaling up of the mineral
processing industry. At the time, the country's smelting capacity did not
extent far beyond nickel, tin and modest quantities of copper.

For exporters of those materials, as well as others typically exported
in raw form, like iron ore, bauxite and manganese, big changes would
be required. For years the government had sought to encourage the
development of downstream industries, with limited success. If a policy
of gentle persuasion has failed, perhaps the industry would respond to a
blunt legal instrument.

While the 2014 ban on the export of raw materials looked menacing
on paper, pragmatic companies who had followed the ebbs and flows
of Indonesian regulation knew better than to rush off to ensure they

were compliant come the deadline. Few companies had existing smelting facilities in Indonesia, and to advance plans to build smelters on the basis of the legislation alone ran the risk of being stuck with a white elephant should the law be watered down through regulation before the start date arrived.

Smelters don't come cheap. A copper smelter costs about US$800 million, while a nickel smelter could cost up to US$2 billion to construct, according to a 2011 estimate from the Indonesian Chamber of Commerce and Industry (Kadin).[489] (One of the few existing smelters, Aneka Tambang's ferronickel processing plant in North Maluku, with an annual capacity of 27,000 tons, was budgeted at US$1.6 billion.[490]) A study by researchers at the Bandung Institute of Technology found it typically took between 24 and 30 years for a smelter to reach financial break-even point.[491] While the legislation allowed miners to outsource the smelting to other companies, the paucity of such companies and facilities in operation meant a major investment would be required. Given the uncertainty, none were rushing off to make it a reality.

Prior to the Indonesian policy's introduction, no substantive analysis of the economic impact was carried out; only afterwards did the US Agency for International Development carry out a study, finding it would be counterproductive in efforts to grow the country's economy. The February 2013 report projected the direct loss to the Indonesian economy from the mining policy would be US$6.3 billion in 2014, with export earnings to fall by US$6 billion per year. The study noted that the net welfare benefits of the ban will only become operational in 2020, but only after tens of billions of dollars of losses, and even then these total net welfare gains will be modest, totaling just US$832 million per year.[492]

Electric blues

For a handful of miners, the policy was advantageous. For Weda Bay Nickel, 90 percent owned by French mining giant Eramet, the policy made its planned US$4.6 billion investment in a new smelter in Halmahera,

North Maluku, all the more fortuitous.[493] For state-controlled tin miner Timah the policy also proved favourable given its 2008 investment in a smelter to produce tin solder for export to South Korea and Japan.

But for most other miners, the policy threatened to be costly and unachievable. Major participants in the resources industry undertook a campaign to raise awareness about just how impractical the proposal was for all raw materials to undergo processing in Indonesia prior to export.

Central to their argument was that smelters were electricity-intensive facilities, and Indonesia simply lacked an adequate or reliable electricity supply to power them. Therefore miners, or their partners building smelters, would also likely need to source their own electricity.

"A mineral processing industry requires a lot of power, which is mainly supplied by the state utility company Perusahaan Listrik Negara," Bambang Sujagad, an official with the Indonesian Chamber of Commerce and Industry (Kadin), told the *Jakarta Globe*. "We can't wait for PLN to build a power plant. Instead private companies should be given leeway to build their own power plants."[494] For miners to become smelter operators, and now power plant builders, was a stretch few were willing to undertake.

Exacerbating the problem of supplying electricity were a pair of other factors. For one thing, a smelter needs to be powered by a specifically modified power plant given smelting operations lead to sudden changes in electrical usage, with the voltage increasing and declining rapidly. For another, the typical approach of smeltering ore close to its source meant these smelters would need to be built in remote regions often lacking an energy source and basic supporting infrastructure.

Smelters also required a long lead time to develop given the finance and infrastructure involved. Syahrir Abubakar, executive director of the Indonesian Mining Association, said it would typically take six or seven years to build a smelter. "We're not ready for these policies," he told *Agence France-Presse*. "If the government doesn't come up with better infrastructure fast, Indonesians will lose jobs."[495]

Freeport Indonesia president director Rozik Soetjipto spelled out what was involved in constructing a new smelter, based on the company's experience as a 25 percent shareholder in Smelting, the company operating Indonesia's only copper smelter and refinery, in Gresik, East Java. It took six years to move from the feasibility study to the end of construction, and cost US$1.2 billion. The challenge would be even greater in building a smelter near its giant copper mine at Grasberg. "If we want to build a smelter in Papua, there must be electrical supply, roads, ports and a waste-dumping facility nearby," he said.[496]

The policy risked eroding one of Indonesia's biggest advantages as a source of resources. "One of the things about Indonesia is that it is a relatively low-cost producer," Gavin Wendt, a Sydney-based analyst at MineLife, told *Reuters*. "If all of a sudden you increase the costs of production, then a lot of mines are probably going to become uneconomic."[497]

Risk advisor Keith Loveard argued that Indonesia's efforts to claim a greater share of the minerals value chain was bound to upset some of the big mining companies, because it would upset their existing global operations. "It is quite reasonable for Indonesia to want to overcome entrenched business practices in order to benefit more from its own economy," the Concord Consulting analyst said in an interview. "The implementation of the ban on unprocessed ores is one clear case where some mining majors are resisting efforts to disturb the current design of the value chain."[498]

While it was the big players in the mining sector who were the most vocal in opposing the policy, it was in fact the smaller players in the sector, most of them locally owned, who had the most to lose. Large miners were more likely to have the capacity to raise the capital and guarantee the stream of raw materials necessary for an economical processing facility. Their smaller counterparts, however, were at risk of collapse, stuck with the right to mine resources they lacked the capacity to process nor the legal right to export.

Worst fears

Come early 2012, the Ministry of Energy and Mineral Resources issued the regulations that gave form to the minerals export ban, and the text confirmed many of the worst fears of the industry. From January 2014, miners would no longer be allowed to export minerals, including copper, gold, silver, nickel, tin, bauxite and zinc, in their raw form. Coal needed to have a calorific value of at least 5,700 kilocalories per kilogram, a threshold that industry figures said was uneconomical with existing technology and excluded the mountains of low-grade coal Indonesia exports to India and China. Minerals, meanwhile, needed to be processed to at least 99 percent before export, so nickel miners, for example, could no longer export nickel ore but needed to convert it to nickel matte first. Even though mining companies were invited to take part in group discussions as the regulation was being formulated, there was little sign of their contribution in the final document.[499]

Fearing that the 2014 ban would encourage companies to rapidly accelerate their exploitation of reserves before the drawbridge came up, the government contemplated interim measures to tamp down resources sector growth. Just how to achieve that was the subject of disagreement among government officials: some were keen on a hefty tax, others pushed for quotas on export volumes and a third group was keen to bring forward the ban itself. Adding to the confusion was the unfortunate habit of bureaucrats, in advocating their preferred policy to the media, of creating the impression their policy was the definitive one, prompting a market shock and then hasty clarification.

Finally in early May a seemingly definitive interim policy emerged: Energy and Mineral Resources Minister Jero Wacik announced that the ban would come into effect within three days, but exemptions would be allowed for 14 mineral commodities (later expanded to 65), which would become subject to an export tax of 20 percent if sold in the form of ore. That list of 14 commodities notably excluded coal.[500]

To qualify for an exemption from the imminent ban and face only a tax, a miner needed to lodge with the government a comprehensive proposal to develop a smelter, either through building one itself or via a partnership, as well as ensuring their existing legal and financial obligations had been fulfilled. This latter requirement, framed as companies being able to declare their mines having a "clean and clear" permit status from all levels of government, was itself rather restrictive, given the thicket of inconsistent regulations and maps meant only about 40 percent of the country's 10,000 mines had achieved it, according to the Indonesian Mining Association.[501]

While adding to the angst for miners because it brought forward the ban, the interim policy did also create a model of compromise, in which a commitment to future plans to process minerals would be adequate grounds to continue to export commodities in raw form in the short-term.

The ban and tax had a swift impact, enough to give exporters whiplash. In June, the first full month in which the rules were in place, exports of bauxite stood at zero, compared to 2.36 million tons a month earlier, while the export of copper plunged 90 percent to 20,000 tons and overseas sales of nickel nose-dived 80 percent to 572,000 tons. Coal exports, which were excluded from the interim ban-or-tax regime, fell just 13 percent to 26.2 million tons over the month.[502]

The exclusion of coal from the early ban-or-tax regime is intriguing given it was included among the other commodities facing a raw export ban under the 2009 legislation and 2012 ministerial regulation. Was this part of a broader government strategy to exclude coal from the ban altogether? Some industry observers noted that the biggest coal exporter was Bumi Resources, controlled by the influential Bakrie family. With the company up to its neck in debt, it would have little prospect of building the smelters necessary to meet the calorie standards required for export. As the debate rolled on, coal, which accounted for about 80 percent of Indonesia's mineral exports by value, remained excluded from the processing requirements.[503]

At this point the industry shifted its strategy. Clearly the government was wedded to the idea of a ban on exports, and seeking to overturn the substance of the policy was doomed to fail. Instead, the industry zeroed in on the question of timing. Keeping the deadline hard and fast would lead to mines across the country falling silent, with hundreds of thousands of jobs and billions of dollars in government mining royalties at stake. But the model used in enforcing the interim restrictions – allowing exceptions in cases where companies had taken steps towards establishing smelters – could form the basis of a useful compromise in enforcing the substantive ban.

Indonesia's trade competitors sought to capitalise on the country's self-inflicted damage. The Mines and Geosciences Bureau of the Philippines predicted that 2012 nickel ore production and exports would be "far better" than the previous year, particularly in shipments to China, as Indonesia's ban created opportunities.[504] Australia's Bureau of Resources and Energy Economics scaled up its forecast of bauxite exports for the 2013-2014 financial year, citing China's search for alternative sources to Indonesia as the "main contributor" to growth.[505]

Freeport Indonesia and Newmont Nusa Tenggara remained convinced that the legal case for them, as Contracts of Work holders, to be subject to the Mining Law was slim. Nonetheless, they made some commitment to local processing while also emphasising its practical limits. The two pledged to make its copper ore available to the Freeport-part-owned Smelting smelter in Gresik. "With the current condition, however, it is not feasible for PT NNT to build its own smelting plants," company spokesman Rubi Purnomo told the *Jakarta Post* in reference to its Batu Hijau gold and copper mine.[506]

Before the year was out, there was yet another legal twist in the tale. The Supreme Court in November ruled that the ministerial regulation issued earlier in the year was invalid in imposing a ban, albeit a partial one, on the export of raw minerals from May 2012. The court found it overstepped the terms of the legislation it was intended to substantiate, which only imposed the ban from January 2014. The ruling provided some short-term relief for miners feeling the squeeze, but had little impact on the longer-term policy settings.[507]

Search for a compromise

As the one-year countdown to the January 12, 2014, start date for the new rules commenced, government ministers started to sweat that the mining industry would indeed grind to a halt. Regularly they trumpeted private sector plans to develop new smelters as evidence that the policy was working. But at the same time they started hinting at a willingness to compromise. Adding to the urgency for compromise was the country's deteriorating trade balance, as falling commodity prices hurt the value of Indonesia's exports.

In April Energy and Mineral Resources Minister Jero Wacik gave a startling insight into the way informal pragmatism is used to trump formal sluggishness. Meeting the 2014 start date for the raw commodities export ban would be "impossible", the minister admitted, "and there's no need to be ashamed about it". So would the minister seek to legislate a change to the terms of the policy? Not a chance. "Do you think it is easy to revise or annul a law? It will take years to be completed." Instead, he said, the government will seek to find "loopholes" in the law that will allow those miners to keep operating. Such loopholes might include allowing limited exports of raw materials and applying a specific export tax.[508]

As these attempts to kick the stone down the road continued, the mining industry started to talk up another way the rules could be made more accommodating. The 2009 Mining Law stated that miners must "process and purify" minerals extracted in Indonesia ahead of export,[509] but what exactly did that require? Much of the discussion so far had focussed on smelting ores, but there are other incremental steps that could more realistically be undertaken before export short of smelting. After all, as Martiono Hadianto, chairman of the Indonesian Mining Association and chief executive of Newmont Nusa Tenggara, noted, metal miners operating in Indonesia generally already process raw materials domestically before export, producing concentrate. This concentrate, he said, represents 90 percent of the price of smelted, fully processed metal on the global market.[510] Minimum purity thresholds offered room for a compromise.

At the same time as it forcefully put its case to legislators, ministers and bureaucrats behind closed doors, the mining industry also sought to explain the consequences to the public. The Indonesian Mineral Entrepreneurs Association (Apemindo) had a crack at quantifying the fallout from the ban as it stood: US$9.8 billion in lost export earnings in the first year and 3.5 million people losing their jobs. "Workers in mining companies, contractors, suppliers, logistics, as well as those with small businesses around the mining area, all stand to lose their livelihood," Poltak Sitanggang, the group's chairman, told the *Jakarta Globe*.[511]

The more respected Indonesian Chamber of Commerce and Industry (Kadin) offered a tamer estimate of 800,000 workers "directly or indirectly in the mining industry" whose jobs were at risk.[512] For Kadin, the mining issue had proven a tricky one given it draws its membership from across the business spectrum. The body established a taskforce to examine the issue, and ultimately decided to back the ban, prompting the resignation of some members. Explaining why Kadin ultimately supported the government's position despite the job losses, chairman Suryo Bambang Sulisto said: "We don't want to look back in a decade or two and see that we don't have anything left." Like so many of his members, Sulisto had made his fortune in the coal and nickel mining business.[513]

Freeport Indonesia warned of the consequences for its operations if it was subject to the ban: output at its Grasberg mine would fall by 60 percent, and it would lay off half of its 15,000 workers. Its revenue would fall about 65 percent to US$5 billion in 2014, depriving government coffers of US$1.6 billion. "We are trying to inform and convince the government how serious this is," Freeport chief executive Rozik Soetjipto told *Reuters*. "What we are trying to convince government and members of parliament is that allowing us to continue exporting our product would not be breaching the law."[514]

Newmont Nusa Tenggara revealed details of a contingency plan if it was forced to halt exports. In essence, it would halt production at Batu Hijau.[515] For the 4,000 workers and 5,000 contractors employed by the miner at the Sumbawa Island site, the threat of redundancy loomed. And for the regency in which the mine is located, which draws between 60 percent and 80 percent of its revenue from the mining industry, a closure would be cataclysmic.[516]

Government numbers appeared to justify the gloom. An Energy and Mineral Resources Ministry official told the media that Indonesia's foreign exchange revenue from ore exports may decline by US$4 billion in 2014, and by US$2.5 billion the next year. An uptick was finally expected in 2017.[517] As taxes and royalties shrunk, so to would government revenue, plunging the national budget further into deficit: Finance Minister Chatib Basri put the hit to government revenue at Rp 10 trillion (US$833 million) in 2014 alone.[518] Consumer confidence and the rupiah, both already fragile, looked set to come under further pressure.

Mining industry lawyer Bill Sullivan also pointed out that the export ban would fuel the black market for smuggling of unprocessed commodities, a persistent problem that has already led to the establishment of sophisticated underground networks in the case of coal. "Indonesia will simply lose a significant part of the royalty revenue it currently earns from unprocessed mineral product exports without any offsetting benefit being generated for the country," Sullivan wrote in *Coal Asia*.[519]

But not all miners were opposed to the raw export restrictions. One voice of support came from Vale Indonesia, the country's largest nickel miner, which already had a smelter online at Sorowako in South Sulawesi and was happy to see the reduction in supply drive up the global price of the commodity. The fact that it was processing its nickel domestically meant it was assured of an export licence to continue its sales to its main market, Japan. "I see the nickel price jumping quite significantly," Peter Poppinga, an executive director of the company, told *Bloomberg*. "I think the authorities in Indonesia are very reasonable and very serious about that."[520]

As the rains of another wet season started to fall in the dying months of 2013, ministers felt the heat from an angry mining sector and a growing number of workers and local communities who feared the fallout of a shutdown. But the ministers also fretted about the optics of them giving concessions to mining companies, many of them foreign owned, with an election in the offing.

So to give themselves some political cover they reached out to the House of Representatives and sought formal approval for more relaxed rules, including allowing those companies that had made firm plans to build smelters to continue exporting raw materials beyond January. The push was led by Energy and Mineral Resources Minister Jero Wacik. Plans were advancing on the construction of smelters, Wacik argued – 177 companies had submitted expressions of interest to build smelters, 28 were under construction and one had reached the commissioning stage – and so the legislation was already having its desired effect.[521]

But the legislators remained unswayed, in December declaring that they would not budge on the law they had passed nearly five years earlier. "We don't want to create a shock in the mineral and coal sector. However, we don't want this law ignored," said Bambang Wuryanto, a legislator from the Indonesian Democratic Party of Struggle (PDI-P).[522] For legislators, the practical impact had to be weighed against the symbolic significance of any shift in position.

Attention then turned to the finer detail about the threshold of processing that a mineral needs to meet to beat the ban, a matter within the scope of regulators and ministers. Explaining that it was economically unfeasible for Newmont Nusa Tenggara to construct a smelter near its

Batu Hijau copper mine, chief executive Martiono Hadianto talked up the processing his company did undertake. "All of the ore from the Batu Hijau mine is processed through crushing, grinding, and flotation systems to produce copper concentrate at our processing facility in West Sumbawa," he said in a statement.[523] But R. Sukhyar, the man appointed in December 2013 as director general of coal and mineral resources at the Energy and Mineral Resources Ministry, was adamant that was not enough. "They must purify the minerals. That means processing the ore into metal, not concentrate," he told the *Jakarta Globe*, citing the terms of the 2009 Mining Law.[524]

Crunch time

As the new year rolled around, more than 100 mining companies trimmed or shut down operations due to the uncertainty surrounding the mineral export ban. Thousands of workers were laid off, prompting protests in Jakarta. "We call on all mining workers to prepare to go on the streets and swarm the presidential palace if the government goes ahead with the implementation of the ban," Juan Forti Silalahi of the National Mine Workers Union implored.[525]

So it came down to government ministers and bureaucrats in the first days of 2014 to use what power they had to take some edge off the impact of the new rules. On January 11, a Saturday, President Susilo Bambang Yudhoyono called together his cabinet for a meeting at his private residence in Cikeas, West Java, that stretched into the evening. The ministers contemplated just how far they wanted to water down the law, and how they would sell it to a public already sceptical of the actions of big mining companies but also nervous about job losses.

The outcome of those discussions came in the form of a presidential regulation issued just hours before the commencement of the ban. President Yudhoyono allowed 66 companies, including Freeport Indonesia and Newmont Nusa Tenggara, to continue to export processed minerals because their assurances that they will soon build smelters were deemed adequate. The companies given the exemption were permitted to export copper, manganese, lead, zinc and iron ore concentrate until 2017.[526]

But nickel ore and bauxite exports, worth more than US$2 billion annually, would still be banned in their raw form because there were deemed to be ample domestic smelters. The government made that decision with its eyes wide open: just a month earlier it forecast that with the policy in place nickel production would sink 78 percent in 2014 compared to two years earlier, while bauxite would dive 97 percent.[527]

The mining industry's campaign to water down the purity level required in a mineral for it to be eligible for export also yielded success. Previously the expectation had emerged that a purity level of 99 percent was required before export, but new regulations set more modest thresholds: copper at 15 percent, ferronickel at 10 percent, iron ore at 58 percent, lead at 57 percent and zinc at 52 percent.[528] The regulation also spelled out the necessary adding of value to non-metals, such as limestone, quartz and marble, before they can be exported.[529]

As welcome as the decision was, it remained a short-term fix. The impracticality of building electricity-hungry smelters in remote parts of the country remains the case, and is very likely to persist to 2017 and beyond. There seems little doubt that the arguments that were made repeatedly and forcefully in the lead up to 2014 will continue.

With the election looming, many miners, including those who committed on paper to constructing smelters, held off on major expenditure until they could see the shape of the new government. Investors already scarred by years of spinning around the policy roulette wheel have plenty of incentive to wait to see where it lands.

Investment Coordinating Board (BKPM) deputy chairman Tamba Hutapea defended the policy as a legitimate attempt by the country to create additional value and maximise the revenue it gets from its natural resources. "God does not create it twice. Once it's consumed, it's consumed," he said with a laugh. He rejected the claim that there had been inadequate consultation before the ban was introduced, arguing that discussions on the law started in 2005 and most of its enforcement will not commence until 2017. He also challenged the idea that there was an inadequate power supply at the likely smelter locations. "If they have clear proposals, we will provide electricity," he said.[530]

Next steps

The suite of policies included in the 2009 Mining Law certainly made Indonesia a tougher place to do business, but pragmatists might argue that it is a sensible response to Indonesia's position of relative strength. Given anyone seeking to extract the resources will have to negotiate with the Indonesian government and the fact that several other resource-rich countries were also tightening the screws on foreign mining investors, perhaps this was the perfect time for the Indonesian government to assert its claim on its bounty.

But there's strong evidence that Indonesia was going well beyond its resources rivals in creating a hostile environment for foreign mining investors. The Fraser Institute, a Canadian free-market think-tank, in 2013 ranked Indonesia last of 96 jurisdictions in a survey of mining companies' assessment of the regulatory environment. Indonesia's position, down from 85th of 93 jurisdictions just a year earlier, reflects the extent to which it has slipped against its peers.[531]

The signs were that Indonesia's mining investment climate was not just worse than it had been in the past – it was worse than the already-deteriorating environment in comparable countries. For investors in boardrooms around the world working out where to invest next, the case for Indonesia got a whole lot tougher.

What makes Indonesia's regulatory environment so unfriendly is not just the tone of the law and regulation, but the piecemeal way in which it is made public. Regulations are often slow to emerge, inconsistent and poorly drafted, adding to costs and anxiety for companies seeking to comply with them.

The Fraser Institute's Fred McMahon noted that frustration from mining executives in high-uncertainty places like Indonesia was not necessarily because the law was unfavourable but instead because it changed frequently. "Countries such as Sweden can be in the top 10 most attractive destination for mining companies, even though they implement high taxes. This is due to the fact that they have stability in terms of their rule of law," he said.[532]

And what does uncertainty on the ground look like? PricewaterhouseCoopers depicted the landscape in a May 2013 report: "Through the enactment of the Mining Law, the government has sought to create more certainty about Indonesia's mining framework. This certainty will only crystallise, however, when all the regulations implementing the law are in place. Four years on, the law still requires some further implementing regulations which have not yet been issued, and as usual the devil is in the detail. Furthermore, some implementing regulations are not entirely clear in addressing the issues and further guidance is required. This may cause further uncertainty for investors."[533]

As for the actual impact of the new rules on mining activity, at the time of writing it is too soon to tell. But if industry estimates of future behaviour under the rules are any guide, the country's resources industry is destined for a tough few years, much of it the product of well-intentioned but short-sighted regulations from Jakarta.

14

Conclusion

In the 1980s Karawang was an unremarkable agricultural village like dozens of others in West Java, a place where many kids were bored and sought opportunities and excitement in big cities like Jakarta, 70 kilometres to the west. But when the place was selected by the national government as a hub for manufacturing, its fortunes changed. Under Suharto's New Order and then the Reformasi leadership that followed, Karawang's new industrial estates attracted a slew of investors both local and foreign to establish factories. A particular focus was the automotive sector: several car-makers, particularly from Japan, opted to construct vehicles there, and other parts makers and suppliers also set up shop.[534]

The outcome was a booming town, where the sons and daughters of farmers from the surrounding area flocked to make a living as part of the automotive supply chain. For more than two decades the companies on site have been flat out producing products for the booming domestic automotive market. And with a critical mass of producers and suppliers there, and the (albeit overwhelmed) Tanjung Priok port within reach, there is great potential for the output from Karawang to be exported.

Several big companies have made major investments in Karawang, and are enjoying the benefits. Toyota each year manufactures tens of thousands of units of its Innova, Fortuner and Avanza models in concert with a local partner; Yahama produces motorcycles; Sharp and Panasonic make semi-conductors. All seem to quietly go about their business, have good relations with government and unions, employ tens of thousands of people between them and deliver solid returns to their shareholders. The industrial parks make a lot of sense for manufacturers given they largely negate the risk of conflicting claims over land.

Despite the gloom that pervades many of the case studies cited in this book, it is important to remember the ethos outlined in the introduction – Indonesia is a high-risk investment destination, but one that also has potential for great reward. The companies who have made a success of their investment in Karawang are among those that have gone on to realise that reward, and illustrate that it can be achieved in a way that is within the ethical, legal and financial limits for international companies.

Just a cycle?

As hostility towards foreign investment has grown in recent years, many observers have attributed it to the upcoming elections, arguing both that politicians have been burnishing their nationalist credentials in order to appeal to a nationalist public, and also seeking to raise funds from deep-pocketed local companies. After the election, the argument goes, things will settle down and more reasoned legislative and bureaucratic decisions will return. Unfortunately, such an argument is merely wishful thinking.

The economic nationalism, as documented in this book, has not been evident just in the year or two leading into the 2014 legislative and presidential polls. Instead, it spans the five-year gap between elections, with major instances of hostility to foreign investment scattered across the period. Big policies, like the food self-sufficiency goals and the Mining Law, involved major decisions on design and enforcement during the supposed off-peak period between visits to the ballot box.

And if the election link is to be believed, the intensification ahead of 2014 should have been less than ahead of either of the previous two elections, given in the latest round there is no presidential incumbent seeking re-election (as opposed to Megawati Sukarnoputri a decade earlier and Susilo Bambang Yudhoyono himself in 2009). With Yudhoyono unable to run for another term in 2014 because of constitutionally imposed term limits, he theoretically had a much freer hand to withstand ill-informed populism and explain to his people the benefits of connecting with the global economy.

Instead, Yudhoyono has proven risk averse in the "lame duck" period of his presidency. On issue after issue he deferred tough decisions, while he seemed to place little faith in his skills of political salesmanship. Come the countdown to 2014, one could argue that electoral politics still dictated Yudhoyono's thinking because of the desire to maintain support for his struggling Democratic Party, but even with that in mind the president showed a lack of fortitude in taking on difficult economic challenges.

Jakarta Governor Joko "Jokowi" Widodo is set to become Indonesia's seventh president. Widodo's views on foreign investment remained murky during the election campaign; while he did little to suggest he would buck the popular antipathy towards it, his strong push for transparency and clearing away the stodgy bureaucracy give cause for optimism. As governor of the capital he has dealt with some major foreign contractors, including drawing on many for the development of public transportation projects. But the stance Widodo, a principled populist, would take as president is difficult to know. Along the way Widodo eclipsed two candidates who inspired little hope for change. Aburizal Bakrie, the Golkar Party hopeful whose party failed to garner enough support for him to land a spot on the ballot, is the billionaire part-owner of the Bakrie Group. Prabowo Subianto, the Great Indonesia Movement Party (Gerindra) nominee who fought a head-to-head battle with Widodo, was a key shareholder in Nusantara Group. Both were part of the Indonesian political establishment stretching back to the New Order era, and were unlikely to dismantle the networks in which they are so central.

Underlying trend

Rather than being a product of electoral cycles, rising economic nationalism in Indonesia is an underlying trend that will likely continue beyond 2014 unless it is confronted. The trend has come about through the combination of several factors – popular sentiment among ordinary people, its cynical exploitation by elites and the rise of global commodity prices.

One of the legacies of colonialism is that many ordinary Indonesians are deeply cynical about foreign intentions towards their country. For centuries, the Dutch (and on occasions the Portuguese, British and Japanese) methodically exploited the islands that now make up Indonesia, through policies such as the cultivation system that demanded a fixed quantity of agricultural output go direct to Dutch authorities, regardless of total yield, sometimes consigning local people to poverty. More recently some foreign companies used the permissiveness of the Suharto era to gain a stranglehold on resources, to the advantage of the ruling elite but not necessarily the people at large. And during the Asian Financial Crisis of the late 1990s, it was foreign institutions that sought to impose their austere policy prescriptions on Indonesia in exchange for a bailout (notably, many European nations resisted embarking on similar policies when they faced financial crises of their own a decade later).

Given these historical realities, it is unsurprising that many Indonesians are instinctively suspicious of foreign companies. But why has it bubbled to the surface only in recent years? Any answer is by definition speculative, but perhaps it might be linked to growing frustration among many people that life remains a painful toil even as people hear about their collective shift towards the middle class. A few key statistics tell a story. Economic growth since the global economic crisis has been moderate (4.6 percent in 2009, peaking at 6.5 percent in 2011) when compared to the 8-plus percent growth that regularly occurred under Suharto's rule. Inflation has remained stubbornly high, beyond 8 percent by the second half of 2013, putting cost-of-living pressures on many people. And a rapidly depreciating rupiah (Asia's fastest falling major currency in 2013, down 21 percent against the US dollar) has limited access to imported goods for many people. Collectively, these factors foster anxiety, and foreign investors prove an easy target.

This is where the second factor plays its part. Many wealthy and politically influential Indonesian business figures have sought to fuel hostility towards foreign investors, establishing legal barriers to a level playing field and stoking localised opposition to big projects. Some local conglomerates appear keen to reserve the spoils of Indonesia's middle class for themselves. They are also keen to drive down the price for lucrative energy and minerals projects by scaring off foreign rivals, thereby reducing competitive tension. The strategy to achieve these objectives involves leveraging connections with politicians and officialdom on one hand, and rallying public support for their cause on the other. It is here that the trend of ownership of media outlets within broader corporate conglomerates becomes particularly powerful. Be it the Bakrie Group's tvOne or the Lippo Group's BeritaSatu media empire, the ability of local corporate interests to shape the popular mood is substantial. These powerful local business interests have successfully made the case that what's good for them is good for Indonesia, when the reality is that ordinary people gain little from their dominance but lose out from the foreign investment retreat.

The third element playing a role is the prolonged rise in commodity prices through to the early part of the 2010s. As insatiable resources demand by China and India hit against supply constraints in some parts of the world, prices headed upward, strengthening the hand of those countries, like Indonesia, that had resources to sell. "Many countries look to Indonesia to source mineral products and other natural resources," Australian lawyer Bill Sullivan said in an interview at his Jakarta office. "Certainly during the mineral commodities boom Indonesia came to realise, 'Hey, we've got some power here that we can exploit. We didn't fully realise how significant our role was in the value chain of mineral production and utilisation and now we do, we can use that to advance our nationalist agenda'."[535] While prices have since eased a little, the long-term trajectory is still upward.

All this suggests economic nationalism, including in the resources sector, is not likely to change course beyond 2014.

When in Jakarta …

Confronted with the volume of evidence of corruption, game rigging and environmental mismanagement in Indonesia, a pragmatic businessperson might ask whether they should in fact go along with it. After all, a single enterprises is unlikely to have much impact in changing an entrenched practice and the spoils available to an outsider who is willing to embrace those entrenched practices can be great. Besides, might run the argument, all these expectations of transparency, probity and strict contract enforcement are foreign-imposed notions that clash with Indonesian values of looking after family and maintaining dignity.

But such an argument is flawed. Great works have been written on the moral questions involved and this text does not seek to add to that debate beyond noting that if a person believes certain practices to be unethical in one context, they owe themselves intellectual consistency such that they hold it to be unethical in all contexts. To pick and choose morality based on circumstances seems highly dubious.

Separate from moral concerns, there are several great strategic reasons why partaking in ethically dubious acts in Indonesia is foolish.

Firstly, efforts to catch wrongdoers are becoming increasingly sophisticated. While the state of law-enforcement in Indonesia is generally poor, one shining light has been the Corruption Eradication Commission (KPK). In the decade since it was formed, the KPK has shown a willingness to pursue cases regardless of the political and economic clout of the suspect, up to and including members of the national cabinet. The body rightly enjoys high levels of public support, and consequently has been given a broad mandate by the government to pursue corruption cases using (almost) any means possible. The KPK's wiretapping capacities are legendary, and the fear of a conversation being heard by the no-nonsense graft-busters on Jalan Rasuna Said has surely given many senior business and political figures pause for thought. With the KPK having an extremely high success rate in prosecutions at the dedicated Anti-Corruption Court, unpleasant futures awaits those who finds themselves on the KPK's radar if the evidence stacks up.

Secondly, law enforcers are not the only people who are dedicating themselves to catching corporate crooks. In the Reformasi era, a slew of civil society groups have emerged to confront major social ills. In many cases, they have the resources and expertise to investigate people and organisations engaged in misdeeds and the media savvy to expose them to a wide audience. The Indonesian Forum for Environment (Walhi), for example, has taken to naming-and-shaming companies and government agencies for which they have evidence of destruction of protected forests and polluting of waterways. Indonesia Corruption Watch, another group, chases down allegations and provides referrals to law-enforcement bodies when they believe they have evidence of graft.

Thirdly, most developed countries have now instituted laws that forbid their nationals from engaging in corruption when abroad. The laws, like the US Foreign Corrupt Practices Act, are targeted at activities in places just like Indonesia, where incentives for corruption are high and law enforcement is patchy. Several people have been pursued at home in recent years for their conduct in Indonesia (among them those affiliated with service machine company Diebold and an offshoot of French power and transportation company Alstom), and the volume of business being conducted in the country makes it probable that more will follow. Typically these laws are framed in such a way that casts a wide net for the conduct they prohibit. One area for particular caution needs to be the practice of using a local agent to "fix" any problems that emerge, with a hefty payment offered for their services. If the agent were to engage in corruption, there's a fair chance the party that hired them could find itself subject to close legal scrutiny. An arm's-length distance from the actions of an agent does not necessarily provide legal cover.

Other international efforts are also yielding results. Indonesia has signed up to the Extractive Industries Transparency Initiative, an integrity program that aims to cut corruption in the resources industry by compelling companies and governments to publish details on payments made and received. The first report, covering 2009, was released in May 2013. It oddly showed that the amount received by the Indonesian government from extractive industries was US$243 million more than the companies acknowledged paying, but given it came within one percent of the total amount received and there were 129 companies reporting, the gap is understandable.[536] The initiative, over time, will be well-placed to expose corrupt payments made by companies that never reach government coffers.

Fourthly, there are long-term benefits in the country's business environment becoming more honest and transparent. A pragmatist seeking quick rupiah may care little about the system they help perpetuate, but an investor who is here for the long haul knows that better governance standards make everyone (bar a few corruptors) better off. Efforts to change established norms can be slow and painful, particularly for the early adopters who feel like they are missing out, but is only through enough people demonstrating the change in practice (mass civil obedience, if you will) that it becomes the norm. An improved business environment – of lower transaction costs, easier contract enforcement and fewer rigged tenders – is a hefty incentive.

President's agenda

With the extent of the problem established, we need to turn our attention to what can be done about it. As discussed earlier this chapter, the issue is a sign of a broader underlying trend that seems likely to stretch beyond the presidential election. Having said that, presidents have tremendous power to shape public perceptions and influence future thinking. They also have the capacity to enact administrative changes that can have real impact both because of the reforms themselves and because of the signals they send to others. In Indonesia, where staff in an organisation study their boss's actions closely for signals on how they themselves should act, the president's role as exemplar-in-chief is a significant one.

So for Joko Widodo, who will occupy Istana Negara beyond October 2014, the following ideas are humbly presented in the interests of creating a better investment climate so that local people can continue to enjoy the fruits of international engagement.

Make fewer promises, but be sure to deliver on those promises made. Too many Indonesian politicians in the past have taken the approach of telling audiences what they want to hear – one thing to ordinary local people, another to the local business community and a third thing to foreign investors – in order to avoid conflict and maximise popularity. With so much "noise" in political debate, and a media not keen to blow the whistle on a senior figure's inconsistencies, candidates have been able to get away with it. The consequence of such an approach is that it is extremely difficult to determine a politician's actual position on a given topic once that person is given executive responsibilities.

Such a disconnect between a politician's words and deeds is a source of great anxiety for investors keen for certainty. The frustration is magnified when there is a disconnect between the laws those politicians choose to enact and the laws they seek to enforce. It is the high expectation of slippage in the enactment and enforcement of law that made the tough lines taken by the Yudhoyono administration on both food self-sufficiency and mining so surprising. Had the government established credibility in following through on previous promises, such tough lines would not have been sources of shock.

The next president has a chance to improve the expectations Indonesians have for their politicians. By only promising things that are achievable, setting out a budget to fund those promises and ensuring that promises are consistent with one another, the president can give himself a fighting chance of implementing them. There may be a short-term political price to pay, particularly if rivals continue to go on the promise-binge that politicians on the stump are known for, but it might also serve to improve the sophistication of political debate.

Seek to govern with a smaller, more focused coalition. Indonesian politics in the Reformasi period is severely fragmented, with nine parties represented in the legislature in the 2009 to 2014 period, six of those in President Yudhoyono's coalition. Such diversity in the cabinet room is in part a product of electoral politics – to get a candidate on the presidential ballot paper requires more support than almost any single party can usually muster, and to steer bills through the legislature usually requires backing from multiple blocs. In Yudhoyono's case, coalition partnerships were largely a product of political horse-trading rather than any shared political agenda – coalition members varied from Yudhoyono's own staunchly nationalist Democratic Party to the Islamist Prosperous Justice Party (PKS). This meant that when the going got tough on issues, such as the need to increase the price of subsidised fuel, Yudhoyono's cabinet members sometimes went missing. So weak was the president's position that he was politically unable to force out of the coalition those parties that defied his stated policies.

To ensure stability and greater certainty in the ability to prosecute his or her agenda, the incoming president should seek to take on as few coalition members as possible. Those that are invited to join the coalition should be encouraged to embrace the core tenets of the president's governing philosophy. If, over the course of the presidency, those parties are no longer committed to the government's policies, they should be relieved of their duties. Once appointed to the cabinet, ministers need to put their country and the presidency first and leave behind the individual agendas of their political parties. Too often under Yudhoyono, different ministers would offer vastly different explanations of the government's position on a given matter, too often because they were substituting in their own party's preference for that of the ruling coalition. Such an approach is a recipe for government instability.

Foster an ethic of accountability. There are some tremendously bright and hard-working people in the senior ranks of the Indonesian bureaucracy, designing sensible policy, consulting with stakeholders and scorning the temptations that come with power. But they rarely get the credit they deserve, nor are they treated more favourably than their colleagues who lack the same the diligence, intellect or integrity. The incoming president needs to celebrate the achievements of the stars in his or midst – and sack the poor performers. He could start with the cabinet, making clear that underperforming ministers will be sent to the exits. It might be an unpopular approach at first among ministers and bureaucrats who have become complacent over the years, but it would be extremely popular among good performers, and most importantly among a frustrated public that depends on decent public services.

Joko Widodo's example of accountability in action is a good one. Soon after being installed as governor of Jakarta in October 2012, Widodo started a series of spot checks on provincial government offices. Unannounced, the governor and a gaggle of journalists would descend on a bureaucratic office to test out the services, seeing how many people were at their desk, how many customers were waiting to be served and how cleanly the environment was being maintained. It didn't take long for the governor's visits, or fear of future visits, to prompt a significant improvement in the functioning of offices under his purview. On a national scale, such an approach could prove a powerful catalyst for improvement.

Apply rigourous analysis to spending from the budget. The list of worthy projects competing for government funds is enormous – the 2011 Masterplan for Acceleration and Expansion of Indonesia's Economic Development (MP3EI) featured dozens of infrastructure, energy, mining and agricultural projects that would each have a positive impact on the economy. But choosing from among them is far trickier, in part because of a lack of evidence on the likely economic impact of a given project. The absence of this data makes spending decisions far more vulnerable to the whims of individual ministers, whose favourites among industries and provinces are usually reflected in their spending preferences. Understanding a project's likely return on investment needs to be a key factor in the government decision-making process. Without it, boondoggle projects will continue to clog up the nation's spending.

Once projects have been given the green light, improved efforts need to be put in place to ensure the project is delivered. An open, competitive tender process should be the norm, with private competitors, both local and foreign owned, competing on a level playing field with Indonesian state-owned rivals. Officials with conflicts of interest should be compelled to excuse themselves from the process or face prosecution. Projects should be thoroughly audited before final payments are made so that citizens can be assured they are getting what they paid for. And a long-term plan needs to be put in place for the ongoing maintenance of infrastructure so that bridges don't collapse and roads don't become potholed within a decade of completion.

Clean up the judiciary. The system for appointing people to senior government positions is a highly politicised one, with candidates typically subjected to scrutiny by the legislature before a short list is compiled for the consideration of the president. The substandard outcome of this process is galling in the case of most offices, but is downright dangerous when it comes to the judiciary. A significant proportion of judges, including senior ones, have a professional history in politics that dwarfs their judicial experience. Indeed, in some instances it seems that a judicial appointment has been a gift to a political ally or a face-saving role for a political rival who would otherwise be out in the cold. It should come as little surprise, therefore, that some judges appear out of their depth when hearing cases, particularly on technical and commercial matters.

To improve the situation, the incoming president should reach out to members of the country's legal establishment and tell them he is keen for them to fill positions on the benches. A mandatory gap should be introduced in the time between when someone leaves a formal political role and when that person can take up a judicial one. Political allies, if they unavoidably need to be looked after, should be parked in places where they can do as little damage as possible. And once this new breed of Indonesian judge is in place, they should take steps towards cleaning up the administration of justice: Rulings should be prompt and made public; the Judicial Commission should be given an opportunity to investigate suspicions of corruption; and police should be compelled to honour the terms of a court finding. Academic Howard Dick makes the fine point that discipline must go beyond judges who receive bribes – "it is also essential to disbar lawyers who offer bribes and either suggest or accept their client's instructions to do so".[537]

Be prepared

For foreign investors keen to push ahead in Indonesia, there are a few measures that can be taken to manage the risk, and thereby bolster the risk-adjusted return. The reality is that one should treat investing in Indonesia as they would gambling at a casino – put on the table only money one is prepared to relinquish. Some may end up very wealthy, but others will end up losing the lot. Risking the company on an Indonesian play, like Churchill has done, is a decision that is hard to justify for all but the most one-eyed Indonesian bull.

So with that in mind, what can foreign investors do to ensure they maximise their chances of benefitting from the riches the country has to offer?

Seek out industries with fewer sunk costs. Many of the problems identified in case studies in this book involved large resources projects that required years of investment before they realised a return. Much of the risk they faced came from those sunk costs, and the progressively decreasing leverage they had over government and other stakeholders as those sunk costs accumulated. Many of the investment success stories, however, involve investment in industries with a lighter footprint, for example retail, banking and professional services.

Those industries can be entered incrementally, starting with a small operation and scaling up as confidence grows. They also give to the investor power over the timing and certainty of advancement, given they usually need fewer licences and permits than do infrastructure-heavy projects. The rates of return in those service sectors rarely match those of the mining and energy industries, but they are far less risky. Similarly, Indonesia can serve as a major customer base without a big operation being established on the ground. Look, for example, at Canadian telecommunications device maker BlackBerry, which has a strong mobile phone market share in Indonesia despite having only a light corporate presence in the country. (It has faced calls to establish a data server in Indonesia, but has so far resisted them.)

Choose a local partner carefully, and don't skimp on the due diligence. Words are cheap, so a local partner needs to establish its credibility with a track record of success and integrity. Local partners should ideally bring to the table a skill set that complements that of the foreign partner, in particular the ability to get things done amid the chaos that is business-as-usual in Indonesia. Many local entrepreneurs seeking out foreign capital have an impressive array of contacts in government, but don't necessarily have the resilience to cope should the personalities change. Be particularly wary of local partners who seek to dazzle with mention of a father/uncle/brother in an influential position. (One Australian mining company, Western Mining Network, engaged the services of Panji Adhikumoro Suharto, the grandson of the former president, to help it open doors. It was unclear how many were slammed in its face.)

There is no shortage of corporate intelligence firms operating in Indonesia with the ability to conduct a thorough due diligence on a prospective partner. It takes extensive experience on the ground in Indonesia to know the relevant people, and to have the connections to winnow out the key information. Formal record keeping in Indonesia can be rather poor, so old tax records, company filings and court rulings can be frustratingly difficult to access, even if they are notionally public documents. Using the expertise of people on the ground can save a lot of heartache later, as Nathaniel Rothschild can probably attest.

As Geoffrey Gold, an Australian who has lived for 15 years in Jakarta, explained over a coffee, "The whole idea of doing market research by buying an air ticket and going to the nearest pub to try to pick the brains of the nearest resident Australian is not good enough." Gold, whose company Gold Group helps new arrivals find their feet, urges companies entering the Indonesian market to place an executive on the ground in the country. "If you make a commitment, you've got to make a board commitment. There's no way known that you can avoid all of the known pitfalls without getting market knowledge and being able to explain what's going on here back to the board."[538]

Build redundancy into investment decisions. Prices will rise, regulations will change, deadlines will be blown – that's the reality of life, not just in Indonesia. Howling at the moon in frustration has so far not proven to be an effective salve, so instead investors need to be prepared. Including some extra fat in plans gives them some robustness to cope with the shocks they will inevitably face. Even the most thorough of risk analysis ahead of time will still be subject to Black Swan surprises that can destroy more fragile plans. The bidders for the Tanjung Priok port expansion, for example, had little clue that the government lacked the funds to follow through on the tender it had initiated.

One trap that can catch out investors is parsing the language of regulations or legal rulings too closely. Many of these documents are written to convey a particular sentiment rather than an exact meaning, and so later changes in wording, or ignoring the words altogether, need to be expected. Establishing a business that operates at the margins of what is permissible under the current rules runs a very high risk of those rules changing at a whim and the business being left stranded on the other side of licit.

Build connections with all levels of government. More than a decade of decentralisation has meant that provincial, regency and district governments are vested with tremendous power to control licences involved in big projects. While most strive to exercise the role with diligence, many simply lack the skilled staff they need to do a proper job of scrutinising the environmental, social and economic impacts of the projects before them. Sometimes corruption is the outcome of this process, but more likely it is confusion and uncertainty, particularly if local people develop a strong view either way on the merits of a project.

Thoughtful companies can maximise the chances of success by building bonds with the regulators at all levels of government. Typically this involves regular briefing of the progress of projects, honesty and openness when plans change and the building of a perception that the success of the project is a shared interest. Dealing with the central government in Jakarta might be easier – at least the agencies usually have the depth of skill they need to perform the job they are changed with carrying out – but it won't yield the results necessary when the decision lies with other levels of government.

Develop grassroots support for projects. In the Reformasi era, Indonesians have come to realise they are entitled to considerable influence over projects, particularly resources projects, operating in their community. A social licence to operate has become a vital conceptual frame for the way that investors need to connect to local people. A corporate social responsibility program is an essential component of gaining such a licence, but their very ubiquity has meant that they no longer are effective on their own. Also necessary is a thorough information campaign so that people can be confident that a given resources project is not going to pollute their lungs, destroy their fisheries or send habitat-destroyed tigers roaming their streets.

It is important to not confuse efforts to attract support among local government officials with those attracting grassroots support. In some instances local officials are in touch with the attitudes of their constituents, but in other instances they are aloof and distant. The support of a kepala desa (village head) will count for little among people who are doubtful about the benevolence of the occupant of the office. One common way to build a closer bond with the local community is to make a job pledge, committing to employ a certain number of local people if they have the appropriate skill set, or train them up if they lack it. An enthusiastic workforce in a small town can do wonders when it comes to building popular support for a project.

"There have been many cases where companies have experienced traumatic and disastrous consequences by failing to communicate properly with the local community," noted Concord Consulting risk analyst Keith Loveard. "This is by no means easy, since many Indonesian communities tend to assume that the arrival of an investor means jobs for everybody. In the oil and gas sector this is not the case, and conflicts can arise. One of the standard practices to avoid problems with the community is to employ personnel from the military or the police, but this can also be fraught with danger."[539]

Cause for hope

For all the gloom about the difficulties of doing business in Indonesia, there are some reasons for optimism that things will improve.

Indonesian youngsters are hyper-connected with each other and with the rest of the world through online technology, and through this are gaining an appreciation of the opportunities available to them as global citizens. Seeing themselves as part of a complex web of interconnections may encourage Indonesians to take a more open attitude towards trade in goods and services, matching the way they have become open to the global exchange of cultures. Japanese and Korean popular culture, packaged as J-pop and K-pop respectively, have given many young Indonesians a sense of affection for those countries, and it is unsurprising that brands from those countries (such as South Korea's Hana Bank) have sought some reflected glory.

Slowly emerging is a generation of technocrats and businesspeople whose values are the product of the Reformasi era rather than of the New Order. Members of this generation have a low tolerance for corruption and patronage and have internalised the need for a strong work ethic and high integrity. In the past, it was tough to be a person of high intellect and skill but few personal connections, because so often the door to professional opportunities was slammed shut. Gradually, more organisations, including government agencies, are hiring and promoting staff on merit, a cycle that is likely to be a self-perpetuating one as those people reach senior ranks and themselves make hiring decisions.

By the end of 2015 the 10 countries of the Association of Southeast Asian Nations have agreed to liberalise rules for investment in one another as part of the Asean Economic Community. Embrace of the more open borders has been slow among some countries, including Indonesia, which fear the competition they will face from more advanced countries in the group. But nonetheless the policy will likely open up possibilities abroad for Indonesian companies and demonstrate that they too can benefit from a freer trade environment. For Indonesia to be a key player in a regional trade agreement bodes well for its willingness to embrace global norms on investment rules. Indonesia has already undertaken efforts to cut tariffs – from 2006 to 2012, the average fell to 7.8 percent from 9.5 percent. This has left Indonesia with tariffs constituting just 4 percent of tax revenue, considerably lower than the average for developing countries, according to the World Trade Organization.[540] This means that liberalised trade will not hurt government finances much, even in the short term.

Final word

As 11 a.m. rolls around each Sunday, the cars and motorcycles rev their engines and start their procession down the Jakarta boulevards of Jalan Thamrin and Jalan Sudirman as another Car-Free Sunday comes to an end. For the rest of the day the traffic is a breeze.

But from a little after dawn the next day, congestion builds up as people from the city and beyond converge on the main artery to head to work for the new week. Tinted-window BMWs compete for road space with rust-bucket Kopaja minibuses, while agile motorcycles glide through every gap they can find. Enterprising young men block a lane of traffic for a moment to let a vehicle slip in, collecting Rp 2,000 for their trouble, while others go door to door in the congestion selling newspapers. A phalanx of police motorcycles blare their sirens and carve open a lane of traffic to allow a black limousine to pass through the throng. Young women and their babies offer themselves to help solo drivers reach the three-person threshold they need to use some main roads in peak hour. Tempers occasionally fray, but most people have come to accept this as a reality of life in Jakarta.

Just how will Indonesia manage the rules of the investment road? Will it allow chaos and confusion to dominate, or will wiser heads prevail and seek to bring order? So far the signs are not encouraging – lots of lurching forward before unexplained stops, opportunists promising an express path that ends up leading nowhere, road-clearing police escorts giving an easy run to officialdom and local partners offering themselves as a way to help things run smoothly. Whether this persists into the future will be a big determinant of Indonesia's future economic prosperity. On the roads and in business, the congestion is a sign of demand running hot. But there are no guarantees that demand will remain strong.

Endnotes

CHAPTER 1

1 Indonesian Investment Coordinating Board (BKPM) marketing material

2 "Domestic and foreign direct investment realization in Quarter IV and January-December 2013", BKPM, 21 January 2014

3 "Unrest tarnishes drive to tap Indonesia's gold riches", *Reuters*, 3 October 2012

4 Anthony Reid, "Economic and Social Change, c. 1400-1800", *The Cambridge History of Southeast Asia*, Volume One, Part Two, Cambridge, 1999, page 137

5 Quoted in ibid, page 140

6 "Indonesia urged to fund more teacher scholarships", *Jakarta Globe*, 25 September 2012

7 "QS World University Rankings 2013", QS data set

8 "Red tape bogs down gas projects", *Jakarta Globe*, 22 October 2013

9 Geoffrey Gold, interview with the author

10 Peter Verhezen and Natalia Soebagjo, "Is there hope for corporate governance in Indonesia?" in *Strategic Review*, Vol. 3, No. 3, 2013

11 "Perils of economic policy-making and the rise of 'nationalism'", *Jakarta Post*, 24 April 2012

12 Bill Sullivan, interview with the author

13 Paul Collier, *The Bottom Billion: Why the poorest countries are failing and what can be done about it*, Oxford, 2007, page 160-1

14 ibid, page 62

15 Norman G. Owen, "Economic and Social Change", *The Cambridge History of Southeast Asia*, Volume Two, Part Two, Cambridge, 1999, page 161

16 Harold Crouch, *Political reform in Indonesia after Soeharto*, Singapore, 2010, page 16

17 N.G. Owen, op. cit., pages 144, 161

18 Cited in Ian Chalmers and Vedi Hadiz, *The Politics of Economic Development in Indonesia: Contending Perspectives*, London, 1997, page 71

19 "Suharto Inc: The Family Firm", *Time Asia*, 24 May 1999

20 H. Crouch, op. cit., page 1

21 M.C. Ricklefs, *A History of Modern Indonesia Since c. 1200*, Stanford, 2001, page 409

22 H. Crouch, op. cit., page ix

23 "Indonesian oil industry wary of change", *Jakarta Globe*, 17 May 2013

24 Richard Robison and Vedi Hadiz, *Reorganizing Power in Indonesia: The politics of oligarchy in the age of markets*, London, 2004, pages 10, 253

25 "We need shock therapy: An interview with Indonesia's new president", *Time Asia*, 8 November 2004

26 John Bresnan, "Economic Recovery and Reform", *Indonesia: The Great Transition*, Oxford, 2005, page 227

27 "Indonesia: where bad politics threatens a good economy", *East Asia Forum*, 15 August 2013

28 "Indonesian boom from Aussie tax gloom?", *Sydney Morning Herald*, 2 June 2010

29 "China's CNOOC to pay more for BP Indonesia gas", *Reuters*, 12 May 2013

30 "Indonesia's new mining policy does little to dent enthusiasm", *Bloomberg*, 16 March 2012

31 "Mining In Indonesia: Investment and Taxation Guide", PwC, May 2013

32 "Domestic and foreign direct investment realization in Quarter IV and January-December 2013", BKPM, 21 January 2014

33 "Direct investment flows in Indonesia", Bank Indonesia, 2014

34 World Bank Doing Business index, 2014

35 "Survey of Mining Companies 2012/13", Fraser Institute, February 2013

36 Corruption Perceptions Index, Transparency International, 2013

37 "Trade Policy Review: Indonesia", World Trade Organization, 10-12 April 2013

38 A. Reid, op. cit., page 140

39 "Policy missteps seen as hurting Indonesia's appeal to investors", *Jakarta Globe*, 5 October 2013

40 "Our investment committee will now involve labor representatives", *Tempo*, 10 November 2013

CHAPTER 2

41 Farid Harianto, interview with the author

42 P. Collier, op. cit., page 111

43 "Red tape bogs down gas projects", *Jakarta Globe*, 22 October 2013

44 ibid

45 "To boost growth, jobs and investment, involve business community in policy-drafting process", *Jakarta Globe*, 17 July 2013

46 "Watchdog slams lawmakers for frequent absences", *Jakarta Globe*, 30 March 2013

47 "Akil Mochtar finally spills the beans and confesses to Rp 3 billion kickback", *Jakarta Globe*, 1 February 2014

48 World Bank Doing Business index, 2014

49 Howard Dick and Simon Butt, *Is Indonesia as corrupt as most people believe and is it getting worse?*, Melbourne, 2013

50 *From Reformasi to Institutional Transformation: A strategic assessment of Indonesia's prospects for growth, equity and democratic governance*, Harvard, 2010

51 "Australia's Intrepid Mines surges on Indonesian share deal", *Reuters*, 1 August 2012

52 Chris Leahy, interview with the author

53 "Trade Policy Review: Indonesia", World Trade Organization, 10-12 April 2013

54 "Indonesian oil industry wary of change", *Jakarta Globe*, 17 May 2013

55 "View Point: Mining investors encounter legal landmines", *Jakarta Post*, 21 July 2013

56 "In big antigraft year, not enough big scalps: ICW", *Jakarta Globe*, 3 February 2014

57 "Disputes over mining to intensify", *Jakarta Post*, 6 December 2012

58 Suryo Bambang Sulisto, interview with the author

59 "Trade Policy Review: Indonesia", World Trade Organization, 10-12 April 2013

60 N.G. Owen, op. cit., pages 149

61 J. Bresnan, op. cit., page 190

62 ibid, page 205

63 Corruption Perceptions Index, Transparency International, 2013

64 H. Dick and S. Butt, op. cit.

65 "In big antigraft year, not enough big scalps: ICW", *Jakarta Globe*, 3 February 2014

66 "KPK breaks ground on new headquarters after years of waiting", *Jakarta Globe*, 9 December 2013

67 Global Corruption Barometer, Transparency International, 2013

68 H. Dick and S. Butt, op. cit.

69 J. Bresnan, op. cit., page 215

70 P. Verhezen and N. Soebagjo, op. cit.

71 "Indonesia Economic Quarterly: Continuing adjustment", World Bank, October 2013

72 "Indonesia: where bad politics threatens a good economy", *East Asia Forum*, 15 August 2013

73 P. Collier, op. cit., page 44

74 "Challenges for Indonesia's future", *Jakarta Globe*, 16 August 2013

75 "Trade Policy Review: Indonesia", World Trade Organization, 10-12 April 2013

76 "Why the worst is yet to come for Indonesia's epic bubble economy", *Forbes*, 3 October 2013

77 T. Hutapea, interview with the author

CHAPTER 3

78 G-Resources company information

79 ibid

80 "Green group protests wooing of Aussie miner", *Jakarta Post*, 13 September 2006

81 "N. Sumatra mine operation expected to start in March", *Jakarta Globe*, 15 January 2012

82 "Miners finding Indonesia a tougher ask", *Sydney Morning Herald*, 7 November 2012

83 G-Resources company information

84 "Work halted at Martabe gold mine after complaints", *Jakarta Post*, 10 September 2012

85 ibid

86 Yatun Sastramidjaja, "Memories of protest; Students, history, space and the loss of agency in post-Suharto Jakarta", *Indonesian Transitions*, Yogyakarta, 2006, page 251

87 "Unrest tarnishes drive to tap Indonesia's gold riches", *Reuters*, 3 October 2012

88 "Work halted at Martabe gold mine after complaints", *Jakarta Post*, 10 September 2012

89 G-Resources statement, Sept. 20, 2012

90 "Martabe gold mine in jeopardy over waste dispute", *Jakarta Post*, 2 October 2012

91 "Thousands of gold mine workers face layoffs", *Jakarta Post*, 20 September 2012

92 "G-Resources begins to lay off workers", *Jakarta Post*, 5 October 2012

93 "Minister to get tough on mining firms over labor", *Jakarta Post*, 8 October 2012

94 G-Resources company statement, Oct. 3, 2012

95 "G-Resources expects stoppage resolution within days", *Bloomberg*, 6 October 2012

96 "Unrest tarnishes drive to tap Indonesia's gold riches", *Reuters*, October 2012

97 "Martabe suspension starts to hurt local businesses", *Jakarta Post*, October 2012

98 "Martabe gold mine workers demand govt intervention", *Jakarta Post*, October 2012

99 "Martabe mine installs pipes to channel waste", *Jakarta Post*, October 2012

100 "Sumatra pipeline resumption sparks fiery protest', *Jakarta Globe*, October 2012

101 "Batang Toru district office empty after demonstration", *Jakarta Post*, 31 October 2012

102 "Martabe mine faces protests over pipeline", *Jakarta Post*, 31 October 2012

103 "Officials test the waters and they taste just like water!", *Jakarta Post*, 21 November 2012

104 "Martabe liquid waste well within limits: Labs", *Jakarta Post*, 22 January 2013

105 "Martabe mine installs pipes to channel waste", *Jakarta Post*, 30 October 2012

106 "Miners finding Indonesia a tougher ask", *Sydney Morning Herald*, 7 November 2012

107 "Talking about energy sovereignty", *Globe Asia*, November 2012

108 "Half of Indonesian mining companies pay no tax", *Tempo*, 10 May 2013

109 B. Sullivan, interview with the author

110 "G-Resources raises output target at North Sumatra mine", *Jakarta Globe*, 5 August 2013

111 "Team to monitor mine wastewater", *Jakarta Post*, 10 October 2013

112 "Gold, gems draw companies to invest", *Jakarta Post*, 18 April 2013

CHAPTER 4

113 "Government calls for change at ExxonMobil", *Jakarta Globe*, 4 January 2013

114 "ExxonMobil chief not fired: Regulator", *Jakarta Globe*, 8 January 2013

115 "RI asks ExxonMobil Indonesia to replace its president director", *Jakarta Post*, 2 January 2013

116 "ExxonMobil vows oil, gas will help empower Bojonegoro people", *Jakarta Post*, 8 September 2008

117 "Exxon risks losing Cepu contract on further delays", *Jakarta Globe*, August 2009

118 "East Java's Cepu oil project taking shape on schedule, Exxon says", *Jakarta Globe*, 28 December 2012

119 "Lawmakers say Exxon 'incapable' of working Cepu block", *Jakarta Globe*, 7 September 2009

120 "Exxon risks losing Cepu contract on further delays", *Jakarta Globe*, 17 August 2009

121 "Exxon lifts Cepu output to 5,000 bpd as BP Migas moves to replace execs", *Jakarta Globe*, 31 August 2009

122 "BPMigas orders Exxon Mobil to raise output", *Jakarta Globe*, 4 January 2012

123 "Securing Bojonegoro's final nod, Banyu Urip's oil now within reach", *Jakarta Post*, 18 August 2012

124 "Banyu Urip's E. Java oil project clears permit hurdle", *Jakarta Globe*, 16 August 2012

125 "East Java's Cepu oil project taking shape on schedule, Exxon says", *Jakarta Globe*, 28 December 2012

126 "Govt says delay behind Exxon's boss replacement", *Jakarta Post*, 29 January 2013

127 "RI asks ExxonMobil Indonesia to replace its president director", *Jakarta Post*, 2 January 2013

128 "Officials bracing for fallout from ExxonMobil saga", *Jakarta Globe*, 29 January 2013

129 "Interventions led to Exxon boss dismissal", *Tempo*, 28 January 2013

130 "SKK Migas denies Exxon boss dismissal related to Arun divestment", *Tempo*, 31 January 2013

131 "Interventions led to Exxon boss dismissal", *Tempo*, 28 January 2013

132 "Govt says it has 'lost face', demands ExxonMobil replace 'uncooperative' boss", *Jakarta Post*, 3 January 2013

133 K. Loveard, correspondence with the author

134 "Officials bracing for fallout from ExxonMobil saga", *Jakarta Globe*, 29 January 2013

135 "Exxon's new boss urged to be more 'flexible'", *Jakarta Post*, 5 June 2013

CHAPTER 5

136 Churchill Mining letter to President Susilo Bambang Yudhoyono, 22 November 2011

137 "Dispute over land after coal is found", *Straits Times Indonesia, Nov. 25, 201*

138 Churchill Mining letter to President Susilo Bambang Yudhoyono, 22 November 2011

139 Churchill Mining company presentation, December 2011

140 "Battle over huge coal deposit highlights risks in Indonesia", *Reuters*, 10 October 2011

141 "Rich seam of conflict over coal discovery", *Sydney Morning Herald*, 4 October 2011

142 Churchill Mining company presentation, November 2010

143 "Rich seam of conflict over coal discovery", *Sydney Morning Herald*, 4 October 2011

144 Churchill Mining company presentation, December 2011

145 "Rich seam of conflict over coal discovery", *Sydney Morning Herald*, 4 October 2011

146 Churchill Mining letter to President Susilo Bambang Yudhoyono, 22 November 2011

147 "Indonesia stands firm in Churchill Mining dispute", *Jakarta Globe*, 26 September 2012

148 "Don't blame us in Churchill mining dispute, East Kutai says", *Jakarta Globe*, 3 July 2012

149 "Rich seam of conflict over coal discovery", *Sydney Morning Herald*, 4 October 2011

150 Churchill Mining company presentation, December 2011

151 Churchill Mining company presentation, November 2010

152 Churchill Mining company presentation, December 2011

153 ibid

154 "Churchill pursues its dreams of coal via arbitration with Indonesia", *Jakarta Globe*, 27 September 2012

155 "Bakrie coal mining partnership turns sour", *Straits Times Indonesia*, 25 November 2011

156 "Indonesia's 'resource nationalism' upsets foreign investors", *Agence France-Presse*, 21 March 2012

157 Churchill Mining company statement, 23 September 2010

158 Churchill Mining company presentation, December 2011

159 Churchill Mining letter to President Susilo Bambang Yudhoyono, 22 November 2011

160 Churchill Mining company presentation, December 2011

161 "Indonesia to map coal mines to avoid overlapping claims", *Straits Times Indonesia*, 14 December 2011

162 P. Collier, op. cit., page 154

163 "The legal monster that lets companies sue countries", *The Guardian*, 4 November 2011

164 "The Trojan treaties", *Globe Asia*, April 2012

165 "British mining firm sues Indonesia for asset seizure", *The New York Times*, 8 June 2012

166 "Yudhoyono ready to face international arbitration over mine dispute", *Jakarta Globe*, 29 June 2012

167 "Churchill pursues its dreams of coal via arbitration with Indonesia", *Jakarta Globe*, 27 September 2012

168 "Churchill Mining update: East Kutai chief not worried about pending $2 billion suit", *Jakarta Globe*, 13 July 2012

169 International Center for the Settlement of Investment Disputes organisation information

170 "Coal confusion confounds RI", *Jakarta Post*, 1 May 2012

171 "SBY warns of time bomb in RI mining", *Jakarta Post*, 8 August 2012

172 "Churchill case reflects weakness of RI mining policy: Analysts", *Jakarta Post*, 30 June 2012

173 "Indonesia to map coal mines to avoid overlapping claims", *Straits Times Indonesia*, 14 December 2011

174 "SBY warns of time bomb in RI mining", *Jakarta Post*, 8 August 2012

175 "Commentary: Churchill's legal suit sends negative signal to investors", *Jakarta Post*, 4 July 2012

176 "British mining firm sues Indonesia for asset seizure", *The New York Times*, 8 June 2012

177 "Battle over huge coal deposit highlights risks in Indonesia", *Reuters*, 10 October 2011

178 David Quinlivan, correspondence with the author

CHAPTER 6

179 Audrey R. Kahin and George McT. Kahin, *Subversion as Foreign Policy: The secret Eisenhower and Dulles debacle in Indonesia*, New York, 1995, page 153

180 Chevron Pacific Indonesia company information

181 "BPMigas bets Chevron can pump more oil", *Jakarta Globe*, 15 January 2012

182 "Indonesia has gallons of optimism, but is it realistic?", *Jakarta Globe*, 13 June 2012

183 Chevron Pacific Indonesia bioremediation factsheet

184 "Bioremediation project is not fictitious: Chevron", *Jakarta Post*, 22 May 2012

185 "Chevron Indonesia graft investigation expands to include BP Migas", *Jakarta Globe*, 30 March 2012

186 "Criminal charges haunt Indonesia's oil industry", *Jakarta Post*, 29 October 2012

187 "2010 Review: Indonesia's rules complicate oil and gas business", Jakarta *Globe*, 28 December 2010

188 "Seven suspects named in Chevron Indonesia graft case", *Jakarta Globe*, 16 March 2012

189 "KPK to assist AGO's investigation in alleged Chevron graft case", *Jakarta Post*, 29 March 2012

190 "AGO investigating BP Migas 'negligence' in Chevron case", *Jakarta Post*, 30 March 2012

191 "Govt threatens to stop cost recovery to Chevron", *Jakarta Post*, 30 March 2012

192 "Bioremediation project is not fictitious: Chevron", *Jakarta Post*, 22 May 2012

193 "Chevron Pacific Indonesia in hot water over toxic cleanup", *Jakarta Globe*, 4 August 2012

194 "AGO has no basis for detaining, charging CPI Workers: Lawyer", *Jakarta Globe*, 27 November 2012

195 "IPA: Chevron bioremedial case may hurt investment", *Jakarta Globe*, 16 October 2012

196 "Criminal charges haunt Indonesia's oil industry", *Jakarta Post*, 29 October 2012

197 "Chevron caused $9.9 million in state losses: AGO", *Jakarta Globe*, 15 November 2012

198 "Four Chevron Indonesia employees released from jail", *Jakarta Globe*, 28 November 2012

199 "Chevron graft suspects file Rp 4b lawsuit demanding compensation for embarrassment", *Jakarta Globe*, Nov. 19, 2012

200 "AGO has no legal right to appeal Chevron ruling: court", *Jakarta Globe*, 5 December 2012

201 "Chevron leads investment in RI's oil and gas sector this year", *Jakarta Post*, 11 January 2013

202 "More intrigue in AGO's Chevron crusade", *Jakarta Globe*, 20 June 2013

203 "Minister says govt will stay out of Chevron legal dispute", *Jakarta Post*, 17 May 2013

204 "Chevron bioremediation contractor sentenced to six years", *Tempo*, 10 May 2013

205 "Indonesia rearrests Chevron exec amid tension with big oil", *Reuters*, 22 May 2013

206 ibid

207 "Chevron staff gets two years in prison for phony environmental program.", *Jakarta Post*, 17 July 2013

208 "Chevron Indonesia graft case spooks investors", *Financial Times*, 9 July 2013

209 "More intrigue in AGO's Chevron crusade", *Jakarta Globe*, 20 June 2013

210 "Minister says govt will stay out of Chevron legal dispute", *Jakarta Post*, 17 May 2013

211 "More intrigue in AGO's Chevron crusade", *Jakarta Globe*, 20 June 2013

212 "Graft prosecutors demand five years for Chevron employee", *Jakarta Post*, 11 June 2013

213 "Another Chevron worker gets two years", *Jakarta Post*, 19 July 2013

214 "Indonesian court jails second Chevron employee in cleanup case", *Jakarta Globe*, 18 July 2013

215 "RI at risk of arbitration by Chevron", *Jakarta Post*, 18 July 2013

216 "Indonesian court jails second Chevron employee in cleanup case", *Jakarta Globe*, 18 July 2013

217 "Court's verdict on Chevron contractors scares investors: Regulator", *Jakarta Post*, 10 May 2013

218 *Reformasi Weekly*, 10 January 2014

219 "Chevron Indonesia graft case spooks investors", *Financial Times*, 9 July 2013

220 T. Hutapea, interview with the author

221 "CPI defends executive convicted in case built on shaky foundation", *Jakarta Globe*, 19 October 2013

CHAPTER 7

222 "Time to take a risk", *Globe Asia*, April 2012

223 "Rent-seekers in Pertamina", *Jakarta Post*, 16 June 2004

224 "Karen Agustiawan: Challenges male domination of oil and gas industry", *Jakarta Post*, 8 February 2009

225 "Pertamina sets ambitious target", *Globe Asia*, September 2012

226 ibid

227 "Pertamina says it will acquire 15% stake in Mahakam block from Total", *Jakarta Globe*, 1 September 2009

228 "Total appears set to get Mahakam block extension", *Jakarta Globe*, 27 March 2011

229 "Pertamina planning to push aside foreign firms to control more blocks", *Jakarta Globe*, 8 June 2011

230 "Supermajordämmerung", *The Economist*, 3 August 2013

231 "Pertamina planning to push aside foreign firms to control more blocks", *Jakarta Globe*, 8 June 2011

232 "Pertamina gets backing to operate Mahakam block", *Jakarta Post*, 14 November 2011

233 "Total appears set to get Mahakam block extension", *Jakarta Globe*, 27 March 2011

234 "Total E&P to spend $16.5b for Mahakam gas block", *Jakarta Post*, 29 March 2011

235 "Total appears set to get Mahakam block extension", *Jakarta Globe*, 27 March 2011

236 "Foreign oil firms don't want to rework contracts", *Jakarta Globe*, 6 June 2011

237 "Oil and gas firms balk at plan to redraw contracts", *Jakarta Globe*, 21 July 2011

238 "New oil law clause to put locals ahead", *Jakarta Globe*, 14 November 2011

239 "Oil companies say govt's output target unrealistic", *Jakarta Post*, 3 June 2011

240 "Production at Mahakam continues to decline", *Jakarta Post*, 2 May 2012

241 "Pertamina gets backing to operate Mahakam block", *Jakarta Post*, 14 November 2011

242 "Total seeks assurance for 2017", *Jakarta Globe*, 22 December 2012

243 "Pertamina taking cautious steps toward takeover of Mahakam block", *Jakarta Globe*, 19 October 2012

244 "No longer 'business as usual' in the Mahakam furor", *Jakarta Post*, 25 March 2013

245 "Total E&P Indonesie's Mahakam block contract extension meets resistance", *Jakarta Post*, 18 January 2013

246 "No longer 'business as usual' in the Mahakam furor", *Jakarta Post*, 25 March 2013

247 "Ministers divided over Mahakam block", *Jakarta Post*, 4 April 2013

248 "Pertamina set to operate Mahakam oil and gas block", *Jakarta Globe*, 23 October 2012

249 "Ministers divided over Mahakam block", *Jakarta Post*, 4 April 2013

250 "Pertamina taking cautious steps toward takeover of Mahakam block", *Jakarta Globe*, 19 October 2012

251 "Total keeps plan in Mahakam block", *Jakarta Post*, 3 November 2012

252 "Pertamina to continue Mahakam block operation", *Jakarta Post*, 1 April 2011

253 "Constitutional Court invalidates BP Migas", *Jakarta Globe*, 13 November 2012

254 "Pertamina may join Total in operating Mahakam block", *Jakarta Post*, 19 February 2013

255 "Total requests incentives for Mahakam block", *Jakarta Post*, 23 March 2013

256 "France to boost RI investment amid Mahakam row", *Jakarta Post*, 2 August 2013

257 "National interests rule in gas-rich Masela block", *Jakarta Post*, 19 September 2013

258 "Total E&P demands decision on future of Mahakam gas block", *Jakarta Globe*, 11 July 2013

259 ibid

260 "Ministers divided over Mahakam block", *Jakarta Post*, 4 April 2013

261 "Hardy Pramono takes charge of Total Indonesie", *Jakarta Post*, 28 January 2014

262 T. Hutapea, interview with the author

263 K. Loveard, correspondence with the author

264 "Time to take a risk", *Globe Asia*, April 2012

CHAPTER 8

265 "Tj. Priok has risen above its humble origins", *Jakarta Post*, 18 November 2000

266 ibid

267 "Lino: Leadership takes guts", *Globe Asia*, May 2013

268 "State of Indonesia Logistics 2013", World Bank, August 2013

269 "Attracting FDI: Indonesia", Japan Development Institute, 2008

270 International Association of Ports and Harbors data

271 "Container traffic expected to increase 27% this year", *Jakarta Post*, 16 November 2012

272 "Land to be cleared for toll road to Tanjung Priok", *Jakarta Post*, 6 March 2008

273 "Four new terminals center of $2.4b Tanjung Priok upgrade", *Jakarta Globe*, 11 August 2010

274 ibid

275 "Four new terminals for Tanjung Priok port", *Jakarta Post*, 12 August 2010

276 "Govt expects Tanjung Priok expansion to begin in April", *Jakarta Post*, 28 March 2011

277 "Master Plan for the Acceleration and Expansion of Indonesia's Economic Development (MP3EI)", National Development Planning Agency, 2011

278 "Priok port a shambles: Agus", *Jakarta Globe*, 21 January 2013

279 "Aborted tender leaves bidders furious at govt", *Jakarta Globe*, 29 January 2012

280 ibid

281 "Indonesia scraps crucial port project", *Asia Sentinel*, 30 January 2012

282 "New Priok port will be more efficient, says developer", *Tempo*, 15 January 2013

283 "Yudhoyono kicks off RI's largest port project", *Jakarta Post*, 23 March 2013

284 "A shot of adrenalin for Indonesian ports", *Globe Asia*, May 2013

285 "Independent committee set up to monitor Kalibaru Port", Indonesia Port Corporation statement, 2013

286 "Priok port a shambles: Agus", *Jakarta Globe*, 21 January 2013

287 "HPI to continue to develop port infrastructure in Indonesia", *Jakarta Post*, 27 April 2012

288 "APM Terminals proposes solutions to Indonesia's infrastructure challenges", APM Terminals statement, 22 July 2011

289 "Cikarang dry port ghost town despite crowded Tanjung Priok port", *Jakarta Post*, 11 July 2013

290 T. Hutapea, interview with the author

291 "Aborted tender leaves bidders furious at govt", *Jakarta Globe*, 29 January 2012

CHAPTER 9

292 "Indar Atmanto: Employees are not productions tools", *Jakarta Post*, 20 August 2008

293 "Calling on new expertise", *Globe Asia*, February 2013

294 "IM2 executive jailed over 3G fee evasion", *Jakarta Globe*, 8 July 2013

295 "IM2 launches new wireless broadband subscription package", *Jakarta Post*, 4 October 2007

296 "Customers rate IM2's internet service: 'It sucks' ", *Jakarta Globe*, 6 April 2009

297 "Telco firms rattled by IM2 verdict", *Jakarta Post*, 9 July 2013

298 "Indonesia's Indosat in hot seat over broadband", *Jakarta Globe*, 14 January 2012

299 "Suspect named in $418 million Indosat frequency fraud case", *Jakarta Globe*, 19 January 2012

300 "Indosat, IM2 deny charges", *Jakarta Post*, 7 January 2013

301 "IM2 ex-chief charged with tax evasion", *Jakarta Globe*, 15 January 2013

302 "Indosat was clear to contract out network: Ministry", *Jakarta Globe*, 23 January 2012

303 "An internet case of fraud, tax evasion", *Jakarta Globe*, 22 February 2013

304 "AGO chases telco over 'routine' spectrum action", *Jakarta Globe*, 3 December 2012

305 "Former chief regulator questioned In Indosat broadband transfer case", *Jakarta Globe*, 28 January 2012

306 "Telcom players report judges over IM2 rulings", *Jakarta Post*, 18 July 2013

307 "Belajar dari Kasus Denny AK dan isu pemerasan Indosat Rp 30 Miliar" ("Lessons from the case of Denny AK and issues from the Rp 30 billion Indosat extortion"), *detik.com*, 30 October 2012

308 "Telecommunication industry outraged at ruling", *Jakarta Globe*, 10 July 2013

309 "AGO chases telco over 'routine' spectrum action", *Jakarta Globe*, 3 December 2012

310 ibid

311 ibid

312 "Telecommunication industry outraged at ruling", *Jakarta Globe*, 10 July 2013

313 ibid

314 "Telco firms rattled by IM2 verdict", *Jakarta Post*, 9 July 2013

315 "Telecommunication industry outraged at ruling", *Jakarta Globe*, 10 July 2013

316 ibid

317 "Editorial: Legal, business uncertainty", *Jakarta Post*, 12 July 2013

318 "The Corruption Court found Indar Atmanto guilty: The verdict creates uncertainty for the telecommunication industry", Indosat statement, 9 July 2013

319 "Indosat could suffer trillions in losses", *Jakarta Post*, 11 July 2013

320 "Telco firms rattled by IM2 verdict", *Jakarta Post*, 9 July 2013

321 "Govt regrets court ruling on IM2", *Jakarta Post*, 11 July 2013

322 "Convicted IM2 director fights ruling", *Jakarta Globe*, 13 July 2013

323 "Minister calls on Indonesian mobile operators to consolidate", *Jakarta Globe*, 16 July 2013

324 "The Corruption Court found Indar Atmanto guilty: The verdict creates uncertainty for the telecommunication industry", Indosat statement, 9 July 2013

325 "Indosat wages a new battle for arbitration after latest IM2 verdict", *Jakarta Post*, 7 January 2014

CHAPTER 10

326 "OECD Review of Agricultural Policies: Indonesia 2012", Organization for Economic Co-operation and Development, 2012

327 "The 1945 Constitution of the Republic of Indonesia", Republic of Indonesia

328 "Indonesia's food security just smoke and mirrors?", *Straits Times*, 27 November 2012

329 N.G. Owen, op. cit., page 170

330 "OECD Review of Agricultural Policies: Indonesia 2012", OECD, 2012

331 "Agriculture sector is falling behind: BPS", *Jakarta Globe*, 9 September 2013

332 "Indonesia to rely on soybean imports beyond 2014", *Reuters*, 27 March 2013

333 "Cow slaughter jeopardizes beef self-sufficiency plan", *Jakarta Globe*, 25 February 2013

334 "The beef conspiracy", *Globe Asia*, May 2011

335 "Indonesia opens door to unlimited live cattle imports, scraps quotas", *Reuters*, 19 July 2013

336 "Indonesia's food security just smoke and mirrors?", *Straits Times*, 27 November 2012

337 "The beef conspiracy", *Globe Asia*, May 2011

338 ibid

339 ibid

340 "Gita, Suswono visits cow ranches", *Tempo*, 28 May 2013

341 "Indonesia's food security just smoke and mirrors?", *Straits Times*, 27 November 2012

342 "Increase meat import quota, says Aspidi", *Tempo*, 7 December 2012

343 "Government urged to be transparent about imports quota", *Tempo*, 21 March 2013

344 "Fathanah sentenced to 14 years in prison for graft", *Jakarta Post*, 5 November 2013

345 "Illegal beef suspected to have entered market", *Tempo*, 9 January 2013

346 "Indonesia: where bad politics threatens a good economy", *East Asia Forum*, 15 August 2013

347 "Indonesia frees up soybean import rules again", *Reuters*, 20 September 2013

348 "SBY scolds errant officials over rising food prices", *Jakarta Globe*, 13 July 2013

349 "Indonesia: where bad politics threatens a good economy", *East Asia Forum*, 15 August 2013

350 "Challenges for Indonesia's future", *Jakarta Globe*, 16 August 2013

351 K. Loveard, correspondence with the author

352 H. Crouch, op. cit., page 20

353 "SBY scolds errant officials over rising food prices", *Jakarta Globe*, 13 July 2013

354 "Indonesia told to scrap food import quotas", *Reuters*, 27 February 2013

355 "OECD review of agricultural policies: Indonesia 2012", OECD, 2012

356 "US Trade Representative Kirk seeks World Trade Organization dispute settlement on Indonesia's import restrictions on horticultural and animal products", US Trade Representative's Office statement, 14 March 2013

357 "Imported fruits three times cheaper", *Tempo*, 13 June 2013

358 "Minister Gita: Imported beef may enter traditional markets", *Tempo*, 21 July 2013

359 "Indonesia plans extra cattle imports, cites 'emergency situation'", *Reuters*, 17 July 2013

360 "Indonesia frees up soybean import rules again", *Reuters*, 20 September 2013

361 "SBY sets ambitious food security targets", *Jakarta Globe*, 31 October 2013

362 "After trade spat, Indonesia puts Australian beef on menu", *Reuters*, 4 July 2013

363 ibid

364 "Indonesia to rely on soybean imports beyond 2014", *Reuters*, 27 March 2013

365 Michael Sheehy, interview with the author

366 "Challenges for Indonesia's future", *Jakarta Globe*, 16 August 2013

CHAPTER 11

367 "Real battle in DBS purchase of Danamon has just begun", *Jakarta Globe*, 4 April 2012

368 "DBS to buy stake in Indonesian Bank Danamon for $4.9b", *Bloomberg*, 2 April 2012

369 "DBS boss faces biggest challenge in Bank Danamon bid", *Reuters*, 1 April 2012

370 "DBS to acquire PT Bank Danamon Indonesia TBK to become fifth-largest in Indonesia", DBS company statement, 2 April 2012

371 "DBS to buy stake in Indonesian Bank Danamon for $4.9b", *Bloomberg*, 2 April 2012

372 "DBS to acquire PT Bank Danamon Indonesia TBK to become fifth-largest in Indonesia", DBS company statement, April 2, 2012

373 "DBS's Danamon deal a 'vote of confidence in Indonesia'", *Jakarta Globe*, 2 April 2012

374 "DBS to buy stake in Indonesian Bank Danamon for $4.9b", *Bloomberg*, 2 April 2012

375 "DBS to acquire PT Bank Danamon Indonesia TBK to become fifth-largest in Indonesia", DBS company statement, April 2, 2012

376 ibid

377 "Danamon announces sale of shares by FFH to DBS", Bank Danamon company statement, 2 April 2012

378 "DBS to acquire PT Bank Danamon Indonesia TBK to become fifth-largest in Indonesia", DBS company statement, 2 April 2012

379 "DBS-Danamon banking takeover teeters over ownership rules", *Bloomberg*, 27 May 2012

380 World Bank financial inclusion data, 2011

381 "Indonesia may shoot own-goal with DBS-Danamon decision", *Reuters*, 6 May 2013

382 "Fate of $10 billion bank deals turns on Indonesia's DBS call", *Bloomberg*, 7 May 2013

383 Darmin Nasution speech to Bankers' Dinner (official transcript), Dec. 9, 2011

384 ibid

385 "DBS acquisition plan 'political'", *Jakarta Post*, 1 December 2012

386 Darmin Nasution speech to Bankers' Dinner (official transcript), 23 November 2012

387 "Decision on DBS deal may become BI's legacy", *Jakarta Post*, 6 April 2013

388 "DBS's Danamon deal a 'vote of confidence in Indonesia'", *Jakarta Globe*, 2 April 2012

389 "Bank Indonesia bows to political pressure on DBS-Danamon deal", *Jakarta Post*, 3 December 2012

390 "DBS, Danamon create RI's fifth-biggest bank", *Jakarta Post*, 3 April 2012

391 "DBS acquisition plan 'political'", *Jakarta Post*, 1 December 2012

392 "Real battle in DBS purchase of Danamon has just begun", *Jakarta Globe*, 4 April 2012

393 "Indonesian politicians criticize Bank Danamon takeover bid", *Reuters*, 4 April 2012

394 "Indonesia may shoot own-goal with DBS-Danamon decision", *Reuters*, 6 May 2013

395 "DBS-Danamon banking takeover teeters over ownership rules", *Bloomberg*, 27 May 2012

396 "New banking ownership rule puts deals on hold", *Jakarta Post*, 28 April 2012

397 "Bank Indonesia uses DBS's Danamon bid to negotiate", *Bloomberg*, 11 April 2012

398 "Banks 'ready' to thrive in S'pore", *Jakarta Post*, 3 December 2012

399 "Indonesian politicians criticize Bank Danamon takeover bid", *Reuters*, 4 April 2012

400 "DBS minority holders voice concerns about Danamon deal", *Reuters*, 25 April 2012

401 "BI limits ownership in banks", *Jakarta Post*, 19 July 2012

402 "Indonesia may shoot own-goal with DBS-Danamon decision", *Reuters*, 6 May 2013

403 "BI limits ownership in banks", *Jakarta Post*, 19 July 2012

404 "Indonesian politicians criticize Bank Danamon takeover bid", *Reuters*, 4 April 2012

405 "DBS 'committed' to Danamon ambitions", *Jakarta Globe*, 4 August 2012

406 "Banks 'ready' to thrive in S'pore", *Jakarta Post*, 3 December 2012

407 "Real battle in DBS purchase Of Danamon has just begun", *Jakarta Globe*, 4 April 2012

408 "DBS acquisition plan 'political'", *Jakarta Post*, 1 December 2012

409 ibid

410 "Bank Indonesia bows to political pressure on DBS-Danamon deal", *Jakarta Post*, 3 December 2012

411 "BI decision looms on DBS bid for Danamon", *Jakarta Globe*, 16 April 2013

412 "Indonesia cental bank says approves DBS bid for Bank Danamon", *Jakarta Globe*, 21 May 2013

413 "Singapore holds key in DBS deal", *Jakarta Post*, 22 May 2013

414 Monetary Authority of Singapore statement, 21 May 2013

415 "Shares of Singapore's DBS fall after Danamon agreement extended", *Reuters*, 3 June 2013

416 "Danamon agreement will lapse", DBS statement, 31 July 2013

417 "DBS faces five-year lag in Indonesia as Danamon bid ends", *Bloomberg*, 1 August 2013

418 "DBS deal lapse likely to curb Indonesian bank M&A", Fitch Ratings statement, 31 July 2013

419 Agus Martowardojo speech to Bankers' Dinner (official transcript), 14 November 2013

420 "Indonesia financial regulator expects new banking law completed in 2014", *Reuters*, 23 May 2013

421 "The politics of banking policy", *Jakarta Post*, 12 August 2013

422 "Fate of $10 billion bank deals turns on Indonesia's DBS call", *Bloomberg*, 7 May 2013

CHAPTER 12

423 "Rothschild heir joins Indonesian billionaire to mine coal boom", *Bloomberg*, 17 November 2010

424 ibid

425 "Nat Rothschild rues 'terrible mistake' in deal gone sour", *Bloomberg*, 8 May 2013

426 "Rothschild buys Indonesian coal stakes for $3 billion", *Bloomberg*, 16 November 2010

427 ibid

428 "Nat Rothschild rues 'terrible mistake' in deal gone sour", *Bloomberg*, 8 May 2013

429 "Rothschild buys Indonesian coal stakes for $3 billion", *Bloomberg*, 16 November 2010

430 "Nat Rothschild rues 'terrible mistake' in deal gone sour", *Bloomberg*, 8 May 2013

431 ibid

432 P. Verhezen and N. Soebagjo, op. cit.

433 "Rothschild buys Indonesian coal stakes for $3 billion", *Bloomberg*, 16 November 2010

434 ibid

435 "Rothschild heir joins Indonesian billionaire to mine coal boom", *Bloomberg*, 17 November 2010

436 ibid

437 "Rothschild mends Bakrie ties after sparring over Bumi debt", *Bloomberg*, 13 January 2012

438 Nathaniel Rothschild letter to Ari Hudaya, Nov. 8, 2011

439 "Interim management statement production report for Q3 2011", Bumi Plc company statement, 17 November 2011

440 "Bumi ex-CEO Hudaya quits board as Indonesia probe starts", *Bloomberg*, 25 September 2012

441 "Rothschild mends Bakrie ties after sparring over Bumi debt", *Bloomberg*, January 2012

442 "Interim management statement production report for Q3 2011", Bumi Plc company statement, 17 November 2011

443 "Bumi chairman's plan to double stake incurs wrath of Rothschild", *Bloomberg*, 12 July 2011

444 "Nat Rothschild rues 'terrible mistake' in deal gone sour", *Bloomberg*, 8 May 2013

445 "Bumi ex-CEO Hudaya quits board as Indonesia probe starts", *Bloomberg*, 25 September 2012

446 Bumi Plc company statement, 24 September 2012

447 "Bumi ex-CEO Hudaya quits board as Indonesia probe starts", *Bloomberg*, 25 September 2012

448 "Nat Rothschild rues 'terrible mistake' in deal gone sour", *Bloomberg*, 8 May 2013

449 "Bumi Resources questions motives of London probe", *Bloomberg*, 28 September 2012

450 ibid

451 "Bumi probes role of advisers in assessing coal assets", *Bloomberg*, 24 January 2013

452 ibid

453 ibid

454 "Bumi says $201 million missing after review of Berau funds", *Bloomberg*, 31 May 2013

455 ibid

456 ibid

457 Bumi Plc company statement, 26 June 2013

458 "Bumi agrees to recover missing $173 million from former director", *Bloomberg*, 27 June 2013

459 "Bumi says Roeslani claims he doesn't owe company funds", *Bloomberg*, 4 December 2013

460 "Bumi's defeat of Rothschild clears way for Bakries split", *Bloomberg*, 22 February 2013

461 "Bakries seek fresh delay to $501 million London exit deal", *Bloomberg*, 16 January 2014

462 "Bumi's largest holders 'confident' of ousting Rothschild", *Bloomberg*, 10 February 2012

463 Bumi Plc company statement, 22 Janruary 2013

464 Anonymous interview with the author

465 P. Verhezen and N. Soebagjo, op. cit.

466 C. Leahy, interview with the author

467 "Aberdeen, Manulife seek more independent boards", *Bloomberg*, 28 March 2013

468 "Indonesia plans scorecards to boost corporate governance", *Bloomberg*, 22 January 2013

469 P. Verhezen and N. Soebagjo, op. cit.

CHAPTER 13

470 "Govt and Freeport feeling their way through foreign ownership rules", *Jakarta Globe*, 5 July 2012

471 "Mining in Indonesia: Investment and Taxation Guide", PwC, May 2013, page 5

472 "Threat issued on mineral firms as govt plans export ban", *Jakarta Post*, 21 February 2012

473 "Mining In Indonesia: Investment and Taxation Guide", PwC, May 2013, page 9

474 "Editorial: Bombarding foreign miners", *Jakarta Post*, 9 March 2012

475 "Future of Coal Mining Industry: New restrictions on foreign investors," Bill Sullivan presentation, 30 October 2013

476 "Govt not interested in Freeport shares: Minister", *Jakarta Post*, 27 July 2012

477 "Reworking mine deals a 'moral' issue: SBY", *Jakarta Globe*, 26 June 2012

478 "Indonesia Trade Minister eyes speedy end to Freeport contract talks", *Jakarta Post*, 2 July 2013

479 "Vale seeks govt vow before Sulawesi plan", *Jakarta Globe*, 10 August 2012

480 "Govt plans to renegotiate all contracts including Freeport", *Jakarta Post*, 24 September 2011

481 "Freeport to pay higher royalties after months of contract talks", *Jakarta Globe*, 23 July 2012

482 "Mine talks may bear fruit in 2013", *Jakarta Globe*, 7 September 2012

483 "14 coal miners sign new deals", *Jakarta Globe*, 3 October 2012

484 "Building a smelter is not economically feasible: Newmont", *Jakarta Post*, 22 September 2012

485 "Freeport and Newmont MoUs not enough: Hatta", *Jakarta Globe*, 27 August 2013

486 "Indonesia Trade Minister eyes speedy end to Freeport contract talks", *Reuters*, 2 July 2013

487 "Freeport and Newmont MoUs not enough: Hatta", *Jakarta Globe*, 27 August 2013

488 "Newsmaker Interview: Vice Trade Minister Bayu Krishnamurthi", AmCham, January 2014

489 "Ban on raw mineral exports begins in 2014", *Jakarta Post*, 16 July 2011

490 "Minister signs ban on metal ore exports", *Jakarta Post*, 11 February 2012

491 "If Newmont closes down, what is the plight of thousands of its employees?", *Antara*, 13 December 2013

492 "Export Restrictions: The economic effects of Indonesia's impending export restrictions on unprocessed mineral resources", United States Agency for International Development, February 2013

493 "Indonesian miners support ban on raw materials exports", *Jakarta Globe*, 18 July 2011

494 "Export ban is making miners dig deep: Govt", *Jakarta Globe*, 23 September 2011

495 "Indonesia's 'resource nationalism' upsets foreign investors", *Agence France-Presse*, 21 March 2012

496 "Export ban regulation not ideal: Executives", *Jakarta Globe*, 6 March 2012

497 "Indonesia plans export tax on coal, base metals in 2012", *Reuters*, 24 December 2011

498 K. Loveard, correspondence with the author

499 "Indonesia plans to impose 50 percent mining tax in 2013", *Reuters*, 4 April 2012

500 "Govt to slap export tax on 14 mineral commodities", *Jakarta Post*, 2 May 2012

501 "Mineral exports take a dive over tighter export rules", *Jakarta Post*, 26 July 2012

502 ibid

503 "Indonesia's mining regulatory regime", *Coal Asia*, December 2013-January 2014

504 "Nickel-ore exports from Philippines seen rising on Indonesia ban", *Bloomberg*, 2 April 2012

505 "Australia seen boosting bauxite exports on Indonesia ore export ban", *Bloomberg*, 18 December 2013

506 "Mining firms may not meet government deadlines", *Jakarta Post*, 6 August 2012

507 "Miners turn to court for clarity on ore ban", *Jakarta Post*, 31 December 2013

508 "Meeting 2014 deadline for export impossible, Jero says", *Jakarta Globe*, 11 April 2013

509 "Ore export ban Is definitive, official says", *Jakarta Globe*, 2 January 2014

510 "Freeport and Newmont MoUs not enough: Hatta", *Jakarta Globe*, 27 August 2013

511 "Indonesian miners see dire outcome of export ban", *Jakarta Globe*, 10 December 2013

512 "Ore export ban in Indonesia seen spurring thousands of job cuts", *Bloomberg*, 16 December 2013

513 S.B. Sulisto, interview with the author

514 "Freeport warns of output cuts, layoffs from Indonesia export ban", *Reuters*, 12 December 2013

515 "Mining shutdown looms", *Jakarta Post*, 6 December 2013

516 "If Newmont closes down, what is the plight of thousands of its employees?", Antara, 13 December 2013

517 "Ore export ban is definitive, official says", *Jakarta Globe*, 2 January 2014

518 "Indonesia braces for impact of mineral export ban, *Reuters*, 10 January 2014

519 "Indonesia's mining regulatory regime", *Coal Asia*, December 2013-January 2014

520 "Vale sees nickel over $20,000 a ton on Indonesia ban", *Bloomberg*, 25 February 2014

521 "Indosmelt set to start as govt plans ore ban", *Jakarta Globe*, 5 December 2013

522 "Mining shutdown looms", *Jakarta Post*, 6 December 2013

523 "PTNNT supports government goals on in-country processing; PTNNT does not export unprocessed ore", Newmont Nusa Tenggara statement, 10 December 2013

524 "Ore export ban is definitive, official says", *Jakarta Globe*, 2 January 2014

525 "Freeport, Newmont exempted as mineral ban comes into effect", *Reuters*, 12 January 2014

526 ibid

527 "Indonesia's mining ministry looks to ease mineral export ban", *Reuters*, 8 January 2014

528 "Small miners squeezed in ore export Ban", *Jakarta Globe*, January 2014

529 "Ore export ban Is definitive, official says", *Jakarta Globe*, 2 January 2014

530 T. Hutapea, interview with the author

531 "Survey of Mining Companies 2012/13", Fraser Institute, February 2013

532 "Legal uncertainty remains big problem in RI mining sector", *Jakarta Post*, 17 June 2013

533 "Mining In Indonesia: Investment and Taxation Guide", PwC, May 2013, page 29

CHAPTER 14

534 "Global value chain and 'poor people' employment: The case of automotive industries in Indonesia", Carolyn Sinulingga honours thesis, 2013

535 B. Sullivan, interview with the author

536 Indonesia 2009 report, Extractive Industries Transparency Initiative, May 2013

537 H. Dick and S. Butt, op. cit.

538 G. Gold, interview with the author

539 K. Loveard, correspondence with the author

540 "Trade Policy Review: Indonesia", World Trade Organization, April 2013

Bibliography

Bresnan, John, "Economic Recovery and Reform", *Indonesia: The Great Transition*, Oxford, 2005.

Chalmers, Ian, and Hadiz, Vedi, *The Politics of Economic Development in Indonesia: Contending Perspectives*, London, 1997.

Collier, Paul, *The Bottom Billion: Why the poorest countries are failing and what can be done about it*, Oxford, 2007.

Collins, Elizabeth F., *Indonesia Betrayed: How Development Fails*. Honolulu, 2007.

Crouch, Harold, *Political Reform in Indonesia After Soeharto*, Singapore, 2010.

Dick, Howard, and Butt, Simon, *Is Indonesia as corrupt as most people believe and is it getting worse?*, Melbourne, 2013.

Hadiz, Vedi, *Localising Power in Post-Authoritarian Indonesia: A Southeast Asia Perspective*, Stanford, 2010.

Kahin, Audrey R., and Kahin, George McT., *Subversion as Foreign Policy: The Secret Eisenhower and Dulles Debacle in Indonesia*, New York, 1995.

Owen, Norman G., "Economic and Social Change", *The Cambridge History of Southeast Asia: Volume Two, Part Two – From World War II to the present*, Cambridge, 1999.

Reid, Anthony, "Economic and Social Change, c. 1400-1800", *The Cambridge History of Southeast Asia: Volume One, Party Two – From c. 1500 to c. 1800*, Cambridge, 1999.

Ricklefs, M. C., *A History of Modern Indonesia Since c.1200 (Third Edition)*, Stanford, 2001.

Robison, Richard, *Indonesia: The Rise of Capital*, Sydney, 1986.

Robison, Richard, and Hadiz, Vedi, *Reorganizing Power in Indonesia: The politics of oligarchy in the age of markets*, London, 2004.

Sastramidjaja, Yatun, "Memories of protest: Students, history, space and the loss of agency in post-Suharto Jakarta", *Indonesian Transitions*, Yogyakarta, 2006.

Taylor, Jean Gelman, *Indonesia: Peoples and Histories*, New Haven, 2003.

Verhezen, Peter, and Soebagjo, Natalia, "Is there hope for corporate governance in Indonesia", *Strategic Review*, Vol. 3, No. 3. 2013.

The Voice of Reason: A Collection of Some of the Best Editorials of the Jakarta Post 1983-2008, Jakarta, 2008.

Acknowledgements

This work would not be possible without the encouragement and insight of many people I have encountered in Jakarta. My initial grounding in all things Indonesian came in my time at the *Jakarta Globe*, which has a newsroom filled with diligent and hardworking multilingual journalists, both local and foreign. I am thankful to Abdul Khalik, Dominic Diongson and their team for making me so welcome and helping to explain the nuances of this complex nation.

Joe Cochrane and the team at the Jakarta Foreign Correspondents Club have done a fantastic job of creating an English-language forum for some of Indonesia's leading thinkers to speak about topics close to their heart. It was through the JFCC's many events that I came to hear many ideas that shaped this book.

Yosef Djakababa, Amelia Liwe and the team at the Center for Southeast Asian Studies in Indonesia have established a wonderful space for learning and discussion, including an expansive library of books on Indonesia at which I spent many hours following my curiosity.

To the numerous businesspeople, diplomats, journalists and academics who responded with a wry smile when I mentioned the premise for the book and volunteered their own experiences, thanks for your openness. It was reassuring to know that I was not alone in identifying the trend at the heart of the book, and that others shared my concerns.

I appreciate the efforts of those thinkers, observers and participants who gave up their time to articulate their ideas in depth: among them are Howard Dick (University of Melbourne), Geoffrey Gold (Gold Group), Farid Harianto, Tamba Hutapea (Indonesian Investment Coordinating Board), Chris Leahy (Asian Corporate Governance Association), Keith Loveard (Concord Consulting), David Plott, Michael Sheehy (Natural Resources Indonesia), Suryo Bambang Sulisto (Indonesian Chamber of Commerce and Industry), Bill Sullivan (Christian Teo Purwono & Partners), Peter Verhezen (Verhezen & Associates) and Maria Monica Wihardja (University of Indonesia).

Thanks also go to the executives, officials and spokespeople involved in the case studies who engaged with my queries and did what they could to ensure their stories were told fairly and accurately. Responsibility for errors and omissions, however, is mine alone.

Thanks to Anthony Cappello and the team at Connor Court Publishing for their support in helping me bring my research to readers.

And from the bottom of my heart, I give thanks to Carla and Michael, my parents, for instilling in me a sense of curiosity, and Melanie Calvert, the love of my life, for wandering with me down the path of discovery.

About the Author

Ari Sharp is an Australian journalist who worked in Indonesia from 2011 to 2014, leading the copy desk of the *Jakarta Globe* newspaper and writing freelance for several outlets. Prior to that, he worked for *The Age* and *Sydney Morning Herald* newspapers in Melbourne and Canberra covering business, economics and politics. He graduated from the University of Melbourne in 2006 with degrees in arts and commerce.

www.ariontheweb.blogspot.com ----- @arisharp

Index

Agustiawan, Karen 119, 121

Albert, Peter 53, 57-8, 60, 63

American Chamber of Commerce in Indonesia (AmCham) 30

Aneka Tambang 52, 54, 239

Anti-Corruption Court 32, 43, 104, 106, 153, 183, 174, 259

Anti-Corruption Law (2001) 104, 106

Arief, Basrief 111, 165

Arsyad, Yanuar 76

Arun (resources block) 68, 74-6

Asian Financial Crisis 23, 35, 40, 90, 155, 170, 186, 196, 256

Asia Resource Minerals Plc – see Bumi Plc

Atmanto, Indar 153, 156-7, 159, 161, 163-4. 166

Attorney General's Office (AGO) 97, 103, 105, 108, 111, 157, 159-60, 162-3, 165

Australia 6, 8, 33, 43, 51-3, 55, 68, 77, 80, 91, 95, 121, 167, 171, 175-6, 180, 182, 197, 229, 244, 257, 266-7

Bakrie Group 48, 125, 206-10, 211-4, 216, 219, 221, 223, 243

Bakrie, Aburizal 220, 255

Bakrie, Achmad 207-8

Bakrie, Indra 211, 213

Bakrie, Nirwan 208

Bandung Institute of Technology 8, 120, 140, 154, 239

Bank Central Asia 45, 195

Bank Indonesia 34-5, 48, 185-6, 190-1, 193-4, 196

Bank Mandiri 144, 148, 195, 199-200

Bank Negara Indonesia 76, 144, 195, 199

Bank Rakyat Indonesia 144, 178, 192, 195, 200, 204

Bank Danamon 35, 185-90, 192-4, 197, 199-200, 202-4

Banyu Urip - see Cepu

Basri, Chatib 111, 247

Batubara, Abdul Hamid 103-4, 128

Batu Hijau (copper and gold mine) 231, 233, 235, 244, 247, 249

beef 168, 170ff, 184

Berau Coal Energy 208-9, 211, 215-9, 223

Berkeley Mafia 14

bioremediation 97, 100-5, 107-10, 112, 114

Borneo Lumbung Energi & Metal 213-4

BP Migas 38, 68-9, 71-5, 77, 99, 102-4, 109, 113, 120, 124-6, 131-4

Bre-X 19-20

Bumi Plc 207-23

Bumi Resources 6, 207-23

cattle – see beef

Cepu (resources block) 28, 69-71, 73-4

Chevron Pacific Indonesia 34, 97ff, 126, 136,

China 6-7, 20-4, 81, 136, 141, 192, 197, 205-6, 213, 242, 244, 257

Churchill Mining 33-4, 79ff, 255, 265

coal 3, 45, 79-81, 84-6, 88-9, 95, 206-11, 213, 224, 226, 242-3, 246-9

conglomerates 9-10, 44, 212, 222, 257

ConocoPhillips 126, 136

Constitutional Court 16, 31-2, 38, 132, 135

consumers 10-11, 118, 138, 159, 163, 167-8, 171-3, 176-80, 183-4, 190, 201, 204

Contract of Work 31, 54, 233, 235-7

Coordinating Ministry for Economic Affairs 162

Coordinating Ministry for Political, Legal and Security Affairs 103, 109, 128, 149, 162

Corruption Eradication Commission 16, 32, 42, 64, 258

DBS Group Holdings 186, 188, 192, 201

decentralisation 35-6, 38, 70, 79, 93-4, 117, 268

Dick, Howard 33, 43, 265, 273

Djojohadikusumo, Hashim 219

Djonoputro, Bernardus 147, 151

East Kutai (coal field) 80-1, 83-4, 86-9, 91-2

ExxonMobil 28, 67ff, 120, 130

Finance and Development Supervisory Agency (BPKP) 104, 106, 160

Financial Services Authority (OJK) 35, 221

Fitch Ratings 23, 193, 204

France 6, 207

Forestry Ministry 84-6

Fraser Institute 22, 251-2

Freeport Indonesia 231-7, 244, 246, 249

Freeport McMoRan Copper & Gold – see Freeport Indonesia

gas/liquefied natural gas 5-6, 20, 28, 37-9, 42, 67-77, 90, 95, 97, 102-3, 106, 109-10, 115ff, 128, 130-6, 143, 146, 149, 269

Gibbs, Jon 77

gold 231-3, 236, 238, 244, 267, 273

Grasberg (copper and gold mine) 231-3, 241, 246

G-Resources 38, 50, 52ff

Gupta, Piyush 188-90, 197, 203

Habibie, B.J. 17

Hadianto, Martiono 246, 249

Harianto, Farid 27, 47, 177, 183-4, 273

Hegarty, Owen 53, 60

Ho, Henry 190

House of Representatives (DPR) 16, 29, 31, 37, 44, 71, 121, 193, 236, 248

Hudaya, Ari 211-2, 215

Hutapea, Hotman Paris 83

Hutapea, Tamba 48, 114, 135, 250, 273

India 24, 39, 196, 242, 257

Indoguna Utama 174

Indonesian Meat Importers Association (Aspidi) 173

Indonesia Port Corporation (Pelabuhan Indonesia II, Pelindo II) 40, 42, 140, 143

Indonesian Chamber of Commerce (Kadin) 3, 38, 49, 143, 239-40, 246

Indonesian Employers Association (Apindo) 3, 143

Indonesian Forum for Environment (Walhi) 52, 259

Indonesian Petroleum Association (IPA) 8, 28, 105, 113, 125

Indosat 34, 113, 152ff

Indosat Mega Media (IM2) – see Indosat

inflation 13-14, 22, 34, 172, 176, 256

infrastructure 36, 46-7, 51, 54, 72, 74, 86, 100, 144-8, 150-6, 183, 189-90, 240, 264, 266

Inpex 116-8, 120, 124, 133-5

Investment Coordinating Board (BKPM) 3-4, 21, 23, 48-9, 135, 151, 176, 250

Ishaaq, Luthfi Hasan 174

Ishak, Awang Faroek 81, 83, 94, 128

Iskan, Dahlan 23, 40, 129, 160

Japan 13, 20, 74, 116, 139, 142, 147

Leahy, Chris 35, 221, 273

Liman, Maria Elizabeth 174

Lino, Richard Joost 141, 149-50

Liong, Liem Sioe 9

Lippo Group 9, 257

Loveard, Keith 77, 136, 177, 241, 269, 273

Lubis, Todung Mulya 16, 66, 112

Mahakam (resources block) 42, 115ff

Mahfoedz, Lukman 6, 28, 113

Malaysia 5, 123, 129, 170, 191, 196

Mandiri Oil 76, 148, 173, 195, 199-200

Martabe (mine) 38, 50ff

Martowardojo, Agus 144, 150, 202, 204

Master Plan for the Acceleration and Expansion of Indonesia's Economic Development (MP3EI) 145, 264

Mazak, Paul 60, 91

MedcoEnergi 75, 125

middle class 3, 7, 24, 171-2, 256-7

mining 29, 31, 33-4, 37, 45, 50-7, 59-60, 63-6, 79-80, 85, 87-95, 127, 209, 217, 224ff, 261, 264, 266

Mining and Coal Mining Law (2009) 21, 31, 225, 227-9, 237, 249, 251-2, 254,

Mining Business Licences (IUP) 7, 226-230

Ministry of Agriculture 173

Ministry of Communications and Information Technology 159, 162

Ministry of Energy and Mineral Resources 67, 86, 131-2, 242

Ministry of Environment 103

Ministry of State Enterprises 40

Ministry of Transportation 147, 150

Muhammadiyah 128, 131

Nasution, Darmin 191-2, 201-2

Natalegawa, Marty 133

National Banks Association (Perbanas) 199-200

National Commission on Human Rights (Komnas HAM) 108-9

natural resources 2, 7-8, 13, 36, 38, 41, 46, 68, 115-6, 131-2, 137, 183-4, 222, 224-5, 251, 257, 273

Netherlands, the/Dutch 7, 13, 32, 39, 118, 139-40, 256

Newmont Mining Corporation – see Newmont Nusa Tenggara

Newmont Nusa Tenggara51, 231, 233, 235-7, 244, 246-9

nickel 52, 63, 224, 226, 233-4, 238-9, 242-6, 250

New Order 15, 17-18, 38, 46, 65, 82, 119, 168, 253, 255, 270

Noor, Isran 84-5, 92

Nusantara Group 80-6, 147, 151, 255

oil 3, 6, 9, 20, 28, 37-9, 42, 47, 67ff, 90, 95, 97ff, 112ff, 120ff, 131, 135-6, 143, 146, 149, 170, 177, 214, 269

Oil and Gas Law (2001) 38, 125, 132

Ooredoo 155, 162

Organisation of the Petroleum Exporting Countries (OPEC) 99, 136

Organization for Economic Co-operation and Development (OECD) 178

Owen, Richard 67-8, 71-3, 77

Panin Bank 195,

Partowidagdo, Widjajono 125-6

Pertamina 42, 70-1, 75, 90, 99, 116, 118-9, 121-4, 126ff

Perusahaan Gas Negara 75

Perusahaan Listrik Negara 54, 113, 240

prices – see inflation

Priyono, Raden 72, 124-5

Proust, Elisabeth 113, 119, 121, 124, 126, 129, 135

public-private partnerships (PPP) 47, 144, 146, 152

Qatar 6, 155, 162

Quinlivan, David 80, 87, 91, 95

quotas (imports) 31, 167, 170ff, 242

Rajasa, Hatta 144, 150, 181, 231, 234, 236

Reformasi 9, 16-17, 29, 40, 46, 57, 70-1, 107, 113, 120, 225, 253, 259, 262, 268, 270

ReforMiner Institute 94, 123

Riady family 9

Ridlatama Group 80-1, 83-9, 91-3

Roeslani, Rosan 209, 211, 217-9

Rothschild, Nathaniel 45, 206ff, 267

Rubiandini, Rudi 38, 64, 68, 72, 131-2, 135

Rusli, Alexander 155, 165

Saleh, Darwin Zahedy 120, 124

Salim, Anthoni 82

Salim Group 9, 45, 82

Sembiring, Tifatul 162, 165, 173

Sheehy, Michael 183, 273

Sihite, Thamrin 89, 234-5

Sinar Mas 9

Singapore 3-4, 6, 35, 38, 87, 93, 134, 138-9, 142, 146, 149, 185-9, 194-7, 199-203, 208, 212, 221

Sjam, Johnny Swandi 160, 165

SKK Migas 38, 77, 102, 109, 113, 132-4

SK Migas 38, 68, 74-5, 102, 132

Soetjipto, Rozik 241, 247

South Korea 9, 20, 74, 116, 123, 240, 270

State Financial Audit Agency (BPK) 83-4, 102, 104, 106, 160

state-owned enterprises (SOEs) 23, 25, 41, 140, 145

State Logistics Agency (Bulog) 176-8, 182

Subianto, Prabowo 82-3, 169, 219, 255

Suharto 9, 13-17, 23, 26-7, 34, 40, 42, 57, 65, 71, 82, 98, 116-7, 119, 168, 177, 225, 231, 233, 253, 256, 266

Sukarno 13-14, 18, 39, 98, 140, 168, 254

Sukarnoputri, Megawati 18, 254

Sullivan, Bill 10, 64, 95, 229-30, 247, 257, 274

Sulisto, Suryo Bambang 37, 246, 273

Supreme Audit Agency (BPK) 83-4

Suswono 172, 174, 177, 180, 183

Suwondo, Gatot 76

Suyanto, Djoko 111

Tan, Samin 213-4, 216

Tanjung Priok (port) 253

Telekomunikasi Indonesia (Telkom) 155, 157, 160

Temasek Holdings 185, 187-9, 200

Thohir, Garibaldi 148

tin 39, 238, 240

Total 42, 113ff, 124, 126ff, 146

Total E&P Indonesie - see Total

Transparency International 42-3, 149

United Kingdom (UK) 90, 211, 216

United States 3, 6, 98, 104, 110, 139,
    171, 174, 179

Vale Indonesia 233-4, 247

Vallar Plc 207-23

Verhezen, Peter 10, 45, 210, 220, 222,
    274

von Schirnding, Nick 217

Wacik, Jero 59, 68, 72, 76, 111, 124,

130, 132-5, 235, 242, 245, 248

Wahid, Abdurrahman/Gus Dur 17,
    63

Widjaja, Eka Tjipta 9, 104

Widodo, Joko 104-5, 110, 112, 255,
    263

Wihardja, Maria Monica 19, 274

Wirjawan, Gita 173, 176-7, 180

World Bank 22, 33, 46, 69, 142, 151,
    191, 204

XL Axiata 104, 155, 157

Yudhoyono, Susilo Bambang 6, 18-
    19, 23, 26, 34, 72, 76, 83, 87-8, 91,
    94, 111, 120, 124-5, 129, 133, 135,
    144, 167, 170, 173, 176-7, 181,
    231-2, 237, 249, 255, 262